BREAK BULK AND CARGO MANAGEMENT

LLOYD'S PRACTICAL SHIPPING GUIDES
Series Editor: Peter J. McArthur

Maritime Law
Sixth Edition
Chris Hill

Risk Management in Port Operations, Logistics and Supply Chain Security
Khalid Bichou, Michel G.H Bell and Andrew Evans

Port Management and Operations
Third Edition
Professor Patrick M. Alderton

Port Operations
Planning and Logistics
Khalid Bichou

Steel
Carriage by Sea
Fifth Edition
Arthur Sparks

Introduction to Marine Cargo Management
Second Edition
Mark Rowbotham

ISM Code
A Practical Guide to the Legal and Insurance Implications
Third Edition
Dr Phil Anderson

Corporate Manslaughter in the Maritime and Aviation Industries
Simon Daniels

Shipbroking and Chartering Practice
Eighth Edition
Evi Plomaritou and Anthony Papadopoulos

Marine Pollution Control
Legal and Managerial Frameworks
Iliana Christodoulou-Varotsi

Break Bulk and Cargo Management
Mark Rowbotham

For more information about this series, please visit: www.routledge.com/Lloyds-Practical-Shipping-Guides/book-series/LPSG

BREAK BULK AND CARGO MANAGEMENT

MARK ROWBOTHAM

informa law
from Routledge

Cover photo © Getty Images

First published 2022
By Informa Law from Routledge
4 Park Square, Milton Park, Abingdon, Oxon OX14 4RN

and by Informa Law from Routledge
605 Third Avenue, New York, NY 10158

Informa Law from Routledge is an imprint of the Taylor & Francis Group, an informa business

British Library Cataloguing-in-Publication Data
A catalogue record for this book is available from the British Library

Library of Congress Cataloging-in-Publication Data
A catalog record for this book has been requested

ISBN: 978-1-032-18804-1 (hbk)
ISBN: 978-1-032-18808-9 (pbk)
ISBN: 978-1-003-25635-9 (ebk)

DOI: 10.4324/9781003256359

Typeset in Times New Roman
by Apex CoVantage, LLC

CONTENTS

DETAILED CONTENTS

Introduction to general cargo shipping

The River Tyne is a reminder of the good old days, and I remember them well, standing on Tyne Commission Quay, just outside North Shields, and watching the Bergen Line and Fred. Olsen ships preparing for yet another North Sea crossing to Norway, as well as the DFDS ships heading out across the North Sea to Denmark. The River Tyne was also full of general cargo ships loading and unloading all kinds of cargoes, as this was the 1960s and early 1970s, before containerisation had taken hold on the global maritime scene.

I come from a maritime family. Two of my mother's cousins ran the Bonded Stores on Ferry Street, South Shields, while several others were either captains or chief engineers in various shipping lines, including the Ben Line, sailing out of the Royal Docks in East London. The Ben Line, represented by the agents Killick Martin, operated general cargo ships, including the *Ben Lawers*, *Ben Albanach* and the *Ben Ledi*, in the days before Ben Line's short-lived entry into the container business with Ben Line Containers, which I used to deal with in my early days in HM Customs & Excise. I was told as a youth that I would follow the rest of the family and go to sea, but I rebelled. Instead, I joined HM Customs & Excise, becoming an Import & Export Landing Controls Officer, formerly known as an OCX (Officer of Customs & Excise), based in the London Port Collection, dealing with the examination of import and export sea cargoes. I also boarded several ships, checking on cargoes and ship's stores, so I didn't entirely escape the family traditions. I was trained partly by HMC&E, and partly by the shipping agencies, and this stood me in good stead when I left the Department and became a Customs and marine cargo specialist consultant. This proved especially useful when I was involved in a long-term contract with a company supplying subsea flowlines to the offshore Oil and Gas sector, setting up a marine logistics department following a major assessment by HM Customs & Excise, later HM Revenue & Customs, over a failure to control exported consignments. This was sink or swim. I was effectively liaising between the company and the shipping agents, and ensuring that all the paperwork and documentation was correctly arranged and submitted prior to the vessels' departures from the Tyne. Back to old times, and it was sheer fun.

For those involved in the shipping business, it still can be. However, the markets have changed over the decades, and general cargo shipping has changed radically

DOI: 10.4324/9781003256359-1

to include specialist and Project Cargoes. The rest has been swallowed up by containerisation, for better or worse. Containerisation itself evolved from the earliest days of shipping metal boxes in the mid to late 1950s from Port Elizabeth at Newark, New Jersey, to the port of Houston, Texas, by the converted tanker *Ideal X* and later the first boxship *Gateway City*, both belonging to the Pan Atlantic Shipping Company, bought out by a certain Malcom McLean, a former US truck owner. The reason for all this was that McLean became increasingly frustrated by sitting several days at the port of New Jersey waiting for his cargoes of cotton bales to be loaded aboard general cargo vessels by inefficient longshoremen (stevedores and wharfingers). He was a believer that time is money, and that the only way that a vessel earns revenue is by being in operation, i.e. sailing across the sea between two ports. He knew that there had to be a better way of carrying general cargoes by maritime means, and, after consulting with a colleague involved in road transport, Roy Fruehauf, came up with the idea of creating metal boxes which could be filled with cargoes, transported by road chassis to a seaport, and then transferred from the road trailer onto a vessel equipped with facilities to carry these boxes, side by side and loaded on top of each other by locking devices, from one port to another. Special cranes were then devised to handle the transfer of these boxes between the trailers and the vessels and vice versa. From its inception in April 1956, the concept developed to the point that, at present, container ships of 20,000 TEU+ (Twenty-Foot Equivalent Unit) plus, the TEU being the standard designation for a Twenty-Foot container, ply the high seas on a constant basis and only spend a minimum number of hours at each port while their containers are loaded and unloaded.

The progression towards global containerisation, however, spelled the end of the traditional general cargo ship as a standard global means of marine cargo transport. General cargo shipping in the form of traditional break bulk declined to the point where it has become very much of a niche market. General cargo break bulk no longer applies to scheduled services, but revolves almost entirely on *ad hoc* charter services, generally spot voyage charters, as well as some time charter contracts applying to Project Cargo contracts, especially in the offshore Oil and Gas sector.

Although containerisation is accepted as the most convenient and economical method of shipping cargoes worldwide, it is not always the only answer to cargo shipping, as it has its disadvantages and drawbacks. These include:

Site constraints

- Large consumption of terminal space (mostly for storage); move to urban periphery;
- Draft issues with larger containerships;
- A large post-panamax containership requires a draft of at least 13 metres, along with the quayside facility of several dedicated container cranes.

Capital intensiveness

- Container handling infrastructures and equipment (giant cranes, warehousing facilities, inland road, rail access) are important capital investments;
- Large investments in such facilities;
- Many ports are unsuitable for such investments.

Stacking

- Complexity of arrangement of containers, both on the ground and on modes (containerships and double-stack trains);
- Restacking difficult to avoid and incur additional costs and time for terminal operators.

Repositioning

- Many containers are moved empty (20% of all flows);
- Either full or empty, a container takes the same amount of space;
- Divergence between production and consumption at the global level requires the repositioning of containerised assets over long distances (transoceanic);
- Dislocation of containers (especially in the present SARS-CoV global pandemic);
- Resulting increase in box rates.

Theft and losses

- High-value goods and a load unit that can be forcefully and illicitly opened or carried (on truck);
- Organised crime and cargo scams;
- Vulnerability between terminal and final destination;
- About 10,000 containers are lost at sea each year (fall overboard).

Illicit trade

- Containers can be instruments used in the illicit trade of goods, drugs and weapons, as well as for illegal immigration;
- Concerns about the usage of containers for terrorism.

Suitability

- Containers are unsuitable for outsize cargoes;
- Restrictions on cargo weights and volumes;
- Cannot be used for bulk or homogeneous cargoes.

General cargo shipping avoids most of these issues. With general cargo shipping, the ship needs to be repositioned, not the container, and it is often the case that because of the *ad hoc* charter arrangements, the ship may have cargoes awaiting it when it arrives at its first destination. However, the drawback to *ad hoc* chartering is that the general cargo ship does not have guaranteed sailings, as it does not operate a fixed schedule of sailings, hence the nature of *ad hoc* chartering. General cargo ships can load and unload at ports which may be unsuitable for container traffic, and indeed use their own gear (cranes and derricks) without the need to rely on custom-built quayside container cranes. General cargoes are generally stowed below deck, thus avoiding problems with cargoes being washed overboard in heavy seas, as well as providing enclosed protection for sensitive cargoes. General cargoes are generally landed into Customs-controlled Transit Sheds (Temporary Storage) for the purposes of Customs clearance and onward despatch to the customer/importer, thus keeping theft to a manageable minimum in most cases. Because Transit Sheds are located within the port area, security is maintained at a high level, meaning that pilferage is more controllable and generally reduced. Because these cargoes are not containerised, they can be examined and checked on an individual basis by Customs and the Port Authorities, thus avoiding much of the threat of the smuggling of illicit goods. The other main issue is that general cargoes can be loaded aboard individual means of road transport, thus obviating the issue of long container trains and container stacking. Also, general cargoes are carried on an individual basis, even where several cargoes are carried in the same vessel, and thus can be separately identified, documented and handled. The other main advantage with break bulk and general cargo is that outsize cargoes that cannot be carried inside containers can be carried as individual cargoes in general cargo ships, even in cases where the consignment takes up the whole of the hold capacity, e.g. railway locomotives and rolling stock, large boilers and large oilfield equipment such as flowlines and wellhead christmas trees and pumping equipment.

That said, the break bulk charter market is considered very specialist, and consequently requires specialist shipbroker services. In most cases, such services apply to commodity bulk traffic, but there is still major demand for *ad hoc* break bulk and Project Cargo charter services, hence the reason for this book, to examine the role of break bulk shipping, break bulk cargoes, Project Cargoes, and the chartering of the vessels carrying these cargoes.

A ship is a ship is a ship . . . or is it? True, all ships float on water, have engines and funnels, and sail from one port to another. Ships carry cargoes or passengers, but they are diverse, of different types and sizes, especially cargo ships, from the short-sea container feeder vessels to the deep-sea mega-container vessels, and the small handysize cargo vessels through panamax and capesize to the gigantic chinamax dry bulk carriers. There are therefore many different ship types, all specially customised to the type of marine cargo requiring transportation. A cargo of crude oil, with its heavy, viscose, toxic and free-flowing properties, will need totally different carriage conditions to a car, for example. Frozen food needs refrigerated carriage and is transported by a completely different ship to wine, just as live animals have very diverse needs to cut flowers. The carriage of boilers needs a very different approach from the carriage of fertilisers, and yet all these can be carried in general cargo ships, as long as they are equipped with the right forms of handling and storage facilities in their cargo holds.

It is therefore easy to be misled by the name assigned to vessels classed as general cargo ships. The tag "general" conjures up an image of a non-descript ship with no real purpose, or, for that matter, a ship that can be used for the marine carriage of anything. In fact, the reverse is true. A general cargo ship is extremely adaptable and can be used to transport virtually every form of dry non-bulk cargo, from railway lines to agricultural machinery and fertilisers, as long as it is equipped to do so. Indeed, many general cargo ships can be converted to carry quantities of bulk commodities, depending upon the nature of these cargoes. The holds of general cargo ships can vary from single individual holds extending from the keel up to the open deck, sealable by hatches, or containing a separate 'tweendeck, namely a deck located between the keel and the upper deck used for the carriage of specific cargoes.

Tweendeckers are general cargo ships with two or sometimes three cargo decks. The upper deck is called the *main deck* or *weather deck*, and the next lower deck is the '*tweendeck*, so called because it is the deck in between the main deck and the bottom of the vessel's hold. In many cases, tweendecks can be removed or opened up to accommodate larger cargoes which occupy the whole of the vessel's hold, hence the need for adaptability in today's general cargo vessels. Cargoes such as bales, bags, or drums can be stacked in the *tweendeck space*, atop the tweendeck, especially as they weigh less, and will therefore exert less burden on the tweendeck itself. Beneath the tweendeck is the *hold space*, used for general cargo. Cargo ships that have fittings to carry standard shipping containers and retractable tweendecks (which can be moved out of the way), so that the ship can carry bulk cargo, are known as *multi-purpose vessels*. These vessels are more versatile and consequently more adaptable, so that they can be used in a variety of maritime trades.

A **multi-purpose vessel** (MPV) is a seagoing ship that is built for the carriage of a wide range of cargoes. Examples of these cargoes are: wood, steel, building materials, rolls of paper and bulk cargo. Multi-purpose vessels can be divided into four categories: vessels with and without cargo gear, coastal trade liners and sea/river vessels. Larger multi-purpose vessels are able to carry different kinds of loading on the same voyage. Smaller multi-purpose vessels do not have this advantage but they are employed to enter smaller harbours because of their limited draught. Because of their varying operating conditions, these ships have complex designs that are difficult to build. Their all-round design must be able to carry heavy loads, large objects and unitised cargo as well as bulk cargo. These cargoes can be rolled or lifted on board vessel, so this requires different types of loading gear, as well. Coastal vessels are specific to coastal voyages within a limited region, whereas larger MPVs such as handysize vessels are more versatile, as they can and do operate in international deep-sea conditions.

General cargo or multi-purpose vessels are designed for flexibility and carry a huge variety of cargo. To get the most from a general cargo ship, it is important to minimise any time spent in port and optimise the efficient use of the vessel's cargo-carrying space. Get these elements right and your vessel will achieve its maximum earning capabilities.

Flexible and efficient cargo handling systems enable a ship to carry a variety of different cargoes and load and unload them within the shortest time possible. There are several companies which can deliver all the components of an efficient cargo handling system and design the best products and configurations possible. For example, to maximise a ship's earning opportunities and potential, it makes sense to consider its readiness for Project Cargoes. Bulkhead positions, partial openings, ability to carry sensitive cargoes and to operate in challenging ambient conditions are all factors that are worth considering, depending on the shipper's operational needs. All factors define the combination of cargo handling equipment that is best suited to a particular ship.

A distinct feature of general cargo ships is that they normally have their own gear, i.e. cranes and derricks, which means that these versatile ships can trade to smaller ports and terminals that do not have shoreside loading and unloading equipment. And while these ships are often employed with abnormal loads that other ships could not accommodate, in lean times general cargo ships can easily be sued for the carriage of containers, bulk or bagged cargo, casks or drums.

There are many different types of cargoes shipped around the world, some more unusual than others. While containers, crude oil and dry bulk attract the most attention, other cargoes that fall outside these categories are just as important to daily life and indeed are vital to it. Oversized goods, such as a non-motorised barges or road sections, are one such cargo, while heavy cargoes, such as industrial generators and reactors, also require special treatment. Another specialist cargo is livestock, classed loosely as self-loading, which needs to be transported in comfortable surroundings so that the cattle or sheep reach their final destination undistressed and in optimum condition. A classic example of this is the carriage of livestock from the Outer Hebrides in Scotland to the mainland ports, for the animals to be herded to the auction rooms for onward sale. The author has personally seen the use of roll-on roll-off ferries belonging to Caledonian MacBrayne for such purposes, because of their spacious vehicle decks. The downside is that the decks need to be copiously washed and cleaned after the carriage of the livestock, such is the residual mess left behind, prior to resuming conventional vehicle carriage services. Not a pretty sight (or smell), it can be safely stated!

Whatever the specialist cargo, one thing is certain: the ships that carry these cargoes are specially designed to serve that purpose. To counteract the loading and discharging of heavy and voluminous items, heavy-lift ships might use ballast to counterbalance the weight of cargoes such as cranes or other vessels being shipped from one port to another, while others use hydraulic feet to clamp on to the quay, while ships designed to carry livestock need climate control, feed dispensers, watering equipment and equipment for the removal of manure, as well as large quantities of bedding and food. Indeed, at one time, there were vessels used for the carriage of barges, or lighters, that could be loaded and unloaded in the estuary or open river, and the barges towed to a smaller port or even simply quayside upriver, and their cargoes unloaded or loaded at that point. These vessels were known as LASH (**L**ighter **A**board **SH**ip), and, had it not been for the rapid progress of containerisation, these vessels could have been a common sight in many rivers and estuaries, as they avoided the need for the use of large port facilities, including dedicated cranes and quaysides. In many ways, they disturbed the port sector, and indeed the unions representing the dock labour forces, as they were capable of moving cargo management away from the large ports to much smaller, less-equipped quaysides further up river, where unionised labour was much less common. Rivers such as the Maas/Rhine Delta, Humber and Mississippi, benefitted greatly from them in their comparatively short lifespan. Furthermore, the LASH system provided significant versatility for the maritime carriage of cargoes, as the lighters could be used to carry either unit cargoes, such as those carried in containers, or bulk homogeneous cargoes such as timber or grain.

With the physical presence of ports and terminals, often close to major cities, and the various vessels that use them for the purpose of loading and discharging cargoes of various kinds, it is easy to overlook the side of the maritime business that takes place offshore, out of the public line of sight. But that does not mean that this side of the business is any less important. Indeed, in the energy sector, this kind of operation is vital to the industry, as it encompasses the lifelines between the shore and offshore operations.

While oil rigs and platforms offer more semi-permanent means of drilling through the depths for crude Oil and Gas reservoirs, often in remote offshore locations, other more flexible options are available. The Floating Production Storage and Offloading vessel, or FPSO, is a floating unit which can receive, treat, store and offload Oil and Gas pumped up from a reservoir that it is directly connected to. A Floating Storage Offloading vessel, or FSO, offers the same functions, without the treatment, and is connected directly to the production facility, rather than the reservoir.

There is also a need for specialist support ships to help at various stages of Oil and Gas extraction. Platform Supply Vessels (PSVs) offer fuel supply, fresh water, equipment and firefighting capabilities, among other things, while Anchor Handling Towage and Supply (AHTS) vessels, which are a cross between offshore cargo vessels and tugs, can lay and retrieve anchors and can also be used for towing offshore units. Other offshore vessels, such as Dive Support Vessels (DSVs), lay cables, help with crane operations, pipeline laying, diver support and rescue operations. These vessels were designed entirely for the offshore Oil and Gas sector, and from the days of the Ulstein UT704 AHTS, the iconic and pioneering breed of AHTS, the sector that encompasses these vessels has advanced significantly over several decades. These operations are covered in a later chapter of this book.

Overall, therefore, the general cargo ship covers a multitude of marine activities. It is far from non-descript, and in reality still provides much of the backbone of global marine shipping operations. It can service ports that are inaccessible to container vessels, it can carry cargoes that cannot be shipped in bulk and cargoes that cannot be shipped in containers, it can provide specialist services, and it can operate on an *ad hoc* basis, with vessels being made available when required for specific voyages between specified ports that are not covered by scheduled services. However, general cargo ship operations are not cheap, as the cost of chartering a vessel must cover the vessel operating costs, fuel costs (bunkering charges) and the crew wages throughout the voyage, laytime spent loading and unloading at the designated ports, and the freight costs involved with the carriage of the cargo itself. All these costs and considerations must be included in any charterparty contract for this kind of carriage, hence the need for extensive knowledge of the vessel charter markets and how they function.

CHAPTER 1

Break bulk shipping

The term "break bulk" relates to trades where the cargoes are carried in unitised form such as palletised, bagged, strapped, bundled, drummed and crated like below and also non unitised general cargo (vehicles, steel etc.). The ships that carry these break bulk cargoes are known as break bulk, multi-purpose or general cargo vessels and come in a variety of sizes and types such as Single Decker, 'Tween Decker, Box Holds.

Break bulk ships are perhaps the oldest variety of cargo-carrying vessels which still operate at the sea. Unlike the present-day versions of cargo vessels, these types of ship were used to, as their name suggests, for bulk cargo without putting the cargo into shipping containers. In historic terms, there were two forms of break bulk shipping, namely the liner trades, based on fixed shipping schedules between designated ports, and the tramp trades, based on *ad hoc* trades between any port where trade was available.

The following table has been derived from the book *Business of Shipping* by Kendall and Buckley, Chapter 1, and ideally illustrates the differences between the liner and tramp shipping trades.

	Liner service	*Tramp shipping*
1.	Sailings are regular and as per a published schedule to and from designated ports on a trade route.	Sailings under voyage charters are based on cargo commitments and are usually different for every voyage. In certain trades a number of repetitive voyages carrying the same commodity can be arranged under time charters or contracts of affreightment (COA).
2.	Liners accept without discrimination any legal cargo which that ship is able to carry. "Break bulk" "general" and "container" (LCL/FCL) are descriptions applied to liners.	Tramps are private carriers which usually carry a full cargo of a single commodity in bulk, or individual cargoes belonging to different owners.

(*Continued*)

DOI: 10.4324/9781003256359-2

(Continued)

	Liner service	*Tramp shipping*
3.	Cargo carried by liners tends to be of a higher value and attracts higher freight rates. Frequently, the cargo carried aboard liners requires special care – e.g. refrigerated cargoes such as chilled meat.	Cargoes carried by tramps can be homogeneous and of low value, e.g. coal, grain and phosphate, etc. They can also comprise general or Project Cargo, depending upon the requirement for cargo carriage.
4.	Freight rates in liner services are stabilised by setting identical charges for a particular item for all shippers. Liner ships are associated with conferences. Although tariffs tend to remain unchanged for as long as possible, CAF and BAF may be applied to the freight tariff to take account of minor changes in rates of exchange and bunker prices.	Freight rates ("freight" in voyage Charter Parties (C/P), and "hire" in time Charter Parties) fluctuate according to the supply of and demand for the vessel. In terms of general or Project Cargo, freight rates are determined by W/M, i.e. freight per ton, or volumetric weight.
5.	A liner company issues a standard B/L, the provisions of which are not negotiable.	The tramp owner has to negotiate a separate C/P for each contractual employment of the vessel. Although there are standard C/P forms many of the details on these forms are negotiated. The final details depend on "supply and demand" (of ship) and the bargaining abilities of the owner and charterer. The resulting Bills of Lading are Charter Party Bills of Lading, and not standard Ocean Bills of Lading.
6.	Drastic changes in established liner operations are infrequent. The ships ply between the same ports at the same regular intervals. Nevertheless, within the year the capabilities of particular ships and ports of call may be adjusted to take account of the shippers' requirements.	Services as well as rates are determined by negotiations between shipowner and charterer.
7.	Vessels deployed on liner routes usually reflect the special requirements applicable to their employment, i.e. the ships are designed as reefer vessels, container vessels and fitted with particular cargo handling gear.	Tramps are intended for general and bulk cargoes on a worldwide basis. Consequently, they are equipped with cargo handling gear to cope with a range of cargoes. Many of the small and medium sized tramp break bulk vessels are fitted with 'tweendecks.

	Liner service	Tramp shipping
8.	Liner companies tend to have large shore organisations at the main ports of call and especially at the company's headquarters.	Tramp owners tend to have small staff in their headquarters' office. Since their services are on a worldwide basis, matters at the port of call are dealt with by agents.
9.	Procurement of cargo is effected by the company's sales staff, supported by advertisements.	Procurement of cargo is effected through brokers. The owner's broker negotiates with cargo brokers. There is virtually no public promotion.
10.	Some cargo liners are fitted with passenger accommodation. However, as the various SOLAS safety regulations place stringent requirements on vessels carrying more than 12 passengers, the number of passengers carried aboard cargo liners is in effect limited to twelve.	Although there may be an owner's cabin suite for exceptional circumstances, passengers are almost never carried on tramps or break bulk vessels.

Essentially, the tramp, or *ad hoc*, market as it is also known, is based on vessels being available to carry *ad hoc* cargoes arranged at short notice on specific voyages from and to specific ports of origin and destination, on an *ad hoc* basis according to specific need. The basis of *ad hoc* states that the market is based on a specific demand for specific dedicated maritime carriage, rather than relying on fixed maritime schedules between a range of ports. This demand takes into account the specific nature of the cargo, rather than containerised cargoes, especially as many break bulk cargoes cannot fit inside a container, and, by nature, are unitised based on the cargo itself. The *ad hoc* market relies significantly on spot charters, based on the principle of specific voyage charters. This means that the specific break bulk vessel is chartered for a specific one-off voyage to carry a specific cargo or set of cargoes to a specific designated destination. Charter costs vary, but a sizeable six-figure sum of US Dollars is commonplace for a typical vessel charter, including freight costs.

A ship engaged in the **tramp trade** is one which does not have a fixed schedule or published ports of call, rather operating on an *ad hoc* basis according to the need to carry cargo from one port to another as such cargo became available for carriage. As opposed to cargo liners, tramp ships trade on the spot market, i.e. the market where commodities are traded on the basis of immediately delivery, with no fixed schedule or itinerary/ports-of-call. A steamship engaged in the tramp trade is sometimes called a **tramp steamer**; the similar terms **tramp freighter** and **tramper** are also used. Chartering is done mainly on the London, New York and Singapore shipbroking exchanges. The Baltic Exchange, based in the City of London, serves as a type of stock market index for the trade.

The term **tramper** is derived from the British meaning of "tramp" as an itinerant beggar or vagrant; in this context it is first documented in the 1880s, along with "ocean tramp" (at the time many sailing vessels engaged in irregular trade as well). The original image of the tramp market was old ships sailing between ports on a chance basis in search of cargoes to carry. The "tramp" notion was based on the image of tramps, or vagrant beggars, wandering the lanes in search of places to stay or jobs to do. This image has since diminished, indeed almost vanished, in favour of ships being chartered on an *ad hoc* (based on the time of need) basis to carry cargoes destined for shipment to a specific destination from a specific port of loading based on a specific requirement. Hence the use of *ad hoc*, or spot, voyage chartering, on the grounds that daily charter or freight rates could vary during and between voyages, resulting in differentials in charter and freight rates between one voyage and another. It must be remembered that charter rates can vary significantly between one day's trading and another, and there is a constant need to refer to the Baltic Dry Index, reported on a daily basis by the London-based Baltic Exchange, on a daily basis to confirm these rates, as well as consult with shipping agents concerning freight rates on a regular basis. Charter rates are based on supply and demand. Where there is a glut of cargo to be carried but few ships available, the daily charter rates rise significantly. Conversely, where there is a glut of cargo vessels available but little cargo to be carried, the charter rates fall significantly.

The tramp trade first emerged in the UK around the mid-19th century, at the time of the development of steamships. The dependability and timeliness of steamships was found to be more cost-effective than sail. Coal was needed for ships' boilers, and the demand created a business opportunity for moving large amounts of best Welsh coal, known for its efficient combustibility, to various seaports in Britain, a trade that was largely instrumental in developing shipping companies such as Cory Brothers, which specialised in the carriage of coal from South Wales. Within a few years, tramp ships became the workhorses of trade, transporting coal and finished products from British cities to the rest of the world.

The size of tramp ships remained relatively constant from 1900 to 1940, between around 7,000 and 10,000 deadweight tons (dwt). However, the British fleets suffered massive losses in the early months of the Second World War owing to U-boat attacks, resulting in the construction by the United States of the "Liberty" ships. These ships had a simple and single design that could be easily built at yards unaccustomed to building cargo ships, and used to carry just about any form of cargo, with a deadweight tonnage of 10,500 dwt. The US produced 2,708 Liberty Ships, and they were used on every international trade route. After the Second World War, economies of scale took over and the size of tramp ships rose rapidly to maintain pace with a booming supply and demand cycle. During this time, new types of cargo vessel were built as replacements for the Liberty ships, including the *Freedom* and *Fortune* classes of cargo vessels built in Japan, and the renowned *SD14* cargo vessels built at the yards of Austin & Pickersgill at Sunderland, in the

North-East of England in the 1960s and 1970s, each at a deadweight tonnage of 14,000 dwt and a cost of around £1 million per vessel. The bulk carrier, which evolved from these general cargo vessels, became the tramp of choice for many owners and operators. The bulk carrier was designed to carry coal, grain and ore, which gave it more flexibility and could service more ports than some of its ancestors, which only carried a single commodity. Today, dry bulk carriers range from the huge chinamax vessels (around 400,000 dwt) through capesize (100,00 dwt+), panamax (60,000 dwt+), supramax and handymax (37,000 dwt–59,000 dwt).

Today the tramp trade includes all types of vessels, from bulk carriers to tankers. Each can be used for a specific market, or ships can be combined like the oil, bulk, ore carriers (OBOs) to accommodate many different markets depending upon where the ship is located and the supply and demand of the area. Tramp ships often carry with them their own gear (booms, cranes, derricks) in case the next port lacks the proper equipment for loading or discharging cargo.

The tramp ship is a contract carrier. Unlike a liner, often called a common carrier, which has a fixed schedule and a published tariff, the ideal tramp vessel can carry anything to anywhere, and freight rates are influenced by supply and demand. To generate business, a contract to lease the vessel known as a *charter-party* is drawn up between the shipowner and the charterer. There are three types of charters, voyage, time and demise.

The concept of "tramp shipping" was readily understood by professionals in the shipping industry some years ago, but there is still the question as to its significance in today's markets, as well as the nature of the key characteristics of this category and the types and sizes of companies involved. These questions are answered in a report published in 2015 by Clarkson Research Services on behalf of the European Community Shipowners' Associations (ECSA), which was an update of the first edition published more than ten years earlier but which still applies today (2021). This text summarises the report and how it relates to today's interpretation of the tramp market.

In the report, entitled "The Tramp Shipping Market", prepared for the ECSA by Clarkson Research Services, detailed statistical profiles of large elements of the bulk and specialised vessel markets are presented, together with a background commentary on prominent features. One especially useful item is the vessel ownership pattern data, identifying sizes and types of owning companies. Seven sectors are profiled – bulk carriers, crude oil tankers, oil products tankers, chemical tankers, liquefied petroleum gas (LPG) carriers, liquefied natural gas (LNG) carriers and roll on-roll off (RO-RO) vessels. Also provided are detailed figures on the world fleet (all vessel types) and world seaborne trade, showing how these have developed over the past three decades.

An accompanying ECSA press release suggests that "in shipping, an industry unknown to many and invisible to most (people), tramp shipping is arguably one of its least known segments". The report fulfils a purpose of making the tramp market more visible, and it will prove valuable for students and academics as well as many industry professionals who may find much of the content revealing. It highlights the vast scale of global shipping activities, their varied nature and their significance for the world economy.

The statistics showing vessel-owning patterns provide useful insights, but the report draws attention to the difficulty of accurately identifying ships' controlling owners. Other data compilers have also emphasised this problem. The task is a highly challenging exercise, reflecting a huge number of ships in the world fleet, owner changes in many cases, and a frequent absence of sufficient definite evidence to identify who is the ultimate shipowner.

Today, the name "tramp shipping" is only infrequently mentioned in current market discussion, as it no longer conveys any specific meaning in common industry parlance. When it was in common usage, many years ago, it had a well-defined meaning, namely that vessels plied the seas in search of cargoes, and were generally used to carry cargo from one port to another on an *ad hoc* basis. Tramp shipping mainly applied to the dry cargo sector, although there were tramp tankers as well as dry cargo tramps. Specialised vessels, by nature of the services rendered, were not normally considered as part of tramping activities. Today's definition, however, includes bulk, tanker or specialised shipping. A reason for retaining the tramp shipping name, for the purpose of this report, appears to be that it has been defined for the purpose of the application of European Union competition rules, and therefore has gained an authoritative status extending its use.

The stated intention of the report is to provide a briefing about how this market sector is organised and an insight into its competitive economic structure. Tramp shipping is defined as comprising the bulk and specialised segments, although these are organised differently and have different competitive processes. Liner (predominantly container services) shipping, while not part of tramping, is included in the discussion because it is a partial competitor. Key aspects discussed in the report are:

(a) Type of product – sea transport service provided;
(b) Structure of demand for seaborne transportation;
(c) Sea transport demand differentiation – price and service aspects;
(d) Supply of sea transport – fleets and transportation capacity;
(e) Sea transport risk and investment strategy;
(f) The companies involved in the shipping business;
(g) Shipping market features and contractual arrangements; and
(h) Cooperative agreements.

Much of the information in the ECSA report covers the entire global merchant ship fleet, and so has value beyond the tramp shipping category which is the principal focus. From the numerous statistical tables, significant shipping industry indicators can be directly extracted, or derived by simple calculations. A selection follows, providing a view of the industry's profile, together with some observations based on these.

World fleet of all cargo-carrying vessels

As at February 2015, the world fleet of all cargo-carrying vessels comprised 53,101 ships totalling 1,672 million deadweight tonnes (equivalent to 1,083 million gross tonnes). These vessels were owned by 14,122 companies each operating an average of four ships. Of these, 11,631 companies owned up to four ships. Only 48 companies owned 100 or more ships. The figures confirm impressions of the fragmented nature of global shipowning business, with many small enterprises contributing. Larger enterprises include Spliethoff and BBC Chartering.

Fleet growth rates

In the ten years from 2004 to 2014, average annual growth in the bulk carrier fleet was 8.9%, while the tanker fleet (all types) grew by 4.7% annually. Alongside this, the container ship fleet expanded by 8.6% annually. Among the specialised fleets, LNG carriers saw the fastest expansion at 11.3% annually. These remarkable average growth rates, over a decade, partly explain why overcapacity has been an enduring feature of several sectors in recent years.

Global fleet ownership

Ownership patterns for the world fleet in seven segments – bulk carriers, crude oil tankers, oil products tankers, chemical tankers, LPG carriers, LNG carriers and RO-RO vessels – are included in the report. Detailed statistical breakdowns are shown based on owning company fleet sizes, and type of ownership.

Owning company sizes

Data shows the distribution of company sizes, based on the number of vessels owned (and corresponding deadweight or other capacity). Relatively large companies are a feature of only one of the seven segments. In the bulk carrier fleet, 21 companies (just 1% of the total 1,721 companies in this segment) owned 50 or more ships. However, these 21 company fleets comprised almost one quarter of the overall world bulk carrier fleet's deadweight capacity, implying that the few large companies owned mainly big bulk carriers. The norm is many companies with small fleets. Companies owning nine or fewer ships comprised between 80% and 98% of the total number of companies in the seven sectors, as shown by the table. These small companies mainly owned relatively small ships. In the bulk carrier sector, for example, companies owning nine or fewer ships comprised 1,475 or 86% of the overall companies total, but the deadweight capacity of the ships owned by the 1,475 companies mentioned comprised only 30% of the overall world fleet volume in that sector. It should also be noted that general cargo Ships are not specifically mentioned, but are included in the section on bulk carriers.

Percentage of number of companies and deadweight capacity in world fleets, at February 2015

Company fleet size	0–9 ships owned		10–49 ships owned		50+ ships owned	
	% of number of companies	*Deadweight % owned*	*% of number of companies*	*Deadweight % owned*	*% of number of companies*	*Deadweight % owned*
bulk carriers	**85.7**	29.9	**13.0**	46.5	**1.3**	23.4
crude oil tankers	**79.8**	31.4	**18.6**	56.2	**1.6**	11.9
oil products tankers	**95.6**	40.9	**4.1**	48.5	**0.2**	9.8
chemical tankers	**95.4**	53.7	**4.4**	35.7	**0.3**	9.4
LPG carriers*	**91.5**	55.7	**8.5**	44.1	**0.0**	0.0
LNG carriers*	**80.6**	44.0	**19.4**	56.0	**0.0**	0.0
roll on-roll off ships	**98.2**	62.4	**1.7**	18.0	**0.0**	19.0

* % of capacity based on cubic metres

Source: calculated by Richard Scott from Clarkson Research Services report for ECSA, "The Tramp Shipping Market" (March 2015), 48–61

Top 20 owners

Another way of observing market concentration is to look at the market share achieved by the group of largest owners in each sector. These shares vary greatly. The biggest fleet proportion owned by the top 20 owners, as at February 2015, was seen in the LNG sector. In this category, the top 20 comprised 68% of the number of ships (284 ships, within an overall world fleet of 419 ships) and 72% of the related cubic metre capacity. This contrasts sharply with bulk carriers, where a relatively low 17% of the number of ships, equivalent to 26% of the entire fleet's deadweight tonnage, was owned by the top 20 companies.

Owning company types

The data also shows what types of ownership are prominent in each sector. Designated ownership types are: independent private companies, public listed companies (quoted on a stock exchange), state interests, cargo interests, financial companies and oil companies. Independent private ownership is highest in the oil products tanker, chemical tanker and RO-RO sectors, where four-fifths of vessel numbers, and 64–75% of the deadweight tonnage is owned by independents. Public listed companies comprised large proportions of the bulk carrier, crude oil tanker, oil products tanker, chemical tanker, LPG and LNG sectors, where 9–26% of the number of vessels and 19–33% of capacity is owned by these companies.

World seaborne trade growth

According to the report, global seaborne trade has been steadily increasing in several sectors in the past few years. Average annual growth since 2010 is 5.3% in the dry bulk sector, although only a modest 0.7% for oil. Container cargoes grew by 6.2% annually, while LNG saw a 3.2% average rise. These figures confirm that this trade has been increasing, contrary to suggestions by some elements of the maritime media that trade has been growing only slowly or has stagnated.

This selection of details derived from the ECSA report emphasises the vast scale of the global merchant cargo-carrying fleet of ships and its composition. Also depicted is the fleet's remarkable growth, amid solid expansion of global seaborne trade in many sectors. A prominent characteristic is that the industry's bulk and specialised vessel sectors are still predominantly owned and controlled by private independent companies, although there is also significant involvement by public listed companies. It should also be remembered that much of this activity is controlled and monitored by the London-based Baltic Exchange. Moreover, the sectors which form what the report describes as "tramp shipping" are highly fragmented, and the typical owning company profile is small, with over four-fifths of companies owning nine or fewer ships.

The **voyage charter** is the most common charter in tramp shipping. The owner of the tramp is obliged under the Hamburg Rules and the Hague-Visby Rules to provide a seaworthy ship and a fully-competent crew, while the charterer is obliged to provide a full load of cargo. This type of charter is the most lucrative, but can be the riskiest due to lack of new charterers. During a voyage charter, a part or all of a vessel is leased to the charterer for a voyage to a port or a set of different ports, i.e. a Partial or Split Charter, or a Full Charter. There are two types of voyage charter – net form and gross form. Under the net form, the cargo a tramp ship carries is loaded, discharged and trimmed at the charterer's expense. Under the gross form, the expense of cargo loading, discharging and trimming is on the owner. The charterer is only responsible to provide the cargo at a specified port and to accept it at the destination port. Time becomes an issue in the voyage charter if the tramp ship is late in her schedule or loading or discharging are delayed. If a tramp ship is delayed the charterer pays *demurrage*, which is a penalty, to the shipowner.

Tramp shipowners and tramp ship charterers rely on brokers to find cargoes for their ships to carry. A shipbroker understands international trade conditions, the movements of goods, market prices and the availability of the owner's ships.

The Baltic Exchange, based in London, is the physical headquarters for tramp ship brokerage. The Baltic Exchange functions like an organised market and provides a meeting place for shipowners, brokers and charterers. It also provides easy access to information on market fluctuations and commodity prices to all the parties involved, using the Baltic Dry Index, encompassing capesize, panamax and supramax bulk carriers, and the Handysize Index, which covers the smallest bulk carriers and general cargo vessels, including Multi-purpose Vessels (MPVs).

Brokers can use it to quickly match a cargo to a ship or ship to a cargo depending on whom they are working for. A committee of owners, brokers and charterers are elected to manage the exchange to ensure everyone's interests are represented. With the speed of today's communications, the floor of the Baltic Exchange is not nearly as populated as it once was, but the information and networking the exchange provides is still an asset to the tramp trade.

Due to the massive rise of liner container services, and in large part, due to containerisation since the 1960s, the tramp trade has decreased, but is by no means ended. A contemporary trend in the shipping business has resulted in renewed interest in tramp shipping. To increase profits, liner companies are looking at investing into tramp ships to create a buffer when the market is down. For example, companies such as the Japanese Mitsui OSK Lines possess large fleets with tramp ships and liners. With both types of shipping covered they are able to service a world economy even in a down market. The advantage of tramp ships is they are relied upon at a moment's notice to service any type of market. Even in a down economy there will be a market for some type of commodity somewhere and the company with the ships able to exploit that market will do better than the company relying on liner services alone.

The Baltic Dry Index (BDI) is a composite of the capesize, panamax and supramax Time-charter Averages. It used to incorporate the index for handysize vessels, but as from 1 March 2018, this index was discontinued. Handymax vessels had contributed just 10% to the BDI, as opposed to 40% capesize, 25% panamax and 25% supramax.

The Baltic Exchange Handysize Index (BHSI) was formally launched in 2007 and is a measure of the strength of spot freight earnings for smaller dry bulk and general cargo/break bulk vessels, currently based on a standard 38,000 dwt bulk carrier. For example, as at 10 January 2019, the BHSI stood at 684, 4 points down from the previous day at 688 points. The 52-week year-on-year range for the BHSI stood at 290–692, reflecting a very significant fluctuation in the handysize vessel market.

The indices can be illustrated as follows:

Baltic Indices

	BHSI 38,000	*%*	*Net TC Avg*	*Net TC Avg (BHSI 28,000)*	*BSI*	*%*	*Net TC Avg*	*BDI*	*Difference*	*%*
6-mths	458	−8.7	–	–		0.0	–	9122	−3050	−33.4
3-mths	662	−36.9	–	–		0.0	–	12794	−6722	−52.5
1-mth	508	−17.7	–	–		0.0	–	9073	−3001	−33.1
1-wk	465	−10.1	–	–	685	−15.2	–	976	−204	−20.9

	BHSI 38,000		*Net TC Avg*	*Net TC Avg*	*BSI*			*BDI*		
		%		*(BHSI 28,000)*		*%*	*Net TC Avg*		*Difference*	*%*
02-Jan-20	465	–	US$7,957	–	685	–	US$7,162	976	–	–
03-Jan-20	452	−2.8	US$7,732	–	662	−3.4	US$6,913	907	−69	−7.1
06-Jan-20	443	−2.0	US$7,576	–	642	−3.0	US$6,712	844	−63	−6.9
07-Jan-20	434	−2.0	US$7,415	–	611	−4.8	US$6,387	791	−53	−6.3
08-Jan-20	426	−1.8	US$7,291	–	593	−2.9	US$6,193	773	−18	−2.3
09-Jan-20	418	−1.9	US$7,154	–	581	−2.0	US$6,072	772	−1	−0.1

Source: The Baltic Exchange

The BDI is reported around the world as a proxy for dry bulk shipping stocks as well as a general shipping market indicator, and is also an assessment of the average price to ship raw materials (such as coal, iron ore, cement and grains) on a number of shipping routes (about 50) and by ship size. It is thus an indicator of the cost paid to ship raw materials on global markets and an important component of input costs. As such, the index is considered as a leading indicator (forward looking) of economic activity since it involves events taking place at the earlier stages of global commodity chains (the procurement and transformation or raw materials). A high BDI index is an indication of a limited shipping supply due to high demand, and is likely to create inflationary pressures along the supply chain. A sudden and sharp decline of the BDI is likely to foretell a recession since producers have substantially curtailed their demand, leaving shippers to substantially reduce their rates in an attempt to attract cargo. Like all market indexes, the BDI is constantly changing, reflecting its price discovery mechanism. The major factors impacting the BDI are:

- **Commodity Demand**. This is mainly a volume impact which could be irrespective of commodity prices. An increase in the demand, particularly if sudden, will likely result in a surge in shipping rates since additional capacity takes time to be brought online (either as new ships or reassignment of existing ones). If expectations about future demand change and producers reduce their raw materials demand accordingly, then the BDI will drop.
- **Ship Supply**. Represents the availability of ships in terms of their capacity and their function. Many bulk carriers, such as tankers, cannot be readily converted to other uses so the bulk market is quite segmented and fairly inflexible. The average ship age can also be taken into account since the useful life of a ship is about 25 years. If the average age becomes too high, there are expectations that significant capacity may be reduced and that this would imply a rise of the BDI. Inversely, the

addition of new capacity in terms of ship orders may trigger a decline of the BDI, particularly if demand is not expected to change significantly in light of this new supply.

- **Seasonality**. The demand for raw materials, such as grain and coal, has a significant seasonality which will create fluctuations in the BDI when the transport of these commodities is in high or low demand.
- **Bunker Oil Prices**. Bunker fuel accounts for about 40% of vessel operating costs with limited opportunities to mitigate them. Thus, a surge in oil prices is directly reflected in shipping rates. The opposite also holds as if energy prices drop, the BDI can also drop accordingly.
- **Port Congestion and Canal Capacity**. Some ports, particularly in the context of seasonality, can become congested and can tie up ships for longer periods than usual. This results in higher shipping rates as port supply is reconciled with shipping demand. Additionally, the Panama and the Suez canals, important bottlenecks in global freight circulation, have a fixed capacity and can impose additional delays.
- **Geopolitics**. Depending on the geopolitical context, there may be a level of risk at calling some locations, which is reflected in insurance rates and consequently in shipping rates. Some chokepoints, such as the straits of Hormuz, Aden and Malacca may involve the risks of political instability, as well as piracy, and capacity constraints to maritime circulation.

The BDI has been very volatile in recent years, particularly between 2005 and 2009 when it behaved as a bubble. The main driver of this surge was linked to commodity prices, particularly oil. The index then plummeted back to historical levels and has remained weak in spite of a recovery in global trade. A factor is that many ships were ordered during the "bubble years" and have entered the market, providing capacity growth above demand growth. In recent years the BDI remains low, underlining a situation of excess capacity in the shipping industry.

Today's general cargo ships are modern, state-of-the-art vessels designed for the rigours of project chartering, with lifting gear designed with a large Safe Working Load (SWL) capacity, capable of lifting large items such as oilfield equipment, major engineering items, or even yachts and other specific means of transport.

Until the late 1960s and the surge in containerisation, these vessels were very much commonplace. However, developments in the domain of cargo vessels and container vessels led to operators' preferences changing in favour of container transport in the liner trades. As containerisation developed, the need for break bulk vessels diminished, especially in the liner trades, and break bulk transport became more associated with Project Cargo, general cargo and vessel chartering.

The dry cargo market is the one which experiences higher interest since the type of vessels are much more. The basic dry cargo vessels are broadly divided into the following main categories: General Cargo vessels, Bulk Carriers, Short Sea (coaster) ships, Containerships and Specialised vessels while each of them consists of several subcategories mainly depending on their technical characteristics and/or sizes.

It is easy to be misled by the name assigned to the general cargo type of ships, as the tag "general" conjures up an image of a non-descript ship with no real purpose. In fact, the reverse is true. A general cargo ship is extremely adaptable and can be used to transport virtually every form of dry non-bulk cargo, from railway lines to agricultural machinery.

A distinct feature of general cargo ships is that they normally have their own gear, which means that these versatile ships can trade to smaller ports and terminals that do not have shoreside loading and unloading equipment. And while these ships are often employed with abnormal loads that other ships could not accommodate, in lean times general cargo ships can easily turn their hand to carrying containers, bulk or bagged cargo.

General cargo vessels were first mass-produced during the Second World War when the 10,000 tons deadweight (dwt) "Liberty" type ships were very famous. These vessels were built in US shipyards to facilitate the supply of goods and materials to the beleaguered population of the UK, as well as supplying troops stationed in the UK fighting against the Axis powers. They were built simply and efficiently, thus enabling them to be built in such numbers as to ensure that even if some vessels were sunk in the Atlantic Ocean by German U-boats, the rest would safely reach the UK and return to the US for reloading with badly-needed supplies for the UK. Indeed, they were partly instrumental in ensuring that the Allies could win the so-called "Battle of the Atlantic" by 1944.

General cargo or multi-purpose vessels are designed for flexibility and carry a huge variety of cargo. To get the most from a general cargo ship, it is important to minimise any time spent in port and optimise the efficient use of the vessel's cargo-carrying space. As long as these elements are considered and acted upon, the vessel will achieve its maximum earning capabilities.

Flexible and efficient cargo handling systems enable a ship to carry a variety of different cargoes and load and unload them within the shortest time possible. The right shipping agency can deliver all the components of an efficient cargo handling system and design the best products and configurations possible. For example, to maximise a ship's earning opportunities it makes sense to consider its readiness for Project Cargoes. Bulkhead positions, partial openings, ability to carry sensitive cargoes and to operate in challenging ambient conditions are all factors that are worth considering, depending on the company's operational needs. All factors define the combination of cargo handling equipment that is best-suited to a particular ship.

General cargo vessels are built in such way that can carry general cargo, bagged/baled cargo as well as bulk cargo and, to a lesser degree, also containers, although in general their container-carrying capacity is significantly limited. These cargo vessels are usually built in small sizes of about 5,000 to about 25,000-ton deadweight (dwt), and they are nearly always built with two decks, and are known as "tweendeckers", owing to the 'tweendeck (between deck) located between the top (open) deck and the deck at the bottom of the hold. In some cargo vessels, this 'tweendeck can be removed where large or outsize cargoes are to be accommodated in the holds. In 'tweendeckers, each cargo hold can be split in two different sub-compartments: Between the main deck and the tweendeck, there is the tweendeck space (or upper cargo hold) while beneath the tweendeck there is the main cargo hold (or lower cargo hold). Tweendeckers face two main advantages against the single decker vessels: (a) they are equipped with more individual cargo compartments and thus they can carry several different cargoes, which can be kept separate from each other so as to avoid contamination and (b) they can accommodate higher tiers of bagged/baled cargoes with sharing their heavy weight in two different decks. At the same time, tweendecks can be retractable and fold against the sides of the hold so as to facilitate the load of bulk commodities into single holds. Modern general cargo ships are also equipped with special container fittings and are able to load containers. So nowadays the general cargo vessels are more accurately called "multi-purpose" vessels. General cargo vessels are equipped with gears with sufficient capacity (about 30–40 tons Safe Working Load – SWL) able to handle containers and other general cargoes.

In spite of the lack of containers used, a wide array of goods is still successfully stowed within a break bulk ship and transported across oceans. This is perhaps the most important feature of this type of a cargo ship. But even while standardised containers are not utilised, there are other storage mediums that are utilised, in case required.

These cargo storing mediums include pallets – which is a movable platform upon which the cargo can be placed. While unloading the cargo from the vessel, the pallets are unloaded with the help of cranes. Along with pallets, casks and barrels, drums and rugged boxes are also extensively used to store the cargo within them after being stored in the bulk carrier. In the case of pallets, casks and rugged boxes not being utilised, the cargo is directly put into the vessel without any medium to contain it.

This is perhaps the biggest disadvantage of a break bulk vessel as compared to a **shipping container** vessel as the latter ensure absolute surety of quantity and quality for the stored cargo. Since the cargo is piled directly, there is a very high chance of it being stolen or filched in case thorough attention is not paid to the stored cargo. Similarly, there are also chances that due to weather and climatic conditions, the cargo might be unfit for utilisation or consumption.

Cargo can be loaded under deck, on deck or between decks (tweendeck) which many of the break bulk ships have as part of their overall construction.

In a break bulk or multi-purpose vessel:

- Cargoes may belong to various customers;
- No dedicated berth or terminal required;
- Can operate from any free berth.

Concerning lifting equipment, break bulk ships have two categories:

1. **Gearless** – meaning the ship doesn't have its own cranes and/or other cargo handling equipment which means these ships can only berth at a terminal which has the required cargo handling equipment.
2. **Geared** – meaning the has its own cranes and/or other cargo handling equipment which means these ships can call at any suitable berth at the port for cargo operations.

Also when compared to a container ship, the loading and unloading operations of the cargo is also quite tricky and difficult to carry out. The process is highly time-consuming, whilst in case of the latter vessels, the loading and unloading operations are able to be carried out much faster. Also since the cargo is merely piled within the vessel, after unloading a particular batch of cargo, the whole vessel needs to be cleansed so that the next haul of cargo can be stored. Lack of thorough cleaning would result in unnecessary commingling, which could cause qualitative problems to the stored cargo.

This type of ship works very well in those docks and ports which are not technologically advanced. Alternatively, the break bulk ships can also be used as intermediary carriers to transport the cargo between larger vessels and ports which have shallower entryways.

Break bulk cargo ships still form a vital element in the shipping sector. Though their usage might have declined, there is question about their redundancy in the everyday maritime scheme of affairs. As such, it has been well speculated that the future of these vessels is very much safe, without any chances of them being made redundant.

Break bulk ships range from 2,000 dwt to 40,000 dwt, but in general they are classed in two types:

- handysize – 10,000–49,000 dwt, draught 10.2 metres, average LOA (Length Overall) 179.9 metres, Beam 28.4 metres; and
- handymax/supramax – 50,000–60,000 dwt, draught 12.2 metres, LOA 199 metres, Beam 32.2 metres.

Handysize is a naval architecture term for smaller bulk and break bulk carriers with up to 50,000 deadweight tonnes, although there is no official definition in terms of exact tonnages. Handysize is also sometimes used to refer to the span of up to 60,000 tons, with the vessels above 35,000 tonnes referred to as handymax or supramax.

Their small size allows handysize vessels to enter smaller ports to pick up cargoes, and because in most cases they are "geared" – i.e. fitted with cranes – they can often load and discharge cargoes at ports which lack cranes or other cargo handling systems. Compared to larger bulk carriers, handysizes carry a wider variety of cargo types. These include steel products, grain, metal ores, phosphate, cement, logs, woodchips and other types of so-called "break bulk cargo". They are numerically the most common size of bulk carrier, with nearly 2,000 units in service totalling about 43 million tons.

Handysize break bulk carriers are built mainly by shipyards in Japan, South Korea, China, Vietnam, the Philippines and India, though a few other countries also have the capacity to build such vessels. Some of the first postwar pioneering break bulk handysize vessels were the result of the famed Algonquin design of vessel produced by the famous British naval engineer George T. R. Campbell, and were built at the IHI yard at Yokohama, Japan, with a 14,000 deadweight tonnage, the first such vessel being the "Freedom" class *Chian Captain*. Many more such vessels were to follow, and they were the competitors to the equally-famous SD14 14,000 dwt break bulk vessels built by the British shipbuilding firm Austin & Pickersgill at their Sunderland yard. The most common industry-standard specification handysize bulker is now about 32,000 deadweight metric tonnes on a summer draught of about 10 metres (33 feet), and features five cargo holds with hydraulically operated hatch covers, with four 30 metric ton cranes for cargo handling. Some handysizes are also fitted with stanchions to enable logs to be loaded in stacks on deck. Such vessels are often referred to as "handy loggers". Despite multiple recent orders for new ships, the handysize sector still has the highest average age profile of the major bulk carrier sectors.

Today, most handysize vessels operate within regional trade routes. These ships are capable of travelling to small ports with length and draught restrictions, as well as lacking the infrastructure for cargo loading and unloading. They are used to carry small bulk cargoes, often in parcel size where individual cargo holds may have a different commodity. Their dry bulk cargo includes iron ore, coal, cement, phosphate, finished steel products, wooden logs, fertiliser, and grains to name a few. However, they have become increasingly important in the Project Cargo trades, where materials and products too large to be loaded into containers which are destined for major projects such as power stations or offshore Oil and Gas installations can be shipped as outsize cargoes on such vessels.

Handymax and **supramax** are naval architecture terms for the larger bulk carriers in the handysize class. They can be used for larger quantities of break bulk cargo, but in general they are more commonly used for the carriage of bulk cargoes, mainly homogeneous in nature. Handysize class consists of supramax (50,000 to 60,000 dwt), handymax (40,000 to 50,000 dwt), and Handy (<40,000 dwt). The ships are used for less voluminous cargoes, and different cargoes can be carried in different holds. Larger capacities for dry bulk include panamax, capesize and Very Large ore carriers (VLOCs) and chinamax.

A handymax ship is typically 150–200 metres (492–656 feet) in length, though certain bulk terminal restrictions, such as those in Japan, mean that many handymax ships are just under 190 metres (623 feet) in overall length. Modern handymax and supramax designs are typically 52,000 58,000 dwt in size, have five cargo holds and four cranes of around 30 tonnes working load, making it easier to use in ports with limited infrastructure. The average speed depends on size and age.

The cost of building a handymax vessel is driven by the laws of supply and demand. In early 2007 the cost building a handymax was around $20 million. As the global economy boomed, the cost doubled to over $40 million, as demand for vessels of all sizes exceeded available yard capacity. After the Global Economic Crisis in 2009, the cost decreased to $20M. As of 2018, the average price for a handymax vessel was £23 million.

Freight rates

Freight rates for break bulk cargoes are worked out on the basis of freight ton or revenue ton, which means freight is charged on the volume (CBM) or weight (MT) of the cargo whichever is higher. One of the most common questions often asked is "how to calculate CBM and freight ton", specially by those clients who get charged per freight ton or revenue ton.

First, CBM stands for **C**u**B**ic **M**etre. This is the most common unit used for the measurement of volumetric cargo. Metric Tons refer to the weight of cargo (1 Metric Ton = 1000 Kilograms).

Freight ton or revenue ton is derived by calculating the weight or volume of the cargo and the freight is charged based on whichever is higher.

When you have the dimensions of the package, first of all convert the measurement into metres.

Normally dimensions are in Length x Width x Height.

If for example the dimensions of a cargo crate is:

3.2 x 1.2 x 2.2 metres then the CBM is simply 3.2 x 1.2 x 2.2 = 8.448 CBM.

As mentioned above, if the rate is quoted as for example US$12/freight ton and the weight of the package is 1200 kgs = 1.2 tons, then the freight rate for this will be:

8.448 cbm x US$12 = US$101.376 or
1.2 tons x US$12 = US$14.4

Since the CBM rate is higher, the freight rate of US$101.376 will apply.

CHAPTER 2

The globalisation of break bulk

There is little doubt that the introduction and subsequent domination of the shipping container enabled the massive expansion of worldwide trade and the rise of globalisation. What is often overlooked is the instrumental role that break bulk shipping played in this global revolution, carrying out-of-gauge, heavy and Project Cargoes to the new production centres in Asia. It has also provided operators of an ever-increasing number of far-flung offshore Oil and Gas fields with the means to extract the liquid and gaseous gold to fuel the new factories.

Break bulk is a broad term used to describe any cargo that does not fit into the standardised form of the rectangular box. While there are striking examples of remarkable heavy load and semi-submersible vessels that carry incredibly vast and heavy cargoes, this segment actually represents a smaller portion of break bulk cargo operations. Think of industrial components, plant, machinery, cranes, as well as wood, aluminium rolls, timber products, iron and steel, to name but a few. The publication details and discusses eleven break bulk cargo categories, comprising over 200 types of commodity.

The operating model of many break bulk shipping companies remains that of traditional tramping, carried out on a global scale. While this may conjure images in one's mind of decrepit, rusty, sea-beaten vessels operating in regions forgotten by the rest of the world, this is far from the case! The current fleet is expanding through the introduction of modern, sophisticated and highly versatile vessels which can perform a variety of functions all the while being operated by highly professional and well-organised, well-equipped carriers.

The break bulk business is global. The nature of *ad hoc* shipping means that although vessels may be owned and operated from one specific country or region such as Europe, they will be operated in many areas of the world, depending upon the nature of the contract they are fulfilling. *Ad hoc* charter shipping means that a vessel must be available to go to any port worldwide where it is required to load a cargo destined for another specific port, regardless of location. In this respect, the globalisation of the break bulk sector has resulted in a greater need for efficiency and cost-effectiveness in the sector, with the need to have vessels available for *ad*

 DOI: 10.4324/9781003256359-3

hoc charter as and when required. Forward planning in terms of *ad hoc* cargo management is nevertheless required, as charter rates have a propensity to fluctuate on a daily basis, as shown by the Baltic Dry Index. That said, the importance of Project Cargo management prevails greatly in the present world of global break bulk shipping, and this means that cargo planning is increasingly important depending upon the size and quantities of the cargoes concerned, and how many shipments will be required. This also means that a vessel based in Germany or the Netherlands may be required at comparatively short notice to ship cargoes to and from areas such as the Far East or West Africa on an *ad hoc* basis depending upon the need for such shipments.

Studies

The Dutch organisation Dynamar is one of the key analysts of the break bulk sector, and publishes a series of reports and studies concerning the market. Dynamar's third break bulk study builds on the structure laid out in its previous editions, with an emphasis on the current market situation and the industry's prospects. Analysis of the main break bulk (including Ro/Ro, project and heavy-lift/load) operators, the capabilities of the current world fleet and orderbook, descriptions of trades and shifting market trends form the backbone of the study. The fifth study, carried out in 2019, consolidates this further and provides updated information on the state of the global break bulk vessel fleets.

It once again provides the popular rankings of the top break bulk, Ro/Ro and Heavy Load operators by deadweight capacity, followed by similar rankings of the largest Container, Reefer and Vehicle carriers – their principle competitors. Furthermore, there are profiles on 40 of the most important players in the industry. For each company, its existing fleet and orderbook by vessel-type is extensively detailed in terms of number of ships, average age, deadweight, heavy-lift capacity, container space, ramp and semi-submersible capabilities.

As perhaps would be expected, there have been notable changes in our ranking of the Top 25 operators in comparison to our 2010 study. Some operators have seen their fleet capacity increase, some decrease, some have appeared and eight have even disappeared altogether. Three years may not be long, it appears to be time enough for the previous ranking to seem almost unrecognisable with, among others, eight "new" entries. In all, only Gearbulk and Coscol have retained their positions at the top of the pile, occupying 1st and 2nd place respectively.

From overcapacity to control

The 2007/2008 break bulk boom induced many operators to splash out ordering a reported 210 multi-purpose ships during these two years. Another seven were added in 2009, when the worldwide financial and economic crisis engulfed everything afloat. This optimism was reflected in the Top 25's orderbook, reaching 34% of their operated deadweight in early 2010.

Despite some known cancellations, most of these ships, in addition to unreported and previously ordered newbuildings, were delivered in 2010/2012 – no less than 400 units in total. These same relatively meagre years have clearly caused break bulk carriers to act more prudently, ordering just 60 multi-purpose units over the past three years. As of January 2013, the deadweight share of the Top 25 orderbook was a very reasonable 10% of the existing fleet.

Looking at the total number of non-cellular general cargo ships as detailed in the 2015 Dynamar report, including multi-purpose and open-hatch-gantry-crane units, around 20% or 10.4 million deadweight tons comprised vessels older than 25 years. The orderbook as at 2015 represented just 6.6 million dwt, while according to the 2019 report, the orderbook stood at 236 units, or just 5% of the operating fleet. In simple terms, the world break bulk fleet is contracting to levels which can be seen as more manageable according to global demand. This contraction amounts to some four million tons deadweight. That said, since 2010 a very large number of elderly general cargo ships built before 1990 have disappeared from the market. In total, 18 million deadweight tonnage has either been scrapped, wrecked or is simply no longer fit for cargo operations. Measures such as the 2020 IMO Directive concerning maritime vessel emissions may well increase this contraction further.

At the same time, it should once again be emphasised that ships built during the last five years in particular are much more productive and fuel efficient than the vessels they replace. Combined, all operators discussed in Dynamar's break bulk III report of 2015 deployed some 400 vessels built in 2008 or thereafter.

Another look at the relevant global fleet reveals that there has been an explosion in the number of vessels built since the turn of the century; through to 2012 over 2,150 ships comprising 28.5 million dwt has hit the water.

What is also impressive is the growing ability of the onboard cranes of the average modern multi-purpose/project ship. In this respect, the 25 largest operators deploy over 500 ships with heavy lift capabilities of over 100 tons, of which nearly 160 can hoist loads of more than 500 tons. They have another 30 ships on order with lifting capacities of between 500 and a herculean 3,000 tons! These vessels are ideal for moving outsize and heavy cargoes, especially with regard to Project Cargoes, where massive items of equipment need to be moved across the globe. Indeed, ever larger and heavier modules continue to drive up the demand for heavier on board cranes and vice versa, saving the project engineers' on-site assembly costs. The 21 vessels operating and on order which are able to handle lifts of over 1,000 tons are controlled by just four different companies, thus making the market much more niche in terms of specialist activities.

Semi-submersible power

It is the semi-submersible vessel that can carry the largest, heaviest and most imaginative loads, often weighing tens of thousands of tons and initially not designed with the intention of transportation by way of a ship! With its 1 January 2013 fleet of 23 open and closed stern semi-submersibles and dock-ships, the Dutch company Dockwise, having acquired its compatriot rival Fairstar, is the undisputed leader in this segment. It took delivery of the world's largest such ship, having an unobstructed open deck space of over 1,300 square metres and capable of carrying large container cranes to their destination at new container port projects. Such vessels are also capable of carrying offshore oil rigs, by way of partially submerging to the extent that the installation can be floated aboard, then allowing the vessel to rise by blowing the ballast out of its tanks, thus enabling it to sail as normal.

However, as in the multi-purpose/heavy-lift/project segment, Asian carriers are making significant inroads into the semi-submersible scene too. CCCC, Cosco Heavy Transport (a joint venture with Dutch NMA), STX Pan Ocean, TPI Mega Line, ZMPC Shipping and another four single-ship operators, all from China and South Korea are all vying for semi-submersible business, competing with six companies from Europe.

It is perhaps no coincidence that South Korean, Japanese and Chinese engineers and EPC (Engineering, Procurement, and Construction) companies have largely taken over from Western technicians and contractors in not only the Middle East region. Moreover, the Far East is increasingly developing as the source of project materials, rather than as a destination alone. The ASEAN area of South-East Asia alone is providing huge potential for both construction of materials as well as being seen as a transit point for large projects located in or close to the region, especially in the offshore Oil and Gas sector.

Western Australia is the present major area for vast projects, all related to this country and continent's efforts to become the world's second largest supplier of Liquefied Natural Gas (LNG) by 2015. Many multi-purpose/project ships and heavy load carriers of all kinds are very busy transporting materials for the construction of processing plants and the related new infrastructure (ports, roads and the like). Mining is big Australian business too, although this sector is taken care of in terms of maritime trade by the large capesize bulk carriers, much of which supply the large Chinese consumer markets for coal and iron ore, the two largest bulk commodities worldwide.

In addition to takeovers such as witnessed in the semi-submersible segment, break bulk shipping has also seen mergers (Intermarine with ScanTrans), bankruptcies (Beluga) and newcomers (Hansa Heavy Lift), these and others all affecting the landscape in this vibrant industry.

However, the current state and outlook of the break bulk, project and heavy-lift market remains somewhat clouded in a lack of transparency. It sometimes appears that there are as many niches as there are operators. All of those niches, within which traditional general cargo behaves differently from projects, have their own dynamics and cycles. Because of this, therefore, there is no prevailing, overall market picture. What all break bulk operator segments have in common is their vicinity to the cargo.

It must be asked if the break bulk heydays of the mid-2000s will simply remain a distant memory. It must not be forgotten that nearly all shipping sectors were reaping the benefits of rapidly increasing demand, with the dry bulk, container and car carrier operators all keenly focused on their principle markets, offering little competition to the break bulk operators. This could, in reality, lead to a scenario in favour of the break bulk industry, and indeed increasing demand for Project Cargo transport would suggest this. Data for the years 2012 and 2019 have been compared for the purposes of this exercise, although the data of 2019 paints a rather better up-to-date picture of the state of the break bulk operators and their fleets, showing somewhat different data in terms of fleet sizes at the end of the decade compared with the beginning of the decade.

Overall, as at 2019 the current multi-purpose fleet consisted of 4,700 ships with total deadweight for 63 million tons. The fleet could broadly be split into two categories: vessels with ramps (Ro/Ro) and those without (Lo-lo). The order book, at 236 units or just 5% of the operating fleet, was considered modest and included all vessels delivered, or due for delivery in 2019.

Following the break bulk boom of the mid-2000s, there was a peak in production between 2007 and 2012, when more than 200 ships were delivered on an annual basis. Such levels had not been seen since 1985. However, since 2015, production decreased again to below a hundred units per year and in 2018 only 66 break bulk vessels were launched.

The 2019 multi-purpose orderbook, including open-hatch ships but excluding RO-RO, amounts to just 4.2% of the existing fleet. From 2009 to 2018, 1,577 vessels were built and 1,831 were scrapped, a clear sign of a diminishing fleet. Additionally, the 2020 IMO fuel sulphur regulation was likely to induce additional scrapping of vessels, especially those that were underused or redundant, or surplus to requirements.

It was anticipated in 2019 that as a result of this IMO regulation, about 2,500 elderly vessels built before 2,000 would be scrapped more quickly, thus reducing the overcapacity that had burdened the break bulk carrier market since the boom of 2005–2008. Indeed, instead of constructing vessels, capacity requirement at present is increasingly sought in the form of pooling vessel resources and other cooperative measures such as joint services.

However, the break bulk market is notorious for its lack of transparency – Dynamar's "BREAK BULK III: Operators, Fleets, Markets" report in particular provided better insight into this dynamic shipping sector, and this was followed up by Dynamar's BREAK BULK V (2019).

Top 10 break bulk operators ranked by deadweight capacity – vessels over 5,000 dwt – as of late December 2012.

Rank	Break bulk	Existing fleet			On Order		
	Operator	*Ships*	*Total dwt*	*Age*	*Ships*	*Total dwt*	*Dwt share*
1	Gearbulk Pool	48	2,182,000	1994	–	–	–
2	Coscol	85	1,805,000	1996	11	303,000	17%
3	BBC	131	1,465,000	2007	9	127,000	9%
4	Saga-Forest	27	1,311,000	2001	5	269,000	21%
5	Grieg Star	25	1,083,000	1994	–	–	–
6	Westfal-Larsen	21	961,000	1998	–	–	–
7	Spliethoff	50	799,000	2002	–	–	–
8	Clipper Projects	41	483,000	2003	2	36,000	8%
9	Chipolbrok	17	460,000	2002	–	–	–
10	Intermarine-ScanTrans	51	452,000	2006	2	20,000	4%
Top 10 Break bulk Operators		496	11,001,000	2001	29	755,000	6%

Source: Dynamar

The break bulk operators

Because of their large OHGC (Open Hatch Gantry Crane) vessels, forest products – very much a break bulk segment-carriers Gearbulk (1), Saga-Forest (4), Grieg Star (5) and Westfal-Larsen (6) take the top spots in this break bulk ranking.

Representing the ad hoc break bulk ("tramping") sector are BBC (3) of Leer/Germany, Dutch Spliethoff (7), Clipper Projects of Copenhagen (8) and recently merged Intermarine-ScanTrans (10) of the USA/Denmark. They deploy growing fleets of generally young, somewhat smaller, although ever growing multi-purpose/ heavy lift/project vessels with ever-higher crane capabilities.

Chinese/Polish semi-liner operator Chipolbrok has recently completed an extensive newbuilding program of 30,000-dwt vessels with a combined heavy lift capacity of 640 tons each.

Top 10 break bulk operators, ranked by lifting capacity – vessels over 100 tons lifting capacity – as of late December 2012

Rank	Carriers	Ships WITH HEAVY LIFT CAPACITY		
		Ships	*>100 tons*	*>500 tons*
1	BBC	131	126	36
2	Hansa Heavy Lift	19	19	13

(*Continued*)

(Continued)

Rank	*Carriers*	*Ships WITH HEAVY LIFT CAPACITY*		
		Ships	*>100 tons*	*>500 tons*
3	Intermarine-ScanTrans	51	41	15
4	Clipper Projects	41	41	0
5	Chipolbrok	17	17	10
6	Spliethoff	59	42	0
7	Coscol	85	27	4
8	Rickmers Linie	15	14	10
9	Hyundai MM	12	12	9
10	Austral Asia Line	5	5	5
Top 10 Break bulk Heavy Lift		435	344	102

Source: Dynamar

Of a total global break bulk fleet of 4,700 vessels as at 2019, the German company BBC Chartering & Logistics was the primary operator of break bulk vessels, with a total of 131 break bulk ships. Of these, 126 are equipped with cranes that can lift cargoes with an individual weight of over 100 tons, as opposed to the 2010 Dynamar review where there were just 76 vessels of this type in operation with the company. Vessel crane capacities range between 60 and 800 tons, with 320 tons being an average lifting capacity. As at 2015, compatriot operator Hansa Heavy Lift came second at a substantial distance with a total heavy lift capability of 16,000 tons on board of a much smaller number of ships: 19 units. Consequently, this Hamburg-based operator had a considerably higher average heavy lift capability of 840 tons. This is also much more than its predecessor Beluga's 320 tons reported in 2010. As at 2019, the aggregate Heavy lift market was dominated by BBC Chartering, while second place was taken by Zeamarine of Hamburg, followed by the Dutch Amsterdam-based operator Spliethoff, with vessel names ending in . . . *gracht*.

As at 2015, Intermarine (now including ScanTrans) remained in 3rd place in the heavy lift ranking of break bulk operators, although its current 370 tons average was lower than the 435 tons assessed in the previous 2010 report. In 2019, this position for aggregate heavy lift ranking was taken by Spliethoff, while for the average heavy lift ranking, the companies occupying the top three positions were HMM, whose four vessels headed the ranking with an average of 640 tons, followed by Chipolbrok with an average of 570 tons, and Singapore's AAL in third place with 470 tons.

The Dynamar studies provide great detail about break bulk and heavy lift ships, but it should be noted that this sector is extremely specialist, and in the present era revolves significantly around Project Cargoes, often related to port projects and the offshore Oil and Gas sector. Since these markets are by no means guaranteed as regular business, the break bulk and Project Cargo market is not necessarily stable or continuous, meaning the charter rates for the use of such vessels fluctuates significantly from year to year. However, such forms of marine transport are still a necessity, and in this respect, the break bulk and Project Cargo market is worth significant investment on the part of shipowners and charterers alike.

As of early March 2019, the ten largest operators, by deadweight, of multi-purpose-project-heavy-lift tonnage deployed a combined fleet of 476 ships with a total deadweight of 8,220,000 million tons and an aggregate lifting capability of 155,000 tons. The ships' average age was ten years.

In 2019, Dynamar B.V. collated the figures in its latest biennial "BREAK BULK – Operators, Fleets, Markets" publication (2019), and in general these figures show something in a reduction in fleet size across the board, reflecting the state of the fleets as at the end of 2018.

Existing fleets (March 2019)

DWT rank	*Multi-purpose operator*	*Ships*	*Total DWT*	*Average DWT/Vessel*	*Average age (Year build)*
1	BBC	144	1,844,000	12,800	2010
2	Cosco SSC	67	1,821,000	27,200	2009
3	Spliethoff	52	834,000	16,000	2006
4	Zeamarine	79	711,000	9,000	2009
5	AAL	24	656,000	27,300	2011
6	Chipolbrok	21	652,000	31,000	2009
7	Thorco	35	533,000	15,200	2013
8	Wagenborg	29	448,000	15,400	2010
9	MACS	13	395,000	30,400	2009
10	PACC Line	12	327,000	27,200	2006
TOTAL		**476**	**8,220,000**	**17,300**	**2009**

Source: Dynamar

The Orderbooks as at 2019 for these fleets are more limited, but still show fleet growth for some of the companies quoted. The 2019 Dynamar report illustrates as follows:

ORDERBOOK

Operator	*Ships*	*Total DWT*	*Average indiv DWT*	*Share*
BBC	2	25,000	12,300	1%
Spliethoff	6	108,000	18,000	13%
Zeamarine	3	42,000	14,000	6%
TOTAL	**11**	**174,700**	**15,900**	**2%**

Source: Dynamar

2019 Heavy lift top 10 operators

Compared with the 2012 figures, the Heavy lift market has also seen significant changes as at the 2019 database issued by Dynamar. The HL tables are as follows:

EXISTING FLEETS (MARCH 2019)

HL rank	*Multi-purpose operator*	*Ships*	*HL*	*Average HL*	*Average age (Year build)*
1	BBC	144	54,500	380	2010
2	Zeamarine	79	31,600	400	2009
3	Cosco SSC	67	19,400	290	2009
4	Chipolbrok	21	12,400	590	2009
5	Spliethoff	52	12,100	230	2006
6	AAL	24	11,300	470	2011
7	Thorco	35	6,100	170	2013
8	Wagenborg	29	3,800	130	2010
9	MACS	13	2,500	200	2008
10	PACC Line	12	1,300	110	2006
TOTAL		**476**	**154,900**	**330**	**2009**

Source: Dynamar

The combined heavy-lift capability ranking of the same ten multi-purpose operators as recorded at early March 2019 slightly differs. The 476 vessels have an aggregate on board lifting capability of 154,900 tons (up 5%) with a rounded average of 330 tons per ship, ranging between 30 tons (Zeamarine) and 1,400 tons (both BBC and Zeamarine).

With a total of 54,500 tons, average 380 tons, and a share of 35%, BBC Chartering remains the top carrier. Zeamarine, the joint venture between Intermarine and Zeaborne, including Rickmers Linie, takes second place with 31,600 tons, a share of 20%, but with a higher individual average of 400 tons. Lifting capacities per vessel range between 30 and 1,400 tons, constituting the widest capability spread of all top ten operators.

As with the break bulk fleets, the Heavy lift Orderbooks as at 2019 for these fleets are more limited, but still show fleet growth for some of the companies quoted. The 2019 Dynamar report illustrates as follows:

ORDERBOOK

Operator	*Ships*	*Total HL*	*Average HL*	*Share*
BBC	2	1,000	500	2%
Zeamarine	3	2,700	900	9%
Spliethoff	6	2,200	360	18%
TOTAL	**11**	**5,900**	**530**	**4%**

Source: Dynamar

As with the break Bulk operators, the same three operators (BBC Chartering, Zeamarine and Spliethoff) show orderbooks for new vessels. The main difference between these figures and the break bulk market share is that the Heavy lift order book accounts for a higher market share than does the break bulk orderbook market share.

A report issued by Dynamar in August 2019 added the emergence of two further operators in the key first and second positions in the tables of top break bulk operators in the later part of 2019. Dynamar compared the multi-purpose vessel operators based on the total deadweight tonnage of their fleets to determine which operator has the largest cargo capacity.

Dynamar's updated report of 2019 paints a rather less gloomy picture than had been anticipated. Previous doomsday reports of the demise of the break bulk sector, have, like Mark Twain's observations on his own life expectancy, have been somewhat exaggerated. Today, the Dynamar report incorporates the major brands of Rickmers Linie with its semi-liner services. Zeamarine is included with its tramp services, along with, *inter alia*, the commercial management of part of the Carisbrooke (UK) fleet and the chartering activities of the HC Group, MCC Marine and NPC Projects. In addition, the company is active in ship management and ship owning. Zeamarine had stated an objective of operating some 100 multipurpose ships by early 2019, although it was reported that as at the start of the fourth quarter 2019, that objective had not yet been achieved.

Because of its large open-hatch gantry crane vessels, which are way bigger than traditional multi-purpose vessels, the operator G2 Ocean took the top position by a large margin. According to Dynamar, the joint venture of Norwegian shipping companies Gearbulk and Griegstar operated in 2019 a fleet of 89 vessels with a total deadweight of 4.8 million tonnes. G2 Ocean itself, however, stated that its total fleet comprises 130 vessels, of which 110 vessels are of the open hatch type. The fleet consisted of a combination of owned vessels and ships on long-term charters. This is standard practice worldwide, the break bulk operators owning core fleets for essential shipping services, and chartering in further vessels according to demand, usually on a time charter basis. Either way, G2 Ocean's fleet is significantly larger than that of runner-up Saga Welco, which has a total capacity of 2.6 million tonnes divided over 52 vessels.

From the third position down, the break bulk top 10 showed a more familiar picture with BBC Chartering leading the group of traditional multi-purpose and heavy-lift shipping companies. The German carrier sits in the third position with a total deadweight of almost 1.9 million tonnes. BBC's fleet comprises no less than 145 vessels with an average deadweight of 12,900 tonnes, clearly showing the difference with G2 Ocean's fleet which has an average vessel size of 54,100 tonnes.

BBC Chartering is followed by Cosco SSC, Zeamarine, Spliethoff, AAL Shipping, Chipolbrok, Swire Shipping and Wagenborg. Looking at the fleet's multi-purpose vessel operators, Cosco SSC, AAL Shipping and Chipolbrok own significantly larger vessels than their direct competitors with an average ship size of 27,800, 29,500 and 31,100 tonnes, respectively. Some of the increase is due to the operator Saga Welco expanding its fleet of forest product carriers. It is likely that the next Dynamar report, to be issued in 2021, may well show further significant changes owing to the state of the break bulk and heavy lift markets in the wake of the SARS-CoV pandemic.

A 2020 report by Christa Sys, Professor of Transport, Logistics and Ports at the University of Antwerp, showed that present challenges concerning the SARS-CoV pandemic and the increased use of technology are influencing the future of the global break bulk sector. Global crises such as the COVID-19 pandemic and megatrends including globalisation, changing demographics, disruptive technologies, sustainability and geopolitical developments are shaping the future of break bulk. As a result, the break bulk labour market must change dramatically in response to these challenges.

The next generation of break bulk professionals will have to be much more knowledgeable in terms of technology, and must be able to respond to advances in technology. Technology is changing every facet of the break bulk sector. This is no longer simply a question of loading materials on to a vessel at one port and unloading them at the port of arrival using manual or mechanical methods. Issues such as the digitalisation of asset management processes, for example, require a level of familiarity with software interfaces – at least enough to allow for fast, intuitive learning. The advent of Big Data will require a level of analytical and interpretive sophistication the likes of which has never been necessary for the average break bulk professional.

The main issue about technology is that it is exponential. The more that advances are made, the faster they are as a consequence. That is why the break bulk professional of the future will also need a specific mindset, one that is conducive and adaptive to learning, thus enabling growth and development.

Much more education and training will be required for the next-generation break bulk professional, and therefore it will be the people who believe they can continue to learn well into their careers, into middle and even old age, who will have the right mindset to undertake the continued development necessary to maintain pace with the shifting landscape.

The final two pre-requisites for the next break bulk generation are commitment and consistency. For the next generation to carry out, and to be, what is necessary to keep the sector afloat during such choppy conditions, they need to have the desire to achieve this throughout their careers as a form of motivation. According to the ancient Greek philosopher Aristotle, "excellence is not an act, it is a habit". Without commitment, one will never be able to start doing what is necessary; without consistency, one will never accomplish what one set out to achieve.

The main requirements for this in order to equip the next generation of break bulk professionals are a working environment that supports these things and an employer that invests in their skills. There is no doubt that disruptions such as the coronavirus pandemic will have a lasting effect on how people want to and should work, so a flexible and agile working environment will also be a must. However, the virus pandemic has changed certain cultures to the extent that it has been established that certain support activities can be carried out by individuals working on a distance basis, as long as they are in communication with everyone else involved in the project.

People in the industry who are already adopting and embodying these practices, either themselves or in the working environment they provide for their staff, are to be seen as beneficial to the break bulk sector. Such practices, including the use of communication technology, have meant that costs can be reduced, especially concerning support and administrative functions, while maintaining the efficiency of the operation. In the break bulk sector, any measure that reduces costs and makes the operation more efficient must be welcomed. The global break bulk sector has to change according to the times if it is to remain a major influence in the marine business, and must adapt to these new challenges, including the increased use of technology.

CHAPTER 3

Break bulk cargo

The introduction and subsequent dominance of the shipping container from the late 1950s facilitated the massive expansion of worldwide trade and the rise of globalisation. However, what is often overlooked is the equally-important role that break bulk shipping played in this global revolution, carrying out-of-gauge, heavy and Project Cargoes to the new production centres in Asia, and therefore changing from a pure general cargo function to one of specialist handling. Break bulk shipping has also provided operators of an ever-increasing number of distant offshore Oil and Gas fields with the means of extracting large quantities of oil to satisfy the insatiable demands of the global economy, by transporting a wide range of equipment and materials to these offshore projects. Break bulk shipping existed long before the concept of the container, and indeed it has been in existence since biblical times, as it was the only means of shipping cargoes from one port to another, as eulogised by John Masefield's famous poem "Cargoes". Only with the introduction of the standardised 20′ and 40′ metal containers in the late 1950s and 1960s, especially through the pioneering work of the former US trucker Malcom McLean and the shipping line that he created, namely Sea-Land, did break bulk shipping lose its global dominance. However, in an era of specialised project management throughout the world, break bulk shipping has found a renaissance and a niche in global shipping.

In shipping, break bulk cargo or general cargo is a term that covers a great variety of goods that do not fit inside a standardised metal container, such as is carried by conventional container vessel. Such cargoes must be loaded aboard vessel individually, and not in multimodal containers nor in bulk as with oil or the dry bulk commodities such as iron ore, coal or grain. Ships which carry this sort of cargo are often called general cargo ships, and are generally of the handysize or handymax/supramax variety. The term *break bulk* derives from the phrase breaking bulk, namely the extraction of a portion of the cargo of a ship or the beginning of the unloading process from the ship's holds. Break bulk cargoes are mainly transported in bags, boxes, crates, drums, or barrels, and unit loads of items secured to a pallet or skid are also used. Furthermore, many cargoes are extremely heavy, or extremely voluminous, and cannot fit on board a conventional cargo vessel. They require the use of specialised vessels, often of a semi-submersible nature to float the cargo off

 DOI: 10.4324/9781003256359-4

into the water, or vessels which can accommodate such loads on specially-designed open decks.

The term *break bulk* derives from the phrase **breaking bulk** – the extraction of a portion of the cargo of a ship or the beginning of the unloading process from the ship's holds. These goods may not be in shipping containers. Break bulk cargo is transported in bags, boxes, crates, drums, or barrels. Unit loads of items secured to a pallet or skid are also used. A break-in-bulk point is a place where goods are transferred from one mode of transport to another, for example the docks where goods transfer from ship to truck or vice versa.

In present-day terms, break bulk cargo is an item that does not fit into a container due to its large size or weight and needs to be loaded individually. It can, however, be loaded on an open-top container and moved from the top by a crane, or a flat-rack container and loaded from the top or side. Conversely, it is more likely that such cargoes are loaded individually aboard vessel and either secured on deck or in the holds, depending upon the size and volume of the cargo. The term break bulk comes from breaking bulk – extracting the portion of the cargo. It can be an oversized machine, construction or mining equipment, manufacturing materials and more. While moving goods in containers is considered to be the cheapest option of transport, in case of oversized equipment break bulk rates are still cheaper than the costs of disassembling, packing, shipping, unpacking and re-assembling of the machine.

Break bulk was the most common form of cargo for most of the history of shipping. Since the late 1960s the volume of break bulk cargo has declined dramatically worldwide as containerisation has grown. Moving cargo on and off ship in containers is much more efficient, allowing ships to spend less time in port. Break bulk cargo also suffered from greater theft and damage.

Although cargo of this sort can be delivered straight from a truck or train onto a ship, the most common way is for the cargo to be delivered to the dock in advance of the arrival of the ship and for the cargo to be stored in warehouses, namely transit sheds, also known as temporary storage. When the ship arrives at port, the cargo is then taken from the warehouse to the quay and then lifted on board by either the ship's gear (derricks or cranes) or by the dockside cranes. The discharge of the ship is the reverse of the loading operation, with the cargo held in temporary storage until it has been cleared through Customs.

Loading and discharging by break bulk is labour-intensive. The cargo is brought to the quay next to the ship and then each individual item is lifted on board separately. Some items such as sacks or bags can be loaded in batches by using a sling or cargo net and others such as cartons can be loaded onto trays before being lifted on board. Once on board each item must be stowed separately.

Before any loading takes place, any signs of the previous cargo are removed. The holds are swept, washed if necessary and any damage to them repaired. Dunnage, i.e. loose material used as cushioning, is laid ready for the cargo or is simply put in bundles ready for the stevedores to lay out as the cargo is loaded.

There are many sorts of break bulk cargo but among them are:

- Bagged cargoes, such as sugar, fertilisers, coffee;
- Baled cargoes;
- Barrels and casks;
- Corrugated boxes;
- Wooden shipping containers;
- Drums;
- Paper reels;
- Steel coils;
- Automotive vehicles, including rail locomotives and carriages;
- Steel girders;
- Unit loads such as boilers.

The above cargoes require specific loading and stowage, mainly using "Dunnage", which is any materials used to cushion the cargoes from surrounding obstacles and vessel fittings, as well as separating the cargoes form the hard surfaces of the vessel, such as the decks and sides of the vessel.

Bagged cargo

Bagged cargo (e.g. coffee in sacks) is stowed on double dunnage and kept clear of the ship's sides and bulk heads. Bags are kept away from pillars and stanchions by covering it with matting or waterproof paper.

Baled goods

Baled goods are stowed on single dunnage at least 50 mm (1.97 in) thick. The bales must be clean with all the bands intact. Stained or oily bales are rejected. All fibres can absorb oil and are liable to spontaneous combustion. As a result, they are kept clear of any new paintwork. Bales close to the deckhead are covered to prevent damage by dripping sweat.

Barrels and casks

Wooden barrels are stowed on their sides on "beds" of dunnage which keeps the middle of the side (the bilge) off the deck, and they are stowed with the bung, i.e. the stopper, at the top. To prevent movement, wedges called quoins are put in on top of the "beds". Barrels should be stowed fore and aft and not athwart ships. Once the first tier has been loaded the next tier of barrels fits into the hollows between the barrels, this is known as stowing "bilge and cantline". Barrels which are also known as casks or tuns are primarily use for transporting liquids such as wine, water, brandy, whiskey and even oil. They are usually built in spherical shape to make it easier to roll and have less friction when changing direction.

Corrugated boxes

Corrugated boxes are stowed on a good layer of dunnage and kept clear of any moisture. Military and weather-resistant grades of corrugated fibreboard are available. They are not overstowed with anything other than similar boxes. They are frequently loaded on pallets to form a unit load; if so, the slings that are used to load the cargo are frequently left on to facilitate discharge.

Wooden shipping containers

Wooden boxes or crates are stowed on double dunnage in the holds and single dunnage in the 'tweendecks. Heavy boxes are given bottom stowage. The loading slings are often left on to aid discharge.

Drums

Metal drums are stowed on end with dunnage between tiers, in the longitudinal space of the ship.

Paper reels

Reels or rolls are generally stowed on their sides and care is taken to make sure they are not crushed.

Motor vehicles

Motor vehicles, such as trucks or cars, or even rail locomotives, are lifted on board and then secured using lashings. Great care is taken to prevent damage. Vehicles are prepared by removing hazardous liquids (fuel, etc.). This is in contrast to roll on-roll-off (RO-RO) vessels where vehicles are driven on and off the ship under their own power. An example of the handling of such items has been the shipment of hovercraft from the production site on the south coast of England to Canada. The hovercraft were loaded into the hold of a general cargo ship after a large quantity of dunnage had previously been loaded into the hold to avoid damage incurred by the side and skirt of the hovercraft bumping into the side and the bottom of the ship's hold. Suffice to say, the hovercraft arrived in Canada totally intact and undamaged.

Steel girders

Any long heavy items are stowed fore and aft. If they are stowed athwart ships they are liable to shift if the ship rolls heavily and pierce the side of the ship. These include steel girders, steel pipes, oilfield drilling equipment etc.

An example of how this can go fearfully wrong is a case experienced by the author during a business trip to a major oil company in Angola. The oil company had taken delivery of a large consignment of drill pipes from Europe, only to find that on delivery the pipes were severely damaged. Further investigation showed that the pipes had been incorrectly and insecurely lashed in the vessel's hold at the time of loading. The vessel encountered the storms of the Bay of Biscay en route to Angola, and as a result, the badly-secured pipes rolled and bashed into each other, resulting in heavy damage incurred to the entire load. The shipping contract had been arranged on an FOB basis, meaning that the oil company was responsible for arranging the load through the shipping line. However, as the load was consolidated with other cargoes destined for the Oil and Gas sector, the oil company had left the loading responsibilities to the shipping agents in the European port of loading, on the assumption that the agency would supervise the loading of the vessel and ensure the security of the load. This appeared not to have been done, or at least, the shipping company had not ensured that the cargo was loaded correctly according to the shipping instructions. Given that the loading had been negligent, the oil company had the right to sue the shipping line for compensation, and the author was involved in directing the case. The shipping company eventually admitted responsibility for the damage, and duly paid the oil company the appropriate compensation based on the terms of the Charter Party Bill of Lading and the Hague-Visby Rules. As a result, the author also had to deliver an *ad hoc* training seminar to the logistics staff of the oil company on the subject of break bulk cargo management, an area in which he is well-versed because of his work with the offshore Oil and Gas industry.

Break bulk shipments

Better known as Less-than Container Load (or LCL) shipment, break bulk shipment is the most likely option to be used by new exporters, since your first orders are likely to be small. This is because your customer wants to test your product in his or her market before committing to a large quantity, such as a full container load or more. To control the expense of small-quantity shipment, find a transport company who specialises in break bulk, goods that must be loaded individually.

Naturally, when the exporter is shipping a small trial order and hoping for repeat business, it will be to their advantage to control their customer's costs by getting the best rate possible. When shipping LTL, the shipper will need to take extra care in packing and marking their cartons. Break bulk shipments suffer from greater theft and damage. They are commonly packed using the following materials:

- **Pallets (or skids)** – Wood or plastic pallets must be durable enough to be stacked on racks and re-used numerous times. One should never let cartons overhang a pallet, as the whole load might collapse. It is wise to inquire with the transportation company to see whether it is necessary to make an official statement that the pallets or skids being used are using are free of insects and pests, as in the CITES certification. The same holds true for importing. The importer should request that the supplier provides a statement indicating the packing crates and wooden pallets have been treated to prevent infestation.

- **Slip sheets** – These sheets are usually made of fibreboard or plastic. They must be strong enough for the forklift operator to clamp onto and pull the cargo to the point of loading. Slip sheets cost less than pallets and eliminate the expense of transporting pallets back to the shipper for reuse. Cartons placed on slip sheets must be cross-stacked, shrink-wrapped or secured with extra-strength strapping.
- **Crates** – Wood crates are still popular with some shippers due to their strength and resistance to humidity, at any temperature and any point in transit. It is necessary to check with a logistics specialist to make sure that the country of destination accepts the type of crate being used. Some countries are requiring environmentally safe crates and others may ban wood altogether due to pest concerns.

All onboard packing materials should be recyclable or reusable. Although they have little value in themselves, they are vital to the loading process, and should be retained and re-used wherever possible. However, it is also prudent to use the minimum amount of material necessary to protect the product, owing to the availability of packing materials. Different cargoes require different forms of packing or dunnage. In general, wooden materials such as planks or beams are pliable and can be used to cushion larger items being shipped. Even empty or used pallets can be used for dunnage purposes if required. If used for actual cargoes, pallets, slip sheets and crates are loaded in the following manner:

- Bulk loading by machine or hand (with bulk commodities, for example);
- Hand-loading individual shipping containers, with or without pallets;
- Unit loading of palletised or slip sheet stacks into containers with forklifts.

Break bulk vs Containerisation

In international ocean freight shipping, there are generally two options for transporting cargo: containers or break bulk. The difference between both options is simply that break bulk refers to individual or loose materials that are loaded, shipped and unloaded from the ship, and containers refers to a storage unit where all of the materials stay. Twenty-foot or 40-foot containers are available, as well as different containers such as **flat rack**, open top and refrigerated for temperature-sensitive shipments. The containers are usually stacked at the terminals and on the **vessels**. This makes the practice of transporting containers easier to ship because it is streamlined. Shippers can also receive ocean freight shipping quotes online for shipping containers.

The disadvantage with break bulk begins with food shipments that need to be refrigerated; reefer containers are temperature-controlled and not break bulk. For break bulk, the whole of the vessel hold area has to be refrigerated. Since the items with break bulk are loose, there is also the safety issue of having broken or stolen goods. A vast amount of personnel and resources must be utilised in order to make break bulk shipments work. That is why shipping by container has far surpassed break bulk shipping. There is some hope for break bulk however. Some products, like large machines, cannot go into containers and have to be transported as break bulk. Some **ports** are not modernised for containers yet, and break bulk can be used there. In addition, there is also some confidence that the break bulk industry will make a comeback this year. It is wise to contact a local freight forwarder to discuss about container shipping vs. break bulk.

The biggest disadvantage with break bulk is that it requires more resources at the wharf at both ends of the transport – longshoremen (the US term for stevedores), loading cranes, warehouses, transport vehicles – and often takes up more dock space due to multiple vessels carrying multiple loads of break bulk cargo. Indeed, the decline of break bulk did not start with containerisation; rather, the advent of tankers and bulk carriers reduced the need for transporting liquids in barrels and grains in sacks. Such tankers and carriers use specialised ships and shore facilities to deliver larger amounts of cargo to the dock and effect faster turnarounds with fewer personnel once the ship arrives; however, they do require large initial investments in ships, machinery, and training, slowing their spread to areas where funds to overhaul port operations and/or training for dock personnel in the handling of cargo on the newer vessels may not be available. As the modernisation of ports and shipping fleets spreads across the world, the advantages of using containerisation and specialised ships over break bulk has hastened the overall decline of break bulk operations around the world. In all, the new systems have reduced costs as well as spillage, loss and turnaround times; in the case of containerisation, damage and pilfering as well.

Break bulk shipping can be more expensive than containerisation. Oversized or overweight cargo takes up more space on a freighter than containerised goods that are stacked on top of each other. It also costs more in terms of labour. In most cases, break bulk cargo requires more stevedores than a shipping container does. In some cases, specialised warehouses, including transit sheds, need to store the break bulk cargo until it is cleared through Customs. Like warehouses, ships and ports also need special equipment to move break bulk cargo.

There are also security and safety issues with break bulk cargo. Break bulk goods are generally bagged, strapped or bundled for shipping. These items can break or burst, allowing the shipment to be damaged, stolen or cause injury. Break bulk also has a disadvantage where certain food items are concerned. Some food needs to be shipped in temperature-controlled spaces or refrigerated ships. This is common in container shipping but less common in break bulk. Where bulk shipments of meat, fish, fruit or vegetables are concerned, the vessels are specifically designed and built to handle such commodities.

However, containerisation is not the full answer to the needs of shipping and cargo management. Break bulk continues to maintain an advantage in areas where port development has not kept pace with shipping technology; break bulk shipping requires relatively minimal shore facilities – a wharf for the ship to tie to, dock workers to assist in unloading, warehouses to store materials for later reloading onto other forms of transport. As a result, there are still some areas where break bulk shipping continues to thrive. Goods shipped break bulk can also be offloaded onto smaller vessels and lighters (barges) for transport into even the most minimally-developed port which the normally large containerships, tankers and bulk carriers might not be able to access due to size and/or water depth. Indeed, the LASH (Lighter Aboard Ship) system was designed for just this form of marine commercial activity, where the lighters could actually be transported by LASH vessel, unloaded into the river close to their ultimate destination, and hauled by tugs to the appropriate wharf where they were unloaded, reloaded (where appropriate), and towed back to the awaiting LASH vessel for onward deep-sea transportation. In addition, some ports capable of accepting larger container ships/tankers/bulk transporters still require goods to be offloaded in break bulk fashion; for example, in the outlying islands of Tuvalu in the Pacific Ocean, fuel oil for the power stations is delivered in bulk, but has to be shipped and offloaded in barrels as there are no specific wharves or jetties facilitating bulk tanker operations. The barrels are carried in a general cargo vessel as a result.

Beyond this, the obvious benefit of break bulk is the ability to ship oversized consignments without breaking them down into smaller shipments. For example, if Company A orders large construction equipment from overseas, the equipment can be shipped in one piece. The alternative is that the machinery is disassembled and shipped in a container, or several containers. In this case, Company A pays for the machinery to be disassembled, packed, shipped, offloaded, delivered and re-assembled. If it is shipped break bulk, it is loaded aboard vessel, offloaded at the port of destination, and is delivered to the customer.

Another benefit is that break bulk cargo can arrive at the majority of ports in the world. Not all ports are modern or even suitable enough for shipping and receiving containers. Hazardous materials with proper paperwork can be shipped break bulk because they have to be separated from other goods on the ship. This means that underdeveloped countries can receive goods and supplies they need for their economic wellbeing. Turbine and generator companies can ship their equipment anywhere in the world without having to dismantle it. Furthermore, the paperwork process is also easier with break bulk cargo. Because containers carry a variety of goods, there can be several Bills of Lading per container, especially in the case of LCLs (Less-than Container Loads), where consignments are consolidated, or grouped, into the container. In break bulk, one bill of lading, usually a Charter Party Bill of Lading, handles the whole shipment.

These are the top four benefits of break bulk shipping:

1. The ability to move oversized and overweight items that will not fit in a container;
2. Reduction in time spent on deconstruction and reconstruction so that items are ready for dispatch;
3. Goods can enter smaller ports that typically would be unable to accommodate larger container ships or tankers;
4. Goods do not have to be combined in a container; therefore, items can be shipped separately.

Equipment or goods that are tedious to break down or oversized can benefit from break bulk shipping. Instead of breaking down the product to fit into a container or bin, the shipper can send the item in its entirety.

Typically, a break bulk ship is equipped with high capacity deck cranes and additional equipment necessary to load and unload these oversized or heavy goods. Additionally, high deck strength barges are sometimes used to facilitate loading this cargo by rolling it on and off the vessel.

Cargo is transported to and from ports by land, which is usually an efficient option for shippers needing inland services. Otherwise, breaking products up into containers tends to be more expensive than wholly containerised goods.

Cargo on a break bulk vessel, such as a barge or ship, does not have to be deconstructed or separated into pieces. Therefore, it may be a more affordable option for shippers with oversized cargo. Ultimately, this leads to a faster delivery time.

Break bulk is deliverable to most ports around the world and requires little to no deconsolidation or reconsolidation. When loading and discharging goods at a port, equipment is already available on the ship, which saves time in transporting products.

Break bulk does not require that goods are separated into containers to be transported. Instead, heavy or oversized items are loaded with special equipment such as cranes to load the ship. This makes bulky items easier to transport.

RO/RO (Roll On-Roll Off) is typically used when transporting break bulk shipments. Most heavy break bulk shipments use RO/RO and avoid fees such as container hire, storage, additional labor and equipment rental. RO/RO liner services also utilise a frequently scheduled time table which results in fewer short notice cancellations or postponing's. If the route to deliver goods is complex, a transshipment will ensure that cargo reaches its destination in a reasonable time. Heavy break bulk is lashed to handling equipment which prevents lifting and no dismantling. As a result, cargo is rolled on to a deck based on its weight and width.

While there are many examples of remarkable heavy load and semi-submersible vessels belonging to companies such as Dockwise, which carry vast and heavy cargoes, such as drilling rigs, boats and quayside container cranes, this segment actually represents a smaller portion of break bulk cargo operations. In reality, break bulk operations cover the shipment of a wide range of industrial components, plant, machinery, cranes, as well as wood, aluminium rolls, drill pipes, subsea equipment, timber products, iron and steel products, to name but a few. Shipping companies involved in such activities include Gearbulk, BBC Chartering of Germany and Spliethoff of the Netherlands.

As the break bulk market has developed, the operating model of many break bulk shipping companies remains that of traditional tramping, carried out on a global scale. While the image of decrepit, rusty, sea-beaten vessels operating in regions forgotten by the rest of the world has disappeared, the tradition of tramp shipping remains, in the sense of an *ad hoc* market relying on the availability of cargoes to be shipped almost at a moment's notice. The current fleet is expanding through the introduction of modern, sophisticated and highly versatile vessels which can perform a variety of functions and which are operated by highly professional and well-organised, well-equipped carriers.

The global fleet of break bulk vessels has expanded rapidly, with a significant increase in the number of vessels built since 2000; up to 2012, over 2,150 break bulk ships comprising 28.5 million dwt have been built and are presently in service. Furthermore, the ability of the onboard cranes on board the average modern geared multi-purpose/project ship to handle increasingly-heavy cargoes has also expanded. In this respect, the 25 largest break bulk/heavy lift/project operators deploy over 500 ships with heavy lift capabilities of over 100 tons, of which nearly 160 can hoist loads of more than 500 tons. As at 2013, another 30 such ships were on order with lifting capacities of between 500 and 3,000 tons.

A break-in-bulk point is a place (i.e. a port) where goods are transferred from one mode of transport to another, for example the docks where the cargo is transferred from ship to truck at the quayside. The same technique applies at the port of loading, where the cargo is transferred from a truck or specialist road vehicle to the ship.

Break bulk was the most common form of cargo for most of the history of shipping. However, since the late 1960s, the volume of break bulk cargo has declined dramatically worldwide as containerisation has become more prevalent. The transfer of cargo on and off ship in containers is much more efficient, allowing ships to spend less time in port. Break bulk cargo, as well as being a time-consuming process, also suffered from greater levels of theft and damage because of its lack of security and its vulnerability to external threats and influences. In many cases, there was the need to store break bulk cargo temporarily in transit sheds for Customs clearance, and this often resulted in losses caused by a variety of circumstances. As containers became the standard international movement of maritime cargo, security became more important, along with the ability to transfer a container to a waiting truck and immediately remove it from the port to an inland destination.

However, the need for break bulk cargo still exists as a niche market. Cargoes such as forest products, plant and machinery, power generation equipment, offshore

Oil and Gas equipment and materials, mining equipment, other capital equipment and vehicles, whether rail or road, still require the use of break bulk operations. There are also many ports where containerisation is difficult to operate, and in many cases, general cargo operations are seen as being more practical than container handling. In these cases, break bulk operations are still the main form of port activity, and account for a significant proportion of maritime trade. This includes the perishable products trade, where large bulk quantities of perishable fruit and vegetables are carried in refrigerated break bulk vessels because of their sheer volume.

Many specialist break bulk vessels are fitted with heavy lift cranes which can manage the heaviest of cargo safely and quicker than dockside cranes, and this can speed up the process of loading and unloading, and can significantly reduce costs for the shipments.

Although break bulk shipping rates are often seen as more expensive than containerised shipping costs, in that they are calculated at the rate per tonne, be it actual or volumetric weight, as opposed to FCL (Full Container Load) box rates or LCL (Less-Than Container Load) consolidated rates for containerised cargoes, when taking into account the costs and time delays of disassembling, packing, shipping, unpacking and re-assembling of complex items, break bulk shipping can often make much better commercial sense. In the case of road vehicles, for example, it is often necessary to disassemble the vehicles in order to stuff them into standard containers, and then re-assemble them at destination. Using break bulk methods, these vehicles, especially commercial vehicles, cane be loaded aboard vessel in their fully-assembled condition, shipped to their destination, unloaded and transported to their onward destination without the complex activities mentioned above. The cost of break bulk shipment might be greater, but it is far more practical.

Although cargo of this kind can be delivered straight from a truck or train onto a ship, the most common way of transport is for the cargo to be delivered to the dock in advance of the arrival of the ship and for the cargo to be stored in warehouses, namely transit sheds next to the quayside. When the ship arrives at port, the cargo is then taken from the warehouse to the quay and is then lifted on board the vessel by either the ship's gear, i.e. derricks or cranes, or by the dockside cranes. The discharge of the ship is the reverse of the loading operation. Loading and discharging by break bulk is labour-intensive. The cargo is brought to the quay next to the ship and then each individual item is lifted on board separately. Some items such as sacks or bags can be loaded in batches by using a sling or cargo net and others such as cartons can be loaded onto trays before being lifted on board. Once on board, each item must be stowed separately.

Before any loading takes place, any signs of the previous cargo should be removed. The holds should be swept, washed if necessary and any damage to them repaired. Dunnage, which is the loose packing used to cushion the cargo in the hold, may be laid ready for the cargo or may simply be arranged in bundles ready for the stevedores to spread out as the cargo is loaded.

Break bulk continues to maintain an advantage in areas where port development has not kept pace with shipping technology, especially in developing countries, where demand for container transport is comparatively low or where the national and port infrastructure is not suited to container operations. Break bulk shipping requires relatively minimal shore facilities, namely a wharf for the ship to moor at and tie to, dock workers to assist in unloading, warehouses to store materials for later reloading onto other forms of transport. As a result, there are still some areas where break bulk shipping continues to thrive. Goods shipped break bulk can also be offloaded onto smaller vessels and lighters for transport into even the most minimally-developed port where the large container ships, tankers and bulk carriers might not be able to access due to size and/or water depth. Furthermore, some ports are not equipped for major container handling operations, and do not have space for the storage and handling of large numbers of containers, as well as lacking in container crane handling equipment. In addition, some ports which are capable of accepting larger container ships, tankers and dry bulk carriers still require goods to be offloaded in break bulk fashion. For example, in the outlying islands of Tuvalu, fuel oil for the power stations is delivered in bulk but has to be offloaded in barrels because of a lack of bulk transfer facilities at the port.

A ship engaged in the tramp trade does not have a fixed schedule or published ports of call, but is available at short notice, or fixture, to load any cargo to transport from any port of loading to any port of destination. For example, a vessel might load with cargo at the port of Rotterdam to transport to Luanda, in Angola. It then takes another shipment to Durban in South Africa, and reloads with another cargo destined for South Korea. It then loads another cargo destined for Oakland, California. At Oakland, it discharges its load and then sails under ballast to the port of Long Beach, further down the Californian coast, where it loads another cargo destined for Hamburg. The freight rates for each cargo will be individually arranged with the shipper prior to the cargo being loaded, as the freight costs may vary according to the date on which the cargo is to be loaded aboard vessel, and may therefore vary from cargo to cargo depending upon the individual voyage.

The term "tramp shipping" is derived from the British meaning of "tramp" as itinerant beggar or vagrant, but in this context it is first documented in the 1880s, along with "ocean tramp", as at the time many sailing vessels were engaged in irregular trade, and sailed from port to port to port on an *ad hoc* basis loaded with cargo that they simply picked up as the need arose. In many cases, the tramp market meant that a ship registered in the UK and crewed by British mariners rarely returned to the UK, as it was permanently sailing between a series of worldwide ports. In many cases, this is still the same scenario, with vessels operating where the need arises, often operating for long periods away from their home port. As opposed to freight liners, tramp ships trade on the spot market with no fixed schedule or itinerary/ports-of-call. The spot market is used because freight is arranged and payable at a fixed date, usually the time of arranging the freight and its loading aboard vessel, rather than being arranged for and paid at a fixed future date. Spot rates are measured daily on an *ad hoc* basis, and therefore are not subject to conventional indices. For example, a company wishes to ship a specific cargo which cannot be containerised to an overseas port. It uses a shipbroker to ascertain the availability of a suitable vessel, either to be used for that shipment only, or which is already arranged to carry other cargo to that same destination. The shipper arranges for the cargo to be shipped on a specific date, and pays the freight rate according to the spot rate ascertained at the time of arrangement. The tramp ship is a contract carrier. Unlike a liner, often called a common carrier, which has a fixed schedule and a published tariff, the ideal tramp can carry anything to anywhere, and freight rates are influenced by supply and demand. To generate business, a charterparty contract to lease the vessel is drawn up between the shipowner and the charterer. For this purpose, there are three types of charters, namely voyage, time and demise.

Project Cargo comprises all kinds of machinery, equipment and materials destined for specific projects worldwide, such as power stations, refineries, offshore Oil and Gas exploration and production, offshore renewables development and other infrastructure projects. This operation requires specific cargo arrangement and handling, and entails the use of tramp vessels hired in on a charter basis, either voyage charter or time charter. Handling Project Cargo takes special care, expertise and attention. Shipments are typically time-sensitive, and usually concern valuable and/or voluminous cargoes. Project Cargo works on the spot market, with freight payable at the time of shipment. In many cases, the charter is arranged by the recipient company or authority, which arranges the consolidation of cargoes at the port[s] of loading, with each cargo supplied by a different supplier. Each cargo is loaded separately onto the vessel, and is covered by a single break bulk bill of lading. At the port of discharge, all the cargoes are unloaded separately, and are transported to their ultimate destination.

Project Cargo management requires somewhat more planning than single break bulk cargo shipments. Many projects, especially those in the offshore sector, last for several years in terms of exploration and development, and require the shipment of a large amount of materials to the country nearest the offshore oilfields. For this reason, the planning of such cargo movements is vital in terms of the quantity and frequency of the movement of materials. The considerations to be taken into account are as follows:

- The duration of the project;
- The location of the project;
- The nature of each consignment, i.e. the type of materials being shipped;
- The size and total weight of the consignment;
- The need for one-off or several shipments;
- The frequency of the shipments;
- The number of vessels required;
- Voyage/time charter arrangements.

In most cases, Project Cargo movements are carried out in batches, with materials for the project moved in as close frequencies as possible, as well as ensuring that freight rates can be fixed for all the consignment shipments where possible.

In some cases a charterer may own cargo and employ a shipbroker to find a ship to deliver the cargo for a certain price, called the freight rate. A charterer may also be a party without a cargo who takes a vessel on charter for a specified period from the owner and then trades the ship to carry cargoes at a profit above the hire rate, or even makes a profit in a rising market by re-letting the ship out to other charterers. Depending on the type of ship and the type of charter, normally a standard contract form called a charterparty is used to record the exact rate, duration and terms agreed between the shipowner and the charterer.

The voyage charter is the most common charter in tramp shipping. The owner of the tramp is obliged to provide a seaworthy ship while the charterer is obliged to provide a full load of cargo. This type of charter is the most lucrative, but can be the riskiest due to lack of new charterers. During a voyage charter a part or all of a vessel is leased to the charterer for a voyage to a port or a set of different ports. There are two types of voyage charter, namely net form and gross form. Under the net form, the cargo a tramp ship carries is loaded, discharged and trimmed at the charterer's expense. Under the gross form the expense of cargo loading, discharging and trimming is on the owner. The charterer is only responsible to provide the cargo at a specified port and to accept it at the destination port. Time becomes an issue in the voyage charter if the tramp ship is late in her schedule or loading or discharging are delayed. If a tramp ship is delayed the charterer pays demurrage, which is a penalty, to the shipowner. The number of days a tramp ship is chartered for is called lay days.

In a time charter, the owner provides a vessel that is fully manned and equipped. The owner provides the crew, but the crew takes orders from the charterer. The owner is also responsible for insuring the vessel, repairs the vessel may need, engine parts and food and refreshments for ship's personnel. The charterer is responsible for everything else. In this respect, the main advantage of the time charter is that it diverts the costs of running a ship to the charterer.

Tramp shipowners and charterers rely on brokers to find cargoes for their ships to carry. A broker understands international trade conditions, the movements of goods, market prices, and the availability of the owner's ships, although the integrated services of specialist brokers and freight forwarders are becoming increasingly sought after, as freight forwarders are facilitators of freight movements and therefore liaise as a matter of course with shipowners, agents and brokers on behalf of shippers.

The Baltic Exchange in London is the physical headquarters for tramp ship, bulk and break bulk vessel brokerage, and works like an organised market, providing a meeting place for shipowners, brokers and charterers. It also provides easy access to information on market fluctuations, and commodity prices to all the parties involved. Brokers can use it to quickly match a cargo to a ship or ship to a cargo depending on whom they are working for. A committee of owners, brokers and charterers are elected to manage the exchange to ensure that the interests of all concerned are represented. With the speed of today's communications, the floor of the Baltic Exchange is nowhere near as populated as it once was, but the information and networking which the exchange provides is still an asset to the tramp trade and is still seen as the major means of maritime trading.

Due to the rapid increase of liner services, and in large part, due to containerisation since the 1960s, the tramp and *ad hoc* charter trade has decreased, but is by no means forgotten. Indeed, far from being forgotten, it has become a niche market, where specific shipping companies have become specialist in the *ad hoc* trade, and have been flourishing as a result. Indeed, such is the specialism of this trade that the staff who work for such shipping companies are extremely well qualified in the shipbroking profession, and are truly experts in their field. Furthermore, a contemporary trend in the shipping business related to the classic marketing mix, which is essentially the formula of the "4 Ps" (Product, Price, Promotion, Place), developed into Shimizu's 4 Cs (Commodity, Cost, Communication, Channel), named after its author, Koichi Shimizu in 1973, has resulted in renewed interest in tramp and *ad hoc* charter shipping. *Ad hoc* charter shipping encompasses individual cargoes booked on to a chartered vessel because of the following factors:

- Specific ports of loading and unloading;
- Nature of Cargo;
- Size of Cargo;
- Convenience of direct shipment;
- The need to charter a vessel, either on a partial or full basis;
- Unsuitability for containerisation.

The "Channel" element of the Shimizu model influences how the mix is structured, as the commodity, cost and channel factors may well determine how the cargo is to be shipped more economically and efficiently. It is pointless shipping a cargo to a container port miles away from the project's location, when the cargo is so specific that it needs to be unloaded at a port local to the project, and in any case, the cargo may not be suitable for containerisation due to its nature and its size.

To increase profits, liner companies are looking at investing in tramp ships to create a revenue cushion when the market is depressed. In this way, although they will still employ container vessels on routes which can guarantee demand, they also employ tramp vessels to carry cargo on an *ad hoc* basis, i.e. where the need requires, rather than on a regular scheduled service, where demand may not always be consistent. For example, Mitsui OSK Lines possesses a large fleet with tramp ships and liners. With both types of shipping covered they are able to service a world economy even in a down market. The beauty of tramp ships is they are relied upon at a moment's notice to service any type of market. Even in a depressed economy there will be a market for some type of commodity somewhere, and the company with the ships able to exploit that market will do better than the company relying on liner services alone. Indeed, in an age where container freight rates fluctuate wildly and the scheduled routes are becoming increasingly depressed, the *ad hoc* tramp market becomes increasingly attractive and practical, even to the point of containers being carried on tramp services on the basis that the specific cargo in question is still required to be shipped to a particular destination.

In ship chartering, freight is the price which a charterer pays a shipowner for the use of a ship in a voyage charter. There is also the **Contract of Affreightment**, which is the expression usually employed to describe the contract between a shipowner and the charterer, by which the shipowner agrees to carry goods of the charterer in his ship, or to give to the charterer the use of the whole or part of the cargo-carrying space of the ship for the carriage of his goods on a specified voyage or voyages or for a specified time. The charterer on his part agrees to pay a specified price, called freight, for the carriage of the goods or the use of the ship.

A ship may be let like a house to a person who takes possession and control of it for a specified term. The person who hires a ship in this way occupies during the specified time the position of shipowner. The contract by which a ship is so let may be called a charterparty; but it is not, properly speaking, a contract of affreightment, and is mentioned here only because it is necessary to remember the distinction between a charterparty of this kind, which is sometimes called a demise of the ship, and a charterparty which is a form of contract of affreightment, and which may be separate from the charter of the vessel itself.

Contracts of affreightment are a commonly used documentary tool in today's modern trading environment. Such contracts are designed to define the mutual obligations of the parties and, in contrast to a charterparty for consecutive voyages, are not linked to any particular vessel, as they can simply refer to the carriage of a specific cargo between two designated ports.

The basic purpose of a contract of affreightment is the provision of transportation for the shipment of large quantities of cargo over an extended period (expressed as an amount or a number of voyages). This type of contract provides a degree of flexibility between the parties to agree on the timings of each shipment and which vessels are to be employed for each lifting. However, the contract may also be for the shipment of a specific cargo on a single voyage between two designated ports, and therefore applies to that cargo alone, rather than a series of cargo shipments, hence the flexibility of the nature of the contract.

Many of the contracts of affreightment (COA) presently in use are very different, and in some cases, lengthy and unclear. BIMCO's own model form of contract of affreightment, VOLCOA, was first published in 1982 to provide a useful framework for the negotiation of contracts of affreightment. GENCOA is an updated version of the original BIMCO form and provides users with a set of clearly worded terms and conditions governing the key aspects of any contract of affreightment. GENCOA has been designed to be used with any dry-cargo charterparty, although BIMCO would highly recommend the use of one of its complementary forms such as GENCON 94, COAL-OREVOY or GRAINCON.

Whereas a Charterparty bill of lading is not seen as evidence of the contract of carriage, a break bulk bill of lading is an Ocean or Marine bill of lading in the same way as a bill of lading issued for a containerised consignment, and indeed has the same functions as an Ocean bill of lading issued for a containerised consignment, but its main difference is that it simply refers to the cargo as loaded aboard vessel, and does not make any reference to a container number given the fact that the break bulk cargo is not containerised. Furthermore, it is never issued as a Combined Transport or Multimodal bill of lading, as it only refers to the shipment of the cargo between one port and another. In this respect, the INCOTERMS used for such shipments are either FOB (Named Port of Loading) or CIF (Named Port of Discharge). Under these terms, the risk and responsibility for the cargo will pass from the seller to the buyer at the time that the cargo is securely loaded aboard vessel, as defined by the INCOTERMS 2010. It should be noted that for break bulk cargo, all movements are made on a port-to-port basis, and hence only the marine INCOTERMS of FAS (Free Alongside Ship), FOB (Free On Board), CFR (Cost & Freight) and CIF (Cost, Insurance, Freight) apply to such shipments. Any inland transportation must be arranged separately.

CHAPTER 4

Break bulk storage

Break bulk warehousing and transit sheds

A break bulk warehouse is a warehouse at the dock where break bulk ships are loaded. Typically the break bulk cargo will be delivered by road or rail to the break bulk warehouse for storage. Once the ship arrives at the dock the goods are taken from the warehouse and loaded aboard the vessel using cranes. These cranes may be situated on the quayside, but it is more likely that in most cases, docksides do not accommodate cranes given that most quayside cranes were installed many decades previously, and are not suitable to handle many of the large or outsized cargoes that are presently carried on break bulk vessels. Consequently, most break bulk vessels are equipped with their own lifting and handling gear that is used to transfer the cargoes from the quayside to the vessel and vice versa.

The break bulk warehouse is otherwise known as a Transit Shed, or, in Customs parlance, temporary storage. The term Transit Shed refers to the fact that cargo is unloaded from a ship in transit to its owner or consignee, and is therefore held in the shed until it can be cleared through Customs. While in the shed, the cargo can be examined for marks, identification, quantity and value, prior to being cleared by Customs. The author spent much of his time as a Customs officer carrying out these functions, as the Transit Shed was the only place where full Customs clearance could take place prior to the cargo being released to the importer. Conversely, a Transit Shed is used for exporting consignments, where the cargo is transported from the exporter's premises to the shed, where it is held until the vessel onto which it is to be loaded arrives at port. Again, given the Customs export clearance of many break bulk consignments takes place at the Transit Shed, any associated cargo examinations and verifications can be carried out by Customs at this point. Even in an age of electronic manifests and Customs clearance, transit sheds are still a necessity in terms of the handling of bulk consignments and Project Cargoes.

Many Customs Authorities allow goods to be stored in a temporary storage facility, i.e. a Transit Shed, located within the port complex or just outside it, for a period of up to 90 days, thus allowing import or export Customs clearance to be carried out at the premises. For specific break bulk or Project Cargoes, the cargo will be accommodated at the Transit Shed in the period immediately before the cargo vessel arrives for loading, as vessel laytime, i.e. the time that the vessel

DOI: 10.4324/9781003256359-5

is berthed at the quay, can be limited according to the terms of the Charterparty arranged between the shipowner and the charterer. It should be noted that the vessel only earns revenue while it is sailing on a voyage, not while it is berthed, as laytime costs are seen as accruing against the revenue-earning period while the vessel is en route between the port of loading and the port of destination. Because of this, it is essential that all the cargoes to be loaded aboard vessel must be accumulated in the Transit Shed or on the quayside, ready to be loaded aboard vessel once it arrives at port.

An "Enhanced Remote Transit Shed" (ERTS) is an approved place situated outside the appointed area of an approved port/airport where non-Community goods may be held until they are declared to Customs for an approved treatment or use. This allows for operators of "groupage" consignments (a single sea container or airline storage unit that contains goods for more than one importer) to remove the consignment from the port/airport, under arrangements with Customs, to the approved warehouse so that unpacking can commence prior to the goods being entered to or cleared by Customs.

Temporary storage, as a generic term defined by Customs, means the situation of Non-Union goods temporarily stored under Customs supervision in the period between their presentation to Customs and their placing under a Customs procedure or re-exported.

Temporary storage is a term used to refer to goods imported from another country and placed within a neutral, authorised warehouse until they are assigned a Customs-approved treatment. Warehouse operators, transport companies, shipping agents and freight forwarders use this procedure, enabling them to defer duty and tax payments on their goods while they are stored in a Customs designated area.

Temporary storage means that goods are placed there for a set period until they are officially declared to Customs and therefore subject to tax and duty payments. They cannot remain there indefinitely. There are time limits imposed by the Customs Authority, in the case of the UK up to 90 days, before the goods must be declared to Customs and either:

- Removed to a designated Customs Warehouse;
- Re-exported;
- Released into Free Circulation.

A temporary storage facility is a place situated inside or outside the approved area of a sea or airport, where imported goods may be placed in storage prior to being placed under a Customs procedure or re-exported.

There are various ways of referring to these premises depending on their location. These are:

- Internal temporary storage facility (ITSF), which is inside the Customs-controlled area of the frontier (port or airport) and within the vicinity of the port or airport;

- Internal temporary storage facility – remote (ITSF-R), which is outside the Customs-controlled area of the frontier (port or airport) but still within the immediate vicinity of the (port or airport);
- External temporary storage facility (ETSF) which is outside the Customs-controlled area of the frontier (port or airport).

All of these facilities are considered to be part of the national frontier and as a result must be approved for this purpose by the Border Force or national Revenue Authority.

It should be noted that many of the explanations detailed in this chapter refer to UK procedures, but similar procedures exist elsewhere in the world.

The standard procedure is for the importer to pay import or excise duty and VAT on goods imported into the UK that are then declared to UK Customs officials. However, there is the option to defer this with "temporary storage". This process enables one to store their goods within a Customs-approved zone such as a transit shed, warehouse or depot that is free from duty payments. Temporary storage also refers to these approved premises. These premises are based at airports and maritime ports around the UK.

Goods coming into the UK from outside the UK are presented to UK Customs via an authorised electronic trade inventory system. Goods have to be shown within three hours of arrival via air or sea followed by a summary declaration within 24 hours of their initial appearance. This is followed by a full Customs declaration that acts as an official handover of the goods for a Customs-approved treatment, i.e. usage. These treatments include free circulation in the UK, being placed under the jurisdiction of HMRC or discarded and passed to the Exchequer. In some cases, they will be destroyed.

With temporary storage, one only has to present goods and make a summary declaration within the timescales. A written "deed of undertaking" has also to be signed that acts as a form of security. Consider this as a guarantee of one's trustworthiness and honourable intentions as regards trade procedures.

Once these have expired, a full Customs declaration is made and duty and taxes paid. The goods are then available for transportation anywhere in the UK.

There are several benefits to using this procedure, and these are:

- Sufficient time to obtain an official import licence or any other relevant documentation to be presented, prior to making a full Customs declaration. Many documents take some time to be produced, and preference certificates can arrive days after the shipment has arrived into the Port or Airport.
- Using temporary storage facilities saves the cost of having to pay for premises. If you are waiting for documents, then why pay storage charges in the airline bond or on quay?
- Defer Customs and excise duty payments, and VAT.

There is the option to speed up this process using HMRC Customs Freight Simplified Procedures (CFSP) subject to conditions.

Temporary storage premises have to meet a set of HMRC criteria that determines their fitness for use. These include:

- Conforming to UK health & safety guidelines;
- Safe, secure and robust;
- Suitable for the storing and loading of goods;
- Have authorised stock records.

As a result, temporary storage premises have to be able to cope with all sizes and types of goods coming into the UK from a non-EU country. Warehouses, depots and transit sheds are permissible as are tanks and other types of premises although in the latter case, their suitability is considered on a case-by-case basis.

Goods placed in temporary storage are subject to a number of restrictions governing their handling. Their original condition must be preserved during their time in storage and prior to their removal. The aim is to prevent any alteration or modification to the appearance of the goods before they are assigned to a Customs-approved treatment. This equally applies to any processing of the goods.

However, there is one exception, in that goods in temporary storage can be broken apart, dismantled or separated for purposes of an essential examination. However, they must be reformed and presented in their original state following the expiration of the timescales. They can then be moved after a full declaration and assignment to a Customs-approved treatment. For break bulk and Project Cargoes, this can be an advantage, in that products and equipment can be examined in detail in the transit shed or a designated area close by within the port confines prior to being cleared through Customs and transported to its final destination.

Goods can be moved between temporary storage facilities, but can only do so if authorised by HMRC. This is carried out using the Community Transit procedure using the Community Transit System (NCTS), which, following the UK's full withdrawal from the EU, will be a national computerised transit system.

There are certain types of imported goods that cannot be moved into temporary storage until they have undergone a series of comprehensive checks by Customs officers. These include firearms, animal products, endangered species of flora and fauna, foodstuffs and plants. Goods come into the UK from overseas countries on a regular basis and it is important that they are checked and approved before they are freely circulated through the country.

Tax and duty payments have to be made, which are a major concern for warehouse operators, transport companies and freight forwarders, even considering Customs facilities such as Duty and VAT Deferment. However, temporary storage is one way of easing these costs, especially where the materials enter the country in bulk or need Customs clearance at the port of arrival, which is especially the case for break bulk, general and Project Cargoes. Such cargoes can be released in stages, allowing for staged duty payments, while the rest of the cargo remains in temporary storage until it is ready for release and delivery to the customer.

Placing goods into a temporary storage facility means that one has time to obtain the necessary documentation and licences without having to pay duties and taxes during this period. In effect, it buys an importer some extra time to allow for Customs clearance.

An External Temporary Storage Facility Approved Depository (ETSFAD) is a temporary storage facility located outside the approved and controlled area of a port or airport where personal and household effects arriving from outside the Union under transfer of residence may be placed in storage prior to being Customs cleared.

A temporary storage area may, in certain circumstances, be allowed inside other UK Customs authority-approved premises. Where premises are multi use, for example storing warehouse freight, the temporary storage area must be clearly demarcated. This area must be visibly identified inside the premises as well as notated on the building plan. The method of identification must meet the requirements of the local Border Force supervising officer.

This allows for quicker movement of cargo through the port/airport and results in the goods being made available to the importer more readily than would otherwise be the case if all consignments had to be cleared at the port/airport before they could be moved.

The following types of business are eligible to apply to have their premises approved as a temporary storage facility and may benefit from such an approval:

- Freight forwarders;
- Customs agents;
- Warehouse keepers; and
- Transport companies.

The temporary storage premises must be maintained, secure and in good repair to the satisfaction of HMRC. The premises must be equipped with suitable facilities for storing, unloading, examining and clearing the goods and for examining the vehicles.

Where temporary storage goods are removed from the port or airport to an ERTS, the ERTS operator must provide security in the form of a Community Transit Guarantee or Guarantee waiver for the goods.

In general, Transit Sheds are located adjacent to a quayside, for the ease of transferring cargoes to and from the vessel. They are always secured premises, and often comprise a large surface area, designed in such a way as to accommodate large quantities of commodities of goods. They are, however, seen as temporary storage, in that they must be cleared through Customs within a designated time limit, hence the period of 90 days (three months) allowed for such storage facilities. Indeed, it is often the case that the period of free temporary storage is limited by the port (in some cases a limited number of days) before demurrage (storage delay) costs are applied, often amounting to a significant charge per day. The principle of charging demurrage is to discourage the use of a transit shed beyond the free period allowed, so that the space can be used for other cargo, and thus more cargo can be handled at the berth. However, there are cases where cargoes could be seized or delayed by Customs because of a lack of or anomalies with the commercial or transport documentation associated with the consignment, and in this case, cargo clearance could be delayed by several hours or even days, in which case demurrage charges are likely to apply to the cargo concerned.

Several factors influence the size of the Transit Shed, namely:

- Nature of the cargo;
- Size of the cargo;
- Quantity of the cargo;
- Space occupied;
- Height of stacking;
- Allowance for movement and other non-storage areas;
- Size/capacity of vessels.

The length and breadth of the shed provides covered space opposite to the entire length of the largest vessel for which a quayside or berth is designed. The principle is to provide quick access from all the vessel's hold hatches. For a vessel length of 180 metres, the shed length is suggested as 165 metres, as this leaves space for an end access roadway to the quayside and shed floor. The breadth of the shed is determined by the area that the shed is designed to occupy, and to this extent, the minimum width of the she should not be less than 50 metres.

To expedite the loading and unloading of cargo to and from vessels, some open space is left in front of the shed, between the shed and the side of the berth. This is known as the "Apron". The apron is utilised for the installation of mechanical equipment such as cranes, and transport agencies such as road trucks or railway lines for rail wagons, facilitating the efficient handling of cargoes. The width of the apron should be determined by the following factors:

- The width should be kept to a minimum necessary for specific handling operations;
- The cost of the construction of the facility should be kept to a minimum;
- To save the travelling time of the carriage of cargo to and from the vessel and transit shed.

For general cargo terminals, the generally-accepted width of the apron is as follows:

- The average is 10 metres, allowing for a single rail track embedded in the apron;
- For two rail tracks, the minimum width is 12 metres;
- For full portal gantry cranes, the minimum apron width is 15 metres;
- In general, the apron width usually varies from 10 metres for ports with light traffic to 25 metres for direct berthing ports with heavy traffic.

Globally, Customs clearance is in the process of being made fully electronic, using electronic technology developed by Port Community system providers. In the UK, such providers include MCP (Maritime Cargo Processing) using their system

Destin8, CCS-UK, and Descartes Ltd, using their system Pentant. Such clearance systems are able to clear cargoes electronically through Customs at Transit Sheds, as well as providing the systems capable of clearing cargoes at a distance, either through Enhanced remote Transit Sheds (ERTS), or even at inland clearance depots or Customs-approved Warehouses. In essence, the purpose of the exercise is to use the Transit Shed as a temporary transit solution, especially where break bulk or general cargo is concerned.

Temporary storage approval

In order for a temporary storage approval to be accepted, the applicant must be a:

- port or airport operator;
- freight forwarder;
- Customs agent;
- warehouse keeper;
- transport company.

They must also be:

- established in the UK or EU;
- involved with the movement of non-Union cargo.

The operator of the proposed temporary storage facility is responsible for the physical acceptance and release of the goods into and out of the actual temporary storage facility, for the collection of data into the temporary storage stock account record on the physical arrival of the goods into the premises.

The Union Customs Code (UCC) states that "The temporary storage of goods should in principle take place in temporary storage facilities, operated exclusively by the holder of an authorisation granted by the Customs authorities." Under the UCC, third party operators will no longer be allowed to operate a temporary storage facility, it is only the approval holder who has agreed to the terms and conditions and is the principle "authorised" to operate temporary storage facilities. Third parties have not been through the approval vetting process.

The applicant should be aware that if they have a history of Customs debt, any outstanding Customs debt or Customs Civil Penalty (CCP), this may result in the approval being refused.

If the applicant and or close associates have an adverse compliance history relating to breaches of Customs regulations or breaches of UK or legislation in respect of the smuggling of prohibited or restricted goods or evasion of national revenue, their application may be refused.

The criteria set out by the Customs Authority comprises two elements – General and Specific. These are:

- General – terms and conditions for internal temporary storage facility that you must meet and are responsible for;

- General – terms and conditions for an external temporary storage facility approval that you must meet and are responsible for;
- Specific – a degree of flexibility to provide bespoke additional terms and conditions is being introduced along with an Annex to exempt an operator from certain terms or conditions where required for that particular commercial business operation. Border Force will instigate and agree these terms and conditions.

Electronic management

The approved temporary storage facility must be physically equipped with a Customs-approved IT record keeping or inventory system which must have an approved anti-smuggling net (ASN). This system must be able to and be used to:

- provide electronic entry of all temporary storage goods entering into the facility (stock account records);
- provide electronic inventory control of all non-Union goods whilst in the facility;
- provide an electronic record of all activity relating to temporary storage goods, particularly arrival; out turn; discrepancies; examinations; sampling; movement within and between facilities; and/or any other authorised activity;
- provide electronic notification and receipt of the removal of goods after Customs clearance;
- provide an electronic log of the actual time goods remained within temporary storage whilst in the facility;
- transmit electronically all Customs declarations for cargo in the temporary storage area within the appropriate timescales;
- be capable of producing a system generated hard copy clearance advice and unit releases.

The temporary storage operator cannot operate remote management of temporary storage facilities and a responsible person must be on-site during the facilities notified opening hours.

The Customs-approved IT record keeping or inventory system must also be resident in the facility and Customs authorities must have access to these records when requested to do so.

As a temporary storage approval holder, the operator is required to choose and have in place at their facility a computerised inventory system provided by a group of companies called Community System Providers (CSPs). In the case of the UK, the following are current operators approved as CSPs:

- Cargo Community Systems UK (CCS-UK);
- Community Network Services (CNS);

- Maritime Cargo Processing (MCP);
- DHL;
- Pentant.

Other similar providers operate in other countries.

Traders wishing to use their own records must comply with the specifications of a CSP.

In the case of the UK, the design and functionality of these companies' systems is closely controlled and monitored by HMRC departmental resources called CSP Liaison officers (CSPLOs).

Temporary storage operators are at liberty to employ and use as many CSP systems as they require for their commercial operational requirements, however only one CSP system is preferred as the nominated facility stock account or inventory record.

If the operator elects to use a CSP system that is not in use at the port or airport into which the majority of your traffic will arrive be aware of the following:

(a) They may be asked to provide the Border Force or Customs Authority with a pre-arrival manifest providing details of the vessel or flight number, container numbers or airway bill numbers and the date or time of expected arrival of freight at their ETSF premises.

(b) A transit declaration using the Community Transit System (CTS) must be raised at the port or airport of arrival for the movement of the goods to the operator's ETSF premises as removals under the TS approval are restricted to movements within the same CSP. More than one may be used if messaging processes are inbuilt. Manual or other system declarations will not be acceptable except in fallback situations. NCTS declaration must be released at the Office of Departure and Transit Accompanying Document (TAD) and the supporting documents must accompany the freight.

(c) The procedure to discharge the TAD at the Office of Destination must be followed. This means that if the operator is not an authorised consignee under the Computerised Transit System, they must submit the transit document – TAD to the Border Force at your parent port immediately on arrival of the freight unless the operator applies to be an Authorised Consignee in order to take control of these movements themselves and avoid presenting documents to the Border Force. Under fallback arrangements, all traders must submit the TADs to the UK Border Force to obtain permission to offload the freight.

The operator is required to provide details of their chosen computerised inventory system at the time of application and if approval is granted they will be allocated with a specific shed identifier code and their Customs Handling of Import and Export Freight (CHIEF) freight location code. In addition, the operator must also apply for a CHIEF Agents badge code and password if they wish to input their own entries to the Customs Computer via the local CSP system.

CHAPTER 5

INCOTERMS 2010 & 2020

INCOTERMS (International Commercial Terms of Delivery) were first introduced in 1936 amid turbulent economic times, and emergent regional and global markets. At the time, various countries were introducing a series of new trade tariffs and negotiating bespoke contracts; there was a recognition that the general climate of trade risk was changing.

Translated into 25 languages globally, INCOTERMS serve to support current global business practice. The aim is to optimise global trade conduct, clearly defining the obligations of a buyer and seller of goods – in encouraging self-regulation and providing a rules-based framework to facilitate trade.

With each revision, the International Chamber of Commerce (ICC) aspires to advance standards and improve the outreach to businesses whose compliance with INCOTERMS is poor. There is a recognition that many businesses do not correctly use INCOTERMS. To this extent, businesses should, as a matter of course, challenge and encourage trade partners to utilise the correct or most appropriate rules to adopt at the outset of any international contractual negotiation and before a dispute arises.

The INCOTERMS or International Commercial Terms are a series of pre-defined commercial terms published by the ICC relating to the movement and delivery of goods according to the requirements of international commercial law. They are widely used in international commercial transactions or procurement processes as the use in international sales is encouraged by trade councils, courts and international lawyers. A series of three-letter trade terms related to common contractual sales practices, the INCOTERMS rules are intended primarily to clearly communicate the tasks, costs, and risks associated with the transportation and delivery of goods. INCOTERMS inform sales contract defining respective obligations, costs and risks involved in the delivery of goods from the seller to the buyer. However, it does not constitute contract or govern law. Also it does not define where titles transfer and does not address the price payable, currency or credit items.

The INCOTERMS rules are accepted by governments, legal authorities, and practitioners worldwide for the interpretation of most commonly used terms in international trade. They are intended to reduce or remove altogether uncertainties arising from different interpretation of the rules in different countries. As such, they are regularly incorporated into sales contracts worldwide.

 DOI: 10.4324/9781003256359-6

The first work published by the ICC on international trade terms was issued in 1923, with the first edition known as INCOTERMS published in 1936. the INCOTERMS rules were amended in 1953, 1967, 1976, 1980, 1990 and 2000, with the eighth version – INCOTERMS 2010 – having been published on 1 January 2011. The ICC have now published the new revision of INCOTERMS, called INCOTERMS 2020. "INCOTERMS" is a registered trademark of the ICC.

Rules for sea and inland waterway transport

FAS – Free Alongside Ship: Risk passes to buyer, including payment of all transportation and insurance costs, once delivered alongside the ship (realistically at named port terminal) by the seller. The export clearance obligation rests with the seller.

For break bulk operations, FAS generally means that the charterer is responsible for the loading of the vessel, as the vessel's lifting gear will be used to lift the cargo from the quayside onto the vessel. The risk will be shouldered by the charterer/buyer, as will all loading costs associated with such activities. However, quay/conservancy charges will be negotiated between the seller and buyer, as these may be apportioned between the two parties.

FOB – Free On Board: Risk passes to buyer, including payment of all transportation and insurance costs, once delivered on board the ship by the seller. A step further than FAS.

For break bulk operations, with FOB, the seller/exporter is responsible for the loading of the vessel, implying that quayside cranes will be used to load the cargo aboard vessel, with the port stevedores and vessel crew responsible for ensuring that the cargo is correctly loaded and secured aboard vessel. In this case, quayside and conservancy charges are the responsibility of the seller, although these charges may be passed on to the buyer as part of the FOB charges.

CFR – Cost and Freight: Seller delivers goods and risk passes to buyer when on board the vessel. Seller arranges and pays cost and freight to the named destination port. A step further than FOB.

For break bulk operations, with CIF, the seller/exporter is responsible for the loading of the vessel and payment of freight costs to the port of loading, implying that quayside cranes will be used to load the cargo aboard vessel, with the port stevedores and vessel crew responsible for ensuring that the cargo is correctly loaded and secured aboard vessel. In this case, quayside and conservancy charges are the responsibility of the seller, although these charges may be passed on to the buyer as part of the FOB charges. Cargo Insurance for the voyage is arranged by the buyer/charterer.

CIF – Cost, Insurance and Freight: Risk passes to buyer when delivered on board the ship. Seller arranges and pays cost, freight and insurance to destination port. Adds insurance costs to CFR.

For break bulk operations, with CIF, the seller/exporter is responsible for the loading of the vessel and payment of freight costs to the port of loading, implying that quayside cranes will be used to load the cargo aboard vessel, with the port stevedores and vessel crew responsible for ensuring that the cargo is correctly loaded and secured aboard vessel. In this case, quayside and conservancy charges are the responsibility of the seller, although these charges may be passed on to the buyer as part of the FOB charges. However, the risk is passed to the buyer/charterer at the point of loading and securing the cargo aboard vessel, as the insurance policy is transferred to the buyer/charterer at that same point. The buyer/charterer is also responsible for the unloading of the vessel at the port of arrival, as well as Import Customs clearance of the cargo at the port of destination.

It should be noted at this point that in general, break bulk cargo management is governed by the marine INCOTERMS, although with integrated transport systems, the following terms for multimodal use can apply depending upon the transport negotiations arranged between buyer and seller.

Rules for any mode or modes of transportation

EXW – Ex Works: Seller delivers (without loading) the goods at disposal of buyer at seller's premises. Long held as the most preferable term for those new-to-export because it represents the minimum liability to the seller. On these routed transactions, the buyer has limited obligation to provide export information to the seller.

FCA – Free Carrier: Seller delivers the goods to the carrier and may be responsible for clearing the goods for export (filing the EEI). More realistic than EXW because it includes loading at pick-up, which is commonly expected, and sellers are more concerned about export violations.

CPT – Carriage Paid To: Seller delivers goods to the carrier at an agreed place, shifting risk to the buyer, but seller must pay cost of carriage to the named place of destination.

CIP – Carriage and Insurance Paid To: Seller delivers goods to the carrier at an agreed place, shifting risk to the buyer, but seller pays carriage and insurance to the named place of destination.

DAT – Delivered At Terminal: Seller bears cost, risk and responsibility until goods are unloaded (delivered) at named quay, warehouse, yard, or terminal at destination. Demurrage or detention charges may apply to seller. Seller clears goods for export, not import. DAT replaces DEQ, DES.

DAP – Delivered At Place: Seller bears cost, risk and responsibility for goods until made available to buyer at named place of destination. Seller clears goods for export, not import. DAP replaces DAF, DDU.

DDP – Delivered Duty Paid: Seller bears cost, risk and responsibility for cleared goods at named place of destination at buyer's disposal. Buyer is responsible for unloading. The seller is responsible for import clearance, duties and taxes so buyer is not "importer of record".

INCOTERMS do not . . .

- Determine ownership or transfer title to the goods, nor evoke payment terms;
- Apply to service contracts, nor define contractual rights or obligations (except for delivery) or breach of contract remedies;
- Protect parties from their own risk or loss, nor cover the goods before or after delivery;
- Specify details of the transfer, transport, and delivery of the goods. Container loading is NOT considered packaging, and must be addressed in the sales contract;
- *Remember, INCOTERMS are not law and there is NO default INCOTERM.*

The multimodal terms are detailed here.

EXW – Ex Works – named place or origin

It should be noted that this term should be used purely for price quotations and not actual movements of goods, as it is not strictly an international term.

The seller makes the goods available at their premises, or at another named place. This term places the maximum obligation on the buyer and minimum obligations on the seller. The Ex Works term is often used while making an initial quotation for the sale of goods without any costs included.

EXW means that a buyer incurs the risks for bringing the goods to their final destination. Either the seller does not load the goods on collecting vehicles and does not clear them for export, or if the seller does load the goods, he does so at buyer's risk and cost. If the parties agree that the seller should be responsible for the loading of the goods on departure and to bear the risk and all costs of such loading, this must be made clear by adding explicit wording to this effect in the contract of sale.

There is no obligation for the seller to make a contract of carriage, but there is also no obligation for the buyer to arrange one either – the buyer may sell the goods on to their own customer for collection from the original seller's warehouse. However, in common practice the buyer arranges the collection of the freight from the designated location, and is responsible for clearing the goods through Customs. The buyer is also responsible for completing all the export documentation, although the seller does have an obligation to obtain information and documents at the buyer's request and cost.

These documentary requirements may result in two principal issues. First, the stipulation for the buyer to complete the export declaration can be an issue in certain jurisdictions (not least the European Union) where the Customs regulations require the declarant to be either an individual or corporation resident within the jurisdiction. If the buyer is based outside of the Customs jurisdiction they will be unable to clear the goods for export, meaning that the goods may be declared in the name of the seller by the buyer, even though the export formalities are the buyer's responsibility under the EXW term.

Second, most national jurisdictions require companies to provide proof of export for tax purposes. In an EXW shipment, the buyer is under no obligation to provide such proof to the seller, or indeed to even export the goods. In a Customs jurisdiction such as the European Union, this would leave the seller liable to a sales tax bill as if the goods were sold to a domestic customer. It is therefore of utmost importance that these matters are discussed with the buyer before the contract is agreed and that the seller receives documentary proof of export and receipt by the buyer in the form of an endorsed copy of the Transport Document, e.g. CMR Consignment Note, from the buyer. It may well be that another INCOTERM, such as FCA seller's premises, may be more suitable, since this puts the burden of responsibility for declaring the goods for export onto the seller, which provides for more control over the export process.

Third, EXW requires the buyer to be VAT-registered in the country of export, as the buyer is responsible for the export declaration. This may not be practical or easy to carry out, as VAT registration in another country can be a laborious process and can take some time to achieve.

FCA – Free Carrier – named place

It is important to note that this incoterm can be used for any mode of transportation.

While it is generally accepted that no single INCOTERM is better than another, this particular INCOTERM allows for a great deal of flexibility as it can be used for either airfreight or seafreight shipments. In order for this incoterm to be used correctly the shipper or consignee must state a named place, i.e. Free Carrier – freight forwarders facility Los Angeles, California. Free Carrier can also technically be stated FCA – shipper's facility. In this scenario the only difference between FCA and EXW would be that the shipper would be responsible for loading the cargo onto a truck at the dock.

Under the terms of FCA, the seller must deliver the goods to a carrier nominated by the buyer at a specified named place. The seller fulfills his obligation to deliver when he has handed over the goods, cleared for export, into the charge of the carrier named by the buyer at the named place or point.

Payment responsibilities outlined below:

Seller's responsibilities

1. Warehouse storage at point of origin;
2. Warehouse labour at point of origin;

3. Export packing;
4. Loading at point of origin.

Buyer's responsibilities

1. Inland freight;
2. Port of receiving charges;
3. Forwarder's fee;
4. Loading on ocean carrier/airline;
5. Ocean/air freight charges;
6. Charges in foreign airport/port;
7. Customs duties and taxes abroad;
8. Delivery charges to final destination.

INCOTERMS: CPT – Carriage Paid To

CPT "Carriage Paid To" is an incoterm that can be used for any kind of shipment. CPT is somewhat similar to CFR and CIF with some differences.

In CPT, like CIF, the seller/exporter arranges for the goods to be delivered to the named port of destination. Unlike both CFR and CIF, the seller's risks end the moment the goods have been delivered to the carrier. Because this incoterm can be used for any mode of transport, a carrier in this case could be a steamship line, a trucker, a railroad or a freight forwarder. The seller is responsible for all costs until the goods have been delivered to the named port of destination. In this case, the named port of destination is domestic to the buyer, meaning that the named port must be a port in the buyer's country, however unlike other similar INCOTERMS the named port of destination is not necessarily the final delivery point: it could be, but it could also be an agreed upon point at the port of destination. So if you were selling cherries to Thailand (can you tell I like this example?) you would use the term "CPT, Carriage Paid to Laem Chabang Port, Thailand", however Laem Chabang might or might not be the final delivery point at the port of destination.

Under CPT terms, the seller's risks end the moment the goods are handed over to the carrier but the seller is responsible for all costs up to the named port of destination:

Seller's responsibilities

1) Produces the goods and commercial documents as required by the sales contract.
2) Arranges for export clearance and all export formalities.
3) Arranges and pays for all costs for the transportation of the goods up to the agreed point in the named port of destination.

4) Assumes all risk to the goods (loss or damage) only up to the point they have been turned over to the carrier. Seller is under no obligation to buy insurance. SPECIAL NOTE: While the seller has no obligation to insure the goods and may not be legally responsible for the goods once they are with the carrier, he may have a vested interest in the goods during the voyage. It may be a wise decision to purchase additional insurance coverage in the case of a loss.
5) Seller must advise the buyer that the goods have been delivered to the carrier.
6) Seller has to provide the buyer with transport documents that will allow the buyer to take possession of the goods at the agreed point in the named port of destination.

Buyer's responsibilities

1) The Buyer must pay for the goods as per the sales contract.
2) The Buyer must obtain all commercial documentation, licences, and authorisations required for import and arrange for import clearance and formalities at own risk and cost.
3) The Buyer takes delivery of the goods after they have been delivered by the seller to the agreed point in the named port of destination.
4) The Buyer must assume all risks for the goods from the time the goods have been handed over to the carrier. SPECIAL NOTE: While neither the seller nor the buyer are required to insure the shipment, the buyer may have a vested interest in the goods during the voyage. It may be a wise decision for the buyer to purchase additional insurance coverage in the case of a loss.
5) The Buyer pays for all costs of transportation, import Customs formalities and duty fees, and all other formalities and charges related to the transportation of the shipment from the time the goods have been delivered to the agreed point in the named port of destination.
6) The Buyer would accept the seller's transport documents provided they conform with the sales contract and will allow the buyer to take possession of the goods after delivery to agreed point in the named port of destination.

INCOTERMS: CIP – Carriage and Insurance Paid to

CIP – "Carriage and Insurance Paid to" is an incoterm that is commonly confused with CIF. Unlike its more common sibling CIF, I rarely see CIP used, with too many companies using CIF for air shipments and other modes of transport when what they really should be using is CIP. CIP, unlike CIF, can be used for any kind of shipment. CIP is very similar to CIF in that it includes insurance as well as cost and freight.

In CIP, the seller/exporter arranges for the goods to be delivered to the named port of destination. Similar to CPT, the seller's risks do not end until the moment the goods have been delivered to the carrier, but typically do not end until the carrier reaches the agreed destination. Because this incoterm can be used for any mode of transport, a carrier in this case could be a steamship line, a trucker, a railroad or a freight forwarder. The seller is responsible for all costs until the goods have been delivered to the named port of destination. In this case, the named port of destination is domestic to the buyer, meaning that the named port must be a port in the buyer's country, however unlike other similar INCOTERMS, the named port of destination is not necessarily the final delivery point: it could be, but it could also be an agreed upon point at the port of destination. So if you were selling cherries to Thailand you would use the term "CIP, Carriage and Insurance Paid to Laem Chabang Port, Thailand", however Laem Chabang might or might not be the final delivery point at the port of destination.

Under CIP terms, the seller's risks end the moment the goods are delivered to the carrier, but typically do not end until the carrier reaches the agreed destination. The seller is responsible for all costs up to the named port or inland clearance depot of destination:

Seller's responsibilities

1) Produces the goods and commercial documents as required by the sales contract.
2) Arranges for export clearance and all export formalities.
3) Arranges and pays for all costs for the transportation "including insurance" – of the goods up to the agreed point in the named port of destination.
4) Assumes all risk to the goods (loss or damage) only up to the point they have been handed over to the carrier, typically, but not always, ending when the carrier reaches the agreed destination.
5) Seller must advise the buyer that the goods have been delivered to the carrier.
6) Seller has to provide the buyer with transport documents that will allow the buyer to take possession of the goods at the agreed point in the named port of destination.

Buyer's responsibilities

1) Buyer must pay for the goods as per the sales contract.
2) Buyer must obtain all commercial documentation, licenses and authorisations required for import and arrange for import clearance and formalities at own risk and cost.
3) Buyer takes delivery of the goods after they have been delivered by the seller to the agreed point in the named port of destination.

4) Buyer must assume all risks for the goods from the time the goods have been handed over to the carrier, typically, but not always, ending when the carrier reaches the agreed destination. SPECIAL NOTE: While the seller is obligated to insure the goods, the buyer may have a vested interest in the goods during the voyage. It may be a wise decision for the buyer to purchase additional insurance coverage in the case of a loss.
5) Buyer pays for all costs of transportation, import Customs formalities and duty fees, and all other formalities and charges related to the transportation of the shipment from the time the goods have been delivered to the agreed point in the named port of destination.
6) Buyer would accept the seller's transport documents provided they conform with the sales contract and will allow the buyer to take possession of the goods after delivery to agreed point in the named port of destination.

DAP – Delivered At Place (named place of destination)

INCOTERMS 2010 defines DAP as "Delivered At Place" – the seller delivers when the goods are placed at the disposal of the buyer on the arriving means of transport ready for unloading at the named place of destination. Under DAP terms, the risk passes from seller to buyer from the point of destination mentioned in the contract of delivery. The seller is also responsible for all the costs involved to deliver the goods to the named place of destination. The seller's risk also does not end until it reaches the names place of destination.

Once the goods are ready for shipment, the necessary packing is carried out by the seller at his own cost, so that the goods reach their final destination safely. All necessary legal formalities in the exporting country are completed by the seller at his own cost and risk to clear the goods for export.

After arrival of the goods in the country of destination, the Customs clearance in the importing country needs to be completed by the buyer at his own cost and risk, including all Customs duties and taxes. However, as with DAT terms, any delay or demurrage charges are to be borne by the seller.

Under DAP terms, all carriage expenses with any terminal expenses are paid by seller up to the agreed destination point. The necessary unloading cost at final destination has to be borne by the buyer under DAP terms.

Under DAP terms the seller's risk and responsibility end once the goods have been made available to the buyer at the named place of destination while still loaded on the vehicle. The buyer is therefore responsible for the unloading of the vehicle. The seller is also responsible for all costs up to the named place of destination, but is not responsible for delivering the goods to their final destination, in the sense of unloading the vehicle at the final destination.

Seller's responsibilities

1) Produces the goods and commercial documents as required by the sales contract.
2) Arranges for export clearance and all export formalities.
3) Arranges and pays for all costs for the transportation of the goods up to named place of destination.
4) Assumes all risk to the goods (loss or damage) up to the point they have been made available to the buyer at the named place of destination. SPECIAL NOTE: Under DAP terms the seller is under no obligation to provide insurance. However, he may have a vested interest in the goods during the voyage. It may be a wise decision to purchase additional insurance coverage in the case of a loss.
5) Seller must advise the buyer that the goods have been delivered to the carrier and the appropriate arrival information.
6) Seller has to provide the buyer with transport documents that will allow the buyer to take possession of the goods at the named place of destination.

Buyer's responsibilities

1) Buyer must pay for the goods as per the sales contract.
2) Buyer must obtain all commercial documentation, licenses and authorisations required for import and arrange for import clearance and formalities at own risk and cost.
3) Buyer takes delivery of the goods after they have been delivered by the seller to the named place of destination.
4) Buyer must assume all risks for the goods from the time the goods have been made available at the named place of destination.
5) Buyer pays for all costs of transportation, import Customs formalities and duty fees and all other formalities and charges related to the transportation of the shipment from the time the goods have been made available at the named place of destination.
6) Buyer would accept the seller's transport documents provided they conform with the sales contract and will allow the buyer to take possession of the goods after delivery to the named place of destination.

DAT – Delivered At Terminal (. . . named terminal at port or place of destination)

The seller delivers when the goods, once unloaded from the arriving means of transport, are placed at the disposal of the buyer at a named terminal at the named port or place of destination. "Terminal" includes quay, warehouse, container yard or road, rail or air terminal.

Both parties should agree the terminal and, if possible, a point within the terminal at which point the risks will transfer from the seller to the buyer of the goods. If it is intended that the seller is to bear all the costs and responsibilities from the terminal to another point, DAP or DDP may apply.

Responsibilities

- Seller is responsible for the costs and risks to bring the goods to the point specified in the contract;
- Seller should ensure that their forwarding contract mirrors the contract of sale;
- Seller is responsible for the export clearance procedures;
- Importer is responsible to clear the goods for import, arrange import Customs formalities, and pay import duty;
- If the parties intend the seller to bear the risks and costs of taking the goods from the terminal to another place then the DAP term may apply.

DDP – Delivered Duty Paid (named place of destination)

The seller is responsible for delivering the goods to the named place in the country of the buyer, and pays all costs in bringing the goods to the destination including import duties and taxes. The seller is not responsible for unloading. This term is often used in place of the non-INCOTERM "Free In Store (FIS)". This term places the maximum obligations on the seller and minimum obligations on the buyer. No risk or responsibility is transferred to the buyer until delivery of the goods at the named place of destination.

The most important consideration for DDP terms is that the seller is responsible for clearing the goods through Customs in the buyer's country, including both paying the duties and taxes, and obtaining the necessary authorisations and registrations from the authorities in that country. Unless the rules and regulations in the buyer's country are very well understood, DDP terms can be a very big risk both in terms of delays and in unforeseen extra costs, including local duties and sales taxes, and should be used with caution.

INCOTERMS 2020 – essential changes

INCOTERMS are soft rules, and are not mandatory. However, they help greatly in defining international contracts, as they enable buyers and sellers to avoid costly disputes when it comes to the responsibilities of each party concerning the international shipment and delivery of goods. There are, however, a number of common misconceptions surrounding INCOTERMS. In line with earlier editions, INCOTERMS 2020 cover the parties' obligations to arrange for the carriage and insurance of the goods. They determine the point at which the goods are delivered, the point at which risk in the goods for loss or damage is transferred from seller to buyer and the various costs associated with the transport of the goods.

> Incoterms® determine the point at which the goods are delivered, the point at which risk in the goods for loss or damage is transferred from seller to buyer and the various costs associated with the transport of the goods

It should be noted that INCOTERMS, however, do not cover the following:

- Ownership or who retains the title to the goods;
- Quality of goods;
- Breaches of contract;
- Method or terms of payment;
- Responsibility to insure the goods (Except CIF & CIP);
- Other services contractually provided;
- Issues around sanctions;
- Governing law and jurisdiction of contract;
- Regulatory compliance requirements such as the provision of VGM, proof of export for VAT zero-rating purposes (for this the term EXW (Ex Works) should **never** be used);
- Remedies in respect of disputes or breaches of contract;
- Responsibilities for Duties and Sales Taxes (Except DDP).

INCOTERMS 2020 in practice came into force on 1 January 2020. The ICC recommend using the most up-to-date terms, best reflecting current trade practices, but use is not obligatory. Businesses can continue to use earlier versions – whichever edition is being used, it is recommended that businesses ensure that this is clearly defined in the contracts.

INCOTERMS per se are not legally binding, unless express reference to the specific INCOTERM is incorporated into an agreement. However, they are commonly included in commercial contracts, as they define the transfer of risk and responsibility for the international carriage of cargoes from seller to buyer, and also determine the responsibility of either party for the payment of freight and insurance costs relating to the international carriage of these cargoes.

The ICC suggests the following template for incorporation:

> [the chosen Incoterms rule] [named port, place or point] Incoterms® 2020
>
> *e.g. FCA (Winsford, Cheshire, United Kingdom) Incoterms 2020®*
> *e.g. DAP (Unit 15, ABC Business Park, Winsford, United Kingdom) Incoterms 2020®*

While it is not necessary to use the trademark symbol, it is essential to state the version of the INCOTERMS used, as not doing so may result in disputes and unintended outcomes.

There is an importance in accurately inserting the correct named port, place or point of delivery, destination or both. This again will increase certainty and avoid potential costly disputes.

Since 1980 the INCOTERMS have consisted of four main groups of terms:

E – Terms – Ex Works
F – Terms – "Free" goods for export
C – Terms – Carriage (similar to F – Terms but seller contracts the carriage and invoices the buyer)
D – Terms – Delivered. Delivers goods into the buyer's country (transit and risk remains with the seller).

Key changes for 2020

INCOTERMS 2020 consist of 11 defined terms. There are four sea freight only rules and seven rules which can be used for any mode, with 15 available options in total, since FOB, FCA, CIF and CIP can be assigned one of two named delivery places. While this revision has witnessed only a small number of substantive changes, there remains an importance in understanding the impact of these changes.

Delivery At Place – Seeking to remove the confusion historically arising between DAT (Delivered At Terminal) and DAP (Delivered At Place), the former has been replaced by DPU (Delivered At Place Unloaded). This serves to clarify that delivery is effected once the goods have been unloaded from the ship or inland means of transport and made available to the buyer at a specified place in the terminal, which can be a temporary storage premises, i.e. a Transit Shed or even a Customs Warehouse.

DPU – Delivered At Place Unloaded

This term replaces DAT, and means that as well as arranging the transport of the goods to the buyer's nominated premises, the seller is also responsible for the unloading of the goods from the means of transport concerned, whether or not using the lifting equipment provided by the buyer. These conditions are similar to those of the original term DAT. The buyer still arranges Customs clearance and the liability and payment of all Customs/Excise Duties and VAT/Sales Tax.

Insurance – Only two INCOTERMS require and include insurance, in each case requiring the seller to purchase insurance in the buyer's name. CIF Seller buys the insurance in the name of the buyer at Cargo Institute Clauses "C" (which are restricted). CIP Seller buys the insurance in the name of the buyer at Cargo Institute Clauses "A" (All Risks). Parties can expressly agree alternative levels of insurance cover under both CIF and CIP.

Costs – INCOTERMS 2020 provides much more detail around costs and their allocation under A9. In general costs up to delivery are for the seller and the costs thereafter are for the buyer.

Security – The 2020 text provides more detail around security. A4/ B4 and A7/ B7 consider security aspects.

Own transport – INCOTERMS 2010 assumed that all transport would be undertaken by a third party. INCOTERMS 2020 recognises the concept of own transport.

FCA, FOB and Bills of Lading – FCA requires the seller to deliver the goods effectively up to the point that the goods are delivered to the quayside; FOB is still widely used (incorrectly) to undertake the same function. FCA is preferential for the seller given that it does not include the risk associated with loading the cargo onto the ship. Delivery is assumed at the point that the cargo is delivered to the named place. This can in practice give rise to difficulties in terms of payment, however, for example where a letter of credit requires an onboard bill of lading. INCOTERMS 2020 adopts further language under the FCA term to allow the seller to require the buyer to procure an onboard bill of lading to alleviate this issue. The FCA Term can now be used with charter Parties where the seller makes the goods available at the quayside for the charterer to arrange loading aboard vessel.

The risk context

Incorporation of INCOTERMS into a sale contract will not bind any third party, or govern any other contract. It remains for the seller or buyer to ensure that the agreed INCOTERM correctly reflects the reality for finance, carriage and insurance. Start with the end in mind!

While in many instances stakeholders in the supply chain have no influence over the sale terms used, the INCOTERM can influence how goods are prepared for carriage, declared and how they are entered into the global supply chain. Where possible therefore it is generally recommended that stakeholders in the supply chain understand the INCOTERM used and perform a risk assessment accordingly.

> Incoterms® can influence how goods are prepared for carriage, declared and how they are entered into the global supply chain

Cargo integrity

Poor packing and securing of goods in cargo transport units (CTU) remains responsible for an alarmingly high percentage of incidents throughout the supply chain, leading to damage, loss, injuries and fatalities. The claims experiences of various P&I Clubs shows that 65% of incidents involving damage to cargo can be attributed to poor or improper packing and securing.

The INCOTERM selected under the sales contract can provide an insight as to how the goods are likely to be entered into the supply chain. If goods are being sold as Ex Works, for example, stakeholders involved in the transport of the consignment might want to seek greater assurance concerning how the goods are packaged, labelled, packed and secured within the CTU prior to carriage. The seller is only required to present the goods in suitable packaging for collection by the buyer. In practice, the seller/shipper is likely to be involved in packing the cargo into the CTU for the entire transit. Unitised trade moved internationally almost inevitably involves multiple modes of transport; this requires understanding of differing physical dynamics and regulatory requirements. Diligence in such aspects will lead to additional cost.

Cargo insurance

Goods in transit are at risk from a range of "perils", including theft, mishap during carriage and general average. Carriers' liabilities are in many cases limited under the contract of carriage; from the perspective of those with an interest in the cargo, it is prudent to ensure that goods are covered with an appropriate cargo policy from departure to arrival. In certain maritime trades it is understood that as much as 40% of goods travel without cargo insurance.

Where goods are not shipped under CIF or CIP, it is advisable for shipping agencies, freight forwarders or carriers to promote the value of cargo insurance – and perhaps be cautious where a shipper is adamant that they do not wish to purchase adequate cover. This is especially true where the value of the consignment is known to be low, which may give rise to issues at destination where cargoes are either not permitted for import or simply abandoned.

Container demurrage and detention

Where cargoes do experience difficulties at destination, costs build quickly. Demurrage is the daily charge applied by the shipping line for laden containers that have arrived at the destination port, but have not been collected within the prescribed free time period. Detention is the daily charge applied by the shipping line where containers that have been emptied of the carried cargo are not returned within the prescribed free time period.

Due diligence in relation to the nature of the supply chain and a knowledge of the sales terms can provide an early red flag to stakeholders that may mitigate such risks.

Due diligence

Performing adequate due diligence on your contractual partners is a fundamental risk management tool for your business. Inevitably freight forwarders, haulage companies and other stakeholders in the supply chain, by the very nature of their businesses, contract with parties on a global scale in the provision of their valuable services.

Given the global nature of the modern supply chain, stakeholders offering their services face a number of key risk factors which should be considered. The INCOTERM incorporated into the sales contract may be indicative of the behaviour of the buyer and seller and how the goods are entered into the supply chain.

Due diligence is often considered in the context of the party seeking a supplier relationship; today's risk exposures require those offering a service to carry out similar validation of the presenting entity and details – and seek assurance that other stakeholders in the supply chain on whom there will be reliance implement similar checks.

Conclusion

The global freight supply chain is a complex structure, with numerous direct and indirect stakeholders, especially for break bulk and Project Cargo operations. The INCOTERMS represent a valuable and valid framework to bring clarity and standardisation in trading internationally, as well as ensuring clarity within the global supply chain. The consequences of decisions made in the context of the relationship between seller and buyer, as with other international trade related requirements, such as those involved in Customs, Crime Prevention or Security, need also to be assessed on the basis of a primary focus on safety and security.

CHAPTER 6

BIMCO & the Baltic Exchange

Vessel chartering is governed by two main international maritime organisations, namely the Baltic and International Maritime Council (BIMCO), based in Denmark, and the Baltic Exchange, based in the City of London. Together, they govern most of the global break bulk and bulk shipping markets, representing, shipowners, shipping agencies and shipbrokers. They are two completely separate organisations, yet they share much in common in that they are primarily involved in the vessel charter market and ensure the efficient organisation of the bulk shipping sector on a global basis.

BIMCO

The Baltic and International Maritime Council (BIMCO) is the largest of the international shipping associations representing shipowners; its membership controls around 65% of the world's tonnage and it has members in more than 120 countries, including managers, brokers and agents. The association's main objective is to protect its global membership through the provision of information and advice, and while promoting fair business practices, facilitate harmonisation and standardisation of commercial shipping practices and contracts.

The organisation's foundation stretches back to 1905, where BIMCO began as a grain shipping cartel under the name "The Baltic and White Sea Conference". Within a couple of years, the cartel was scrapped, but the collaboration on standard contracts remained. Since then, BIMCO has become more involved in the regulatory side of shipping and is now a leading voice in shipping.

In support of its commitment to promote the development and application of global regulatory instruments, BIMCO is accredited as a Non-Governmental Organisation (NGO) with all relevant United Nations organs. In an effort to promote its agenda and objectives, the association maintains a close dialogue with governments and diplomatic representations around the world, including maritime administrations, regulatory institutions and other stakeholders within the areas of the EU, the United States and Asia.

BIMCO also conducts various training programmes around the world for the Maritime Community.

 DOI: 10.4324/9781003256359-7

BIMCO is the world's largest direct-membership organisation for shipowners, charterers, shipbrokers and agents. In total, around 60% of the world's merchant fleet is a BIMCO member, measured by tonnage (weight of the unloaded ships).

The organisation has NGO status and is based in Bagsvaerd, near Copenhagen, Denmark, with offices in Athens, Singapore and Shanghai. With around 1,900 member companies across 120 countries – from the largest shipowners in the world to small local port agents and law firms – BIMCO represents a wide range of maritime companies and organisations.

BIMCO's goal is to secure a level playing field for the global shipping industry. BIMCO therefore works to promote and secure global standards and regulations for the maritime sector. The organisation's century-long effort into creating standard contracts and clauses is an expression of that aim. Furthermore, BIMCO wants workable and realistic regulations that, among other things, drive the industry towards the target of reducing CO_2 emission by 50% by 2050. Ultimately, the goal is a zero-emissions industry in this century. To achieve its goals, BIMCO organises and funds committees to discuss and deliver new or revised standard contracts and clauses. The documents are used within the entire shipping industry, including containers, dry bulk, tankers, financing, offshore and shipbuilding. Through working groups, BIMCO also develops suggestions for new regulation or industry standards – such as the international standard for underwater hull cleaning.

The aim of the organisation is to produce flexible commercial agreements that are fair to both parties. BIMCO works with industry experts to produce modern contracts tailored to specific trades and activities. BIMCO's contracts are recognised around the world and widely used.

On a political level, BIMCO participates as an NGO at the International Maritime Organization (IMO), where BIMCO advises the member states, on behalf of the shipping industry, on the consequences of proposed regulation and suggests solutions to making regulation effective and practicable. The direction is set by BIMCO's Board of Directors.

As a BIMCO member, a company becomes part of an organisation that brings shipping people together to work for shared goals. Members receive news and access to exclusive hands-on guides and a helpdesk for contractual issues. The BIMCO website contains a broad range of information dealing with the day-to-day operation of a shipping company, such as contracts and contractual issues, port information, a cargo database, maritime security updates and much more.

Members furthermore receive discounts on several BIMCO products including:

- SmartCon;
- Shipping KPI;
- Training;
- Publications, such as the Ship Master's Security Manual.

BIMCO's products include BIMCO's world leading standard contracts and clauses for the shipping industry and our contract editing tool SmartCon. We also run the BIMCO Shipping KPI System which can be used to benchmark ships' operational performance.

Regulation: BIMCO takes an active role on behalf of shipowners during discussions and decisions with global and regional regulators. We work towards a level playing field for shipping – including fair trade and open access to markets.

Information and advice: BIMCO deals with 10,000 queries every year on many issues and see over three million page views on our website each year. Its staff share their expert knowledge with members, giving practical advice to safeguard and add value to their businesses.

The Organisation's *training* activities include face-to-face courses, webinars and tailor-made courses for companies.

All of BIMCO's most widely used charter parties, bills of lading and other standard agreements are available in an electronic format using BIMCO's online pay-as-you-go charterparty editing system, SmartCon.

BIMCO has developed a large number of standalone clauses to supplement the standard contracts. These clauses address a wide range of topics and can be downloaded free of charge.

The Baltic and International Maritime Council (BIMCO) is one of the largest and most diverse private shipping organisations in the world. Its goal is to unite shipping interests to proactively and rapidly respond to issues that affect its members arising in a fast-changing maritime environment. BIMCO provides a forum for international debates on maritime issues. As a private, independent, non-political organisation, BIMCO represents the interests of its members by being a participant in the regulatory process plus issuing media pronouncements to espouse its causes. The organisation is a strong advocate of free trade, open access to markets, a preference for international rather than local or regional regulation, high quality standards of ship operation and effective measures to ensure ship and cargo security.

BIMCO also offers practical and specific services to shipowners, managers, brokers, agents, ship operators, maritime associations and other entities connected with the international shipping industry. Headquartered in Denmark, BIMCO's 1,900 member companies are from over 120 countries resulting in representation of 60% of the world's merchant fleet.

The history of BIMCO dates back to the beginning of the 20th century, and started its life in two very traditional shipping areas, namely the North-East of England and Denmark, areas which have shared common history and interests since the days of the Viking occupation of much of England.

Thomas Cairns, a shipowner based in the city of Newcastle-upon-Tyne, and Johan Hansen of the Danish capital, Copenhagen, were the founders of the organisation which preceded BIMCO. It is also an interesting detail, although not directly associated with this text, that the name "Baltic" is still associated with

Newcastle; the former Baltic Mill is located in Gateshead, on the south side of the River Tyne, and is now a centre for cultural activities on Tyneside.

Thomas Cairns suggested the formation of an organisation to create "a movement based on goodwill and understanding" to advance the interests of shipowners involved with the Baltic Sea trades. This idea gave birth to the 1905 Baltic and White Sea Conference held in Copenhagen with an assembly of 112 shipping people to discuss how to deal with the problems associated with the carriage of forest products in Northwest Europe. The response to the conference was so positive that membership expanded beyond the confines of the Baltic Sea. Ten months after the first meeting, member owners' fleets controlled 1,056 ships of 1.62 million gross registered tons of shipping. Four years after its foundation, membership of the organisation had become representative of much of the entire industry. By 1925, there were 404 owner members from 19 nations representing 8.34 million gross tons of shipping. The changing nature of the membership necessitated a name change in 1927 to the Baltic and International Maritime Conference followed in 1985 to the Baltic and International Maritime Council (BIMCO). More than a century later, the principle of "goodwill and understanding" remains true despite shipping becoming more complex and more geographically dispersed; scarcely recognisable from the small, simple craft carrying forest products around the littoral of the Baltic Sea at the start of the 20th century.

Under its first president, Adolf Carl of Copenhagen, the Baltic and White Sea Conference addressed the need for fair and balanced documents for ship operators by beginning to publish uniform charter parties for arranging the chartering (contracting) of ships and the carriage of cargoes between shippers and shipowners. In 1908, the first standard Charter Party BALTCON was adopted, thus establishing a precedent for the creation of chartering documents which would be acceptable to the shipper and shipowner that protected the integrity and position of both. This eventually became a BIMCO trademark, and today BIMCO publishes over 40 different types of voyage and time charters and bills of lading which are standardised for particular types of cargoes, ships, and conditions. In addition, there are over 70 standardised clauses covering all phases of the loading, carriage and discharging of cargoes that shippers and owners can incorporate in their charter agreements.

It was clear from the beginning of these activities that there was a dearth of information available to shipowners for operating and chartering their vessels. Initial dissemination of important information was carried out by means of a newsletter on port information, contractual and documentary matters along with data on weather and ice conditions. This developed over the years to the point that today the *BIMCO Bulletin* is published every two months with details on new or revised charter parties and other documents, reports on actions or hearings being taken by regulatory bodies with commentaries on new or proposed legislation and other pertinent matters on shipping. *A Handbook of Baltic and White Sea Ports*, published in 1913, was the start of the BIMCO's "brand" to provide clear and concise information in a publication format. Publications now cover freight taxes, ice conditions at sea, security matters affecting shipmasters, the Panama Canal expansion, technical specification guide for new bulk carriers, manpower needs for the maritime industry, ship recycling and a global holiday calendar. The global holiday calendar is a necessity for members who operate ships calling on ports throughout the world where time in port is a cost, not a source of revenue. National holidays are a crucial element of shipping layovers and laytime, as port activities tend to stop over such holiday periods, and this can add significant costs to vessel operations, especially where charter contracts are involved, as such contracts include provisions for vessel laytime.

Membership

BIMCO's membership is open to companies involved in various sectors of shipping. BIMCO membership provides a platform for all those involved in the shipping industry to work together to improve and develop the overall industry. In general, members stay up to date on all news as well as having access to exclusive hands-on guides and a helpdesk for contractual issues. BIMCO website has a broad range of information dealing with the day-to-day operation of a shipping company such as contracts and contractual issues, port information, a cargo database, maritime security updates and other matters.

BIMCO membership is classified into five different groups, including:

- Associate membership;
- Agent membership;
- Club membership;
- Broker membership; and
- Owner membership.

Associate membership allows for members from the industry's major classification societies, maritime law firms, financial institutions, shippers, shipyards, marine consultants and others servicing the shipping industry to join together for a common approach to maritime matters. There are four categories of Associate membership: Plus, Standard, Educational Institution, and PMSC representing port security companies. Associate members benefit with online comprehensive information on 1,800+ ports around the world including holidays, latest shipping market analysis, information on contractual and commercial issues, such as charter parties or bills of lading and access to the BIMCO members' directory.

Agent membership is open to companies operating as ship agents. Applicants who own, manage or operate ships on time charter are obliged to register as owner members. Some of the benefits of membership include having access to direct advice from in-house experts on contractual and commercial issues, specific company information and debt recovery along with availability of online comprehensive information. Port information is available on berthing delays, strikes and lock-out warnings, holidays and working hours, availability of cargo handling equipment and other details.

Club membership is open to Protection and Indemnity (P&I) Insurance associations, freight, demurrage and defence associations and national associations. Members are able to utilise BIMCO's online comprehensive information on 1,800+ ports around the world, including holidays, latest shipping market analysis and reports, information on contractual and commercial issues, such as charter parties or bills of lading, and last, access to the BIMCO members' directory.

Broker membership is for companies operating as shipbrokers or chartering agents. Some of the benefits include direct advice from BIMCO's in-house experts on contractual and commercial issues, such as charter parties or bills of lading guidance on pre/post fixing documentation, business partner company information, and debt recovery. Additionally, online comprehensive information is available on over 1,800 ports around the world including holidays, updates on security warnings and war risk including piracy and drug smuggling, latest shipping market analysis and reports and access to the BIMCO members' directory.

Owner membership in BIMCO is open to companies that own or manage ships, operate ships on bareboat, time and voyage charters or provide scheduled liner services with chartered ships. Some of the benefits of having Owner membership include access to direct advice from BIMCO's in-house experts on issues such as contractual and commercial issues. These would include charter parties and bills of lading, environment, safety, security and navigation issues related to ship operation, ability to obtain business partner company information and debt recovery. Furthermore, members also have access to online comprehensive information on 1,800+ ports around the world including holidays, updates on security warnings and war risk including piracy and drug smuggling, latest shipping market analysis and reports and access to BIMCO members' directory.

Organisation

BIMCO leadership and management consists of the Secretary General, three Deputy Secretary Generals, who manage BIMCO products, regulation and information and advice, Chief Financial Officer, CIO, and Communications Director. In addition to collaborating with others in the industry, BIMCO also supports and participates in the Round Table of international shipping associations with the International Chamber of Shipping, the International Association of Independent Tanker owners and the International Association of Dry Cargo Shipowners. Senior officers in BIMCO and the Secretariat staff meet regularly with these international shipping organisations for an exchange of views on important issues and to coordinate actions to avoid duplication of effort. In addition, the Round Table dialogue has also been successful over the years in assisting to produce improved and more efficient vessel designs.

Finance

BIMCO's financing primarily comes from its various membership fees plus additional revenue from publications, conferences and public events and courses on various aspects of shipping, maritime commerce and law.

Transitional economic governance

BIMCO plays several roles in the transnational economic governance to ensure that the shipping industry does not violate or threaten the global community. One such challenge faced by BIMCO is autonomous ship operation.

Standard contracts for autonomous ship operation

Given the ravages of the global 2020 SARS-CoV pandemic, digitisation and a reduction in crew manning requirements has become much more prevalent, and this has reflected in the adaptation of various BIMCO Agreements. The SHIPMAN 2009 agreement is currently being used for the concept of autonomous ships, although the irony is that, at present, there are no autonomous ships in operation, as traditional crewing is still the main means of vessel operation and control. However, the means of vessel control, including automated distance control, has to progress with pioneering projects that require ongoing adjustments, given the need for global shipping to adapt to present challenges.

BIMCO believes that technological developments have reached a level that autonomous shipping is becoming a real prospect for international trade. An autonomous ship can operate for extended periods with various degrees of reduced human input. Autonomous shipping is characterised by three dimensions: the automated systems in operation, the level of remote control and the level of manning. At the London-based International Maritime Organization (IMO), the following three dimensions have been classified in four degrees of autonomy:

- **Degree One**: Ship with automated processes and decision support: Seafarers are on board to operate and control shipboard systems and functions. Some operations may be automated and at times be unsupervised but with seafarers on board ready to take control.
- **Degree Two**: Remotely controlled ship with seafarers on board: The ship is controlled and operated from another location. Seafarers are available on board to take control and to operate the shipboard systems and functions.
- **Degree Three**: Remotely controlled ship without seafarers on board: The ship is controlled and operated from another location. There are no seafarers on board.
- **Degree Four**: Fully autonomous ship: The operating system of the ship can make decisions and determine actions by itself.

Cyber risk management will be increasingly important for automated ships. A cyber attack on a critical system in Maritime Autonomous Surface Ships (MASS) may adversely affect the safety of the ship, crew and cargo.

BIMCO's position

BIMCO also takes the following position concerning the use of autonomous ships:

- BIMCO takes a leading role in facilitating the use of autonomous ships in international trade including the development of a standard ship management agreement for autonomous ships.
- BIMCO will contribute to the development of a common understanding of the risks and opportunities of autonomous ships.
- BIMCO participates in the initiatives taken by the IMO and CMI (Comité Maritime International) to assess the need for changes to international conventions and national laws for autonomous ships to operate worldwide.

BIMCO recognises the importance of the human element, the need to focus on new competences for seafarers, and the need for human relations' initiatives to overcome problems such as potential loneliness following the reduction of personnel onboard.

BIMCO supports the international interim guidelines for MASS trials to ensure operational reliability, safety and protection of the environment.

BIMCO's extensive website (www.BIMCO.org) provides ready access to information and guidance for members to gain a competitive advantage. BIMCO Online handles thousands of requests for assistance every year in addition to thousands of other enquiries made through the BIMCO website. BIMCO Online offers extensive details of ports around the world, including costs, cargo handling equipment, delays, strikes and various warnings such as boycotts and embargoes. Additionally, BIMCO keeps track of those companies known for their less-than-desirable business practices and assists members in the collection of undisputed outstanding balances.

Anti-drug smuggling

In 1994, BIMCO initiated an anti-drug smuggling co-operation program with the United Kingdom via the first BIMCO sponsored Memorandum of Understanding (MoU). Today, BIMCO has established MoUs with other European Customs authorities and is involved with the Sea Carrier Initiative Agreement established by US Customs though the US Customs and Border Protection (CBP) Agency. BIMCO owner members participating in these agreements must implement anti-smuggling measures on board their vessels. In return, members benefit by being allowed to sail their vessels from port with a minimum of delay should illegal narcotics be discovered on board despite the requisite security measures that have been taken by the owner member.

Security

BIMCO is constantly attentive to security issues such as the increasing threat of stowaways and armed attacks on ships, including global piracy. Warnings and reports are regularly distributed to members and posted on the BIMCO website. Furthermore, BIMCO actively and regularly participates in IMO discussions on security issues and is working within the international shipping industry for a proper response to these threats. BIMCO's policy objective is for initiatives against terrorism to be pursued in an efficient and pragmatic matter with the burden of new responsibilities being shared between the maritime industry and national governments.

Trends and challenges

BIMCO is engaged in many issues in the technical and regulatory areas. BIMCO has a strong presence at the International Maritime Organisation (IMO) in its consultative status since 1969. The practical ship operating experience of its members is highly valued by the IMO, the International Labour Organization, the European Union and the US Coast Guard in their deliberations on the regulation of international shipping. BIMCO remains heavily committed to the principle of internationalism in all forms of regulation necessary for an effective global logistics system and opposes regional regulation that fractures the operational flexibility of global shipping. BIMCO is a strong supporter of IMO as the pre-eminent maritime regulatory body. BIMCO has demonstrated throughout its history the capacity to sense changing trends and to take a proactive role in determining the future course of shipping on behalf of its members.

The Baltic Exchange

The **Baltic Exchange** (incorporated as **The Baltic Exchange Limited**) is a membership organisation for the maritime industry, and freight market information provider for the trading and settlement of physical and derivative contracts. It was originally located at 24–28 St Mary Axe, in the City of London, until the building was destroyed by an IRA bomb in 1992, and is now located further along the same street at 38 St Mary Axe. It has further offices in Europe, across Asia, and in the United States.

Its international community of 650 member companies encompasses the majority of world shipping interests and commits to a code of business conduct overseen by the Baltic. Baltic Exchange members are responsible for a large proportion of all dry cargo and tanker fixtures as well as the sale and purchase of merchant vessels.

The roots of the Baltic Exchange stem from 1744 and the Virginia and Baltick Coffee House in Threadneedle Street, close to the Bank of England. English coffeehouses in the 17th and 18th centuries were important places for merchants and captains to exchange news, and indeed the famous Lloyd's of London Insurance organisation, as well as Lloyd's Register, originated in Edward Lloyd's Coffee House, also located in the City of London. The Baltic Exchange was incorporated as a private limited company with shares owned by its members on 17 January 1900. In November 2016, the Singapore Exchange (SGX) acquired the Baltic Exchange, although it remains headquartered in London.

The Baltic, as it is commonly known, is the world's oldest shipping market. It traces its name to the Virginia and Baltick Coffee House, established in 1744. At this time, it was used mainly by merchants who had a major trade in tallow from the Baltic seaboard. The Baltic Exchange was reorganised into its modern corporate form at the time of the construction of the original Baltic Exchange building in St Mary Axe which opened in 1903. After this building was destroyed by an IRA bomb in 1992, the Baltic Exchange moved into its current headquarters at 38 St Mary Axe. The Baltic developed into the world's most prestigious and only international, self-regulated market for matching ships and cargoes and buying and selling ships. Although in the light of modern business practice and international communications, a trading floor is no longer necessary, the Baltic's global members continue to operate as a shipping marketplace and to apply the highest standards of ethics.

A large part of the world's ship chartering and Sale & Purchase business is negotiated at some stage by members of the Baltic. The Baltic publishes numerous daily indices which are representative of the state of the markets. As well as providing guidance to brokers, these form the settlement mechanisms in the Forward Freight Agreement (FFA) market which is used for risk management. The Baltic Exchange Expert Witness Association (BEWA) is a body of experienced professionals which can provide independent judgments on a wide range of maritime related disputes.

At the time of writing, Baltic members represent worldwide shipping-related interests through over 650 companies. Members include shipowners and charterers, ship operators and traders, physical and derivative brokers and related maritime services companies. More than 3,000 individuals represent these companies globally.

The exchange provides daily freight market prices and maritime shipping cost indices which are used to guide freight traders as to the current level of various global shipping markets, as well as being used to set freight contract rates and settle freight futures (known as forward freight agreements or FFAs). Originally operating a trading floor, the exchange's members' transactions are today mainly conducted by telephone or by electronic means.

The exchange is the source of market-wide information and publishes seven daily indices made up from a suite of wet and dry bench-marked time-charter and voyage routes:

- Baltic Dry Index (BDI);
- Baltic Panamax Index (BPI);
- Baltic Capesize Index (BCI);
- Baltic Supramax Index (BSI);
- Baltic Handysize Index (BHSI);
- Baltic Dirty Tanker Index (BDTI);
- Baltic Clean Tanker Index (BCTI);
- Baltic LNG Tanker Index (BLNG).

In April 2018, the Baltic Exchange announced a global container index (FBX) in partnership with Freightos. Liquified Natural Gas (LNG) assessments launched in 2019.

The exchange also provides forward curves, a dry cargo fixture list, sale and purchase values, LPG & LNG assessments, daily market news and the market settlement data for freight derivative contracts.

As of 2019, the current management includes:

- Chief Executive: Mark Jackson;
- Chairman, Baltic Exchange Council: Denis Petropolous;
- Chief Financial Officer and Company Secretary: Mark Read;
- Chief Commercial Officer: Janet Sykes;
- Communications: Bill Lines.

BIFFEX, the Baltic International Freight Futures Exchange, was a London-based exchange for trading ocean freight futures contracts with settlement based on the **Baltic Freight Index**. It started trading dry cargo freight futures contracts in 1985, and was modestly successful for some years. All contracts were cleared by the ICCH (International Commodity Clearing House), later renamed LCH Clearnet (London Clearing House). A tanker freight futures contract was introduced in 1986, but never became popular and was suspended indefinitely the same year. Volumes in the dry cargo contracts dwindled over the years, and the contracts ceased trading due to lack of liquidity in 2001.

The exchange was originally located at 24–28 St Mary Axe in the City of London until it was destroyed in a 1992 bomb planted by the IRA, and is now located at 38 St Mary Axe, London. It has further offices in Europe, Asia and the United States.

The Baltic Exchange's international community of over 3000 encompasses the world's maritime interests including the dry bulk, tanker, gas and container shipping markets. Members include shipowners, shipbrokers and charterers as well as maritime lawyers, arbitrators, P&I Clubs and other shipping associations. Each member commits to a code of business conduct – known as the Baltic Code – which is summed up by the motto "Our Word Our Bond".

A significant proportion of the world's ship chartering and Sale & Purchase business is negotiated and handled by members of the Baltic Exchange.

The organisation adds value to its members' businesses through supporting services such as escrow, dispute resolution, networking opportunities and education. It has regional offices in Singapore, Shanghai, Athens, Stamford and Houston, and is the world's leading source of independent maritime market data. Our information is used by shipbrokers, owners & operators, traders, financiers and charterers as a reliable and independent view of the dry bulk, tanker, gas, container and air freight markets.

The Baltic Exchange's indices and assessments are used as a settlement tool for freight derivative trades, for benchmarking physical contracts and as a general indicator of the freight markets' performance. Its comprehensive information services cover voyage and time charter rates for capesize, panamax, supramax (handymax) and handysize bulk carriers; Worldscale and time charter equivalent rates for VLCC, Suezmax, Aframax and MR tankers; time charter rates for LPG and LNG vessels; container freight rates; air cargo rates; as well as forward assessments, sale and purchase values, OPEX assessments and ship recycling prices; market reports and fixtures.

The Baltic Code

"Our Word Our Bond" is at the heart of what the Baltic Exchange and its global membership stands for. It provides the basis for ethical conduct and integrity for Member companies and their employees. Adherence to the Baltic Code is one way that many shipping companies differentiate themselves from those who are not Baltic Exchange members and it is referenced widely in arbitration cases and provides a basis for how many organisations govern themselves.

The Baltic Code 2020 provides guidance to shipbrokers and principals on ethical conduct in the physical freight and freight derivatives markets. The physical shipping markets are not regulated by central government authorities, but since the 19th century, the Baltic Exchange has set out a Code of Conduct which sets out market standards. Today the Baltic Code plays an important role by providing guidance and acting as a reference point. It is used by those working the markets on trading desks and referenced at legal hearings. It underpins the ethical approach taken by Baltic members globally in dry cargo, tanker, gas, container, sale & purchase, demolition and freight derivative markets.

Baltic Code objectives

1. Preserve confidence in and the integrity of physical freight and freight derivative markets;
2. Establish and execute ethical business practices and eliminate unacceptable practices in these markets;
3. Ensure the role of the Baltic Exchange remains at the centre of these markets.

A guide to the new Baltic Code (2020)

"Our Word Our Bond" is at the heart of what the Baltic Exchange and its global membership stands for. It provides the basis for ethical conduct and integrity for Member companies and their employees. Adherence to the Baltic Code is one way that many shipping companies differentiate themselves from those who are not Baltic Exchange members and it is referenced widely in arbitration cases and provides a basis for how many organisations govern themselves.

The Baltic Code has been invaluable in providing informal regulation to practitioners. Previous versions of the Baltic Code have been confined to only two pages and provided a short overview of Ethics and Market Practice. Providing guidance that was both specific to the shipping (chartering) market and too general for the more complex markets of today, it formed part of a larger document which provided detail about the practicalities of chartering a vessel and explanatory information about the wider shipping markets. This information has been updated and retained as part of this guide.

In 2018, the Bank of England gave its support to Codes of Conduct produced by unregulated markets. As both a response to this, and in recognition of the compliance and operational challenges created by constantly evolving legal, regulatory and policy developments in all jurisdictions where Baltic Exchange members operate or do business, the Baltic decided that a review of the Baltic Code was necessary. The result is the New Baltic Code (2020).

The objectives of the New Baltic Code are to:

1. Preserve confidence in and the integrity of physical freight and freight derivative markets.
2. Establish and execute ethical business practices and eliminate unacceptable practices in these markets.
3. Ensure the role of the Baltic Exchange remains at the centre of these markets.

Underpinning this was an intention to develop a universally accepted set of principles and good practices that will be applicable not only to members but also to any physical freight and freight derivatives market participants.

The Code is built around five key principles:

1. Integrity of Markets;
2. Fairness and Competition;
3. Ethical Business;
4. Good Market Conduct;
5. Robust and Credible Benchmarks.

The new guide to the New Baltic Code is intended to be a "living document", and that it will be updated regularly as the underlying tenets are applied in the context of the shipping markets. It will be reviewed regularly by the Baltic Membership

Council and, where necessary, by the members themselves (if substantive changes are required).

All members are required to conduct themselves and their businesses in line with the New Baltic Code. Any breaches of the New Baltic Code will be brought before the membership Council for review and ultimately before the Baltic Exchange Council.

Any member deemed to be in breach of the Code may ultimately be expelled from membership.

Membership

Membership of the Baltic Exchange is available in one of four categories:

- Principals who trade on their own account. They either own or control ships or have cargoes to move;
- Brokers, who act as intermediaries between shipowners and cargo interests, and do not trade on their own behalf;
- Freight derivative Trading members who may be in either of the above categories but are also participants in the FFA market.

Non-market members who, while not trading in the Baltic Exchange market, can still be associated with this hub of international shipping. They include maritime services, comprising lawyers, arbitrators, ship financiers, insurers and other maritime institutions and associations.

The Baltic categorises its members so that all those in the market know the status of those with whom they trade. For example, members who will be acting as an intermediary only, and will not trade on their own behalf, sign an undertaking to trade in the market only as a broker. Those who are principals may act both on their own behalf, and as brokers.

Those acting as brokers can represent:

- Shipowners, sometimes exclusively, in which case they are referred to as "owners' brokers";
- Charterers, sometimes exclusively, in which case they are referred to as "charterers' brokers";
- Either shipowners or charterers on a non-exclusive basis, when they are referred to as "competitive brokers";
- FFA traders on an exclusive or non-exclusive basis, in which case they are referred to as "FFA brokers".

Each company elected as a Member is required to demonstrate to the satisfaction of the Baltic Membership Council (BMC), and at any time subsequently, that they are of sufficient financial standing to carry out with confidence the business in which they are engaged. At the time of their election to membership, the BMC considers the reputation and standing in the market of the company and individual prospective members and usually consults the existing membership before approving the new Member.

The Baltic Exchange Council (BEC)

The Baltic Exchange is governed by the Baltic Exchange Council (BEC) which provides oversight of its strategy for membership services, social responsibility and its relationship with its members, governments, regulatory bodies and the global shipping community.

The BEC is composed of 12 individuals. Five of these are nominated by the BEC, two by the Baltic Membership Council (BMC) and two by the directors of Baltic Exchange Ltd (BEL). Such nominations are vetted by the incumbent BEC and approved by BEL. The Chairman of the BIC and BMC and the CEO of the Baltic are Ex officio members of the BEC. The BEC elects its Chairman and Vice Chairman from among its Member Representatives.

The Baltic Index Council (BIC)

The Baltic Index Council (BIC) provides effective scrutiny of the Baltic's index production and particularly its subsidiary, Baltic Exchange Information Services Limited (BEISL), on all aspects of its benchmark determination process in accordance with the applicable law, regulation and guidelines including (without limitation) the EU Benchmarks Regulation 1 (although the UK's exit from the EU at the end of 2020 may require some amendment) and the Baltic's Guide to Market Benchmarks (available on www.balticexchange.com).

The BIC comprises five representatives of the appropriate segments of the market (including at least a dry bulk, a wet bulk and a freight derivatives broker panellist) the participants of the BIC are referred to as the "Market Representatives" and one director of the Board of the Baltic or of one of the Baltic's subsidiaries. Market Representatives are nominated by members of the Baltic Exchange, vetted by the incumbent BIC and approved by the Baltic.

The Chairman of the BIC Governance Council is one of the Market Representatives, nominated by the incumbent BIC. The Chairman is expected to have an intimate understanding of the physical and financial shipping markets as well as a deep understanding of the Baltic itself. The Chief Executive Officer of the Baltic is invited to attend all meetings of the BIC but does not have a vote on any decisions taken by the BIC.

The Baltic Membership Council (BMC)

The BMC considers new membership applications, sports associations and social activities. It may co-opt members who are not BMC participants to provide additional expertise and shipping experience in support of its work.

The BMC has disciplinary powers of censure, suspension and expulsion over members and is responsible for maintaining proper, ethical standards in trading. Should a Member dispute such a decision by the BMC, they have the right to appeal to the BEC.

Advisory Councils

Advisory Councils provide forums through which the Baltic can engage with its membership operating in different geographic locations and market sectors. They serve as a conduit through which the Baltic can discuss the development of the Baltic indices and receive feedback to proposed changes and new products.

At the time of writing of the updated Code, four such Advisory Councils had been formed:

- The Baltic European Advisory Council – dry (BEAC-dry);
- The Baltic European Advisory Council – wet (BEAC-wet);
- The Baltic Asia Advisory Council – dry (BAAC-dry);
- The Baltic Asia Advisory Council – wet (BAAC-wet).

Each Advisory Council is comprised of not more than 12 individuals representing a cross-section of all stakeholders involved in the relevant market(s) including brokers, shipowning, cargo and freight derivatives interests and representatives from panellist companies.

Administration and management of the Baltic Exchange

The Board appoints a Chief Executive to manage the membership administration, organisation of the Baltic Exchange and its staff, the club facilities and the other services for members and facilities for non-members.

The Baltic derives its income from membership subscriptions, the sale of its market data, transaction revenue from the provision of its data for the clearing of FFAs, rents for offices in its building at 38 St Mary Axe and its catering/function facilities for members.

CHAPTER 7

Vessel ownership & chartering

What's in a contract?

We often sail on or see vessels of various kinds operating into and out of port. These will be ferries, cruise liners, container ships, general cargo ships and bulk carriers, be they dry bulk carriers or tankers. They will always sport particular hull and superstructure colours, as well as having specific motifs and colours on their funnels. But who owns them, and are they sailing for their owners?

The answer may not be as clear-cut as it seems. In an age of tighter economies and vessel operation based on absolute need, it is often the case that vessel fleets are managed and operated by the shipping company, but may be owned by another concern. Such practices can be applied to any aspect of the boat business, and also can refer to the use of yachts and private vessels.

Let us take an example. A European ferry operator sailing out of the UK to Northern Europe operates several ferries on a variety of routes. The ferries are all painted in the colours of the ferry company, and to the casual onlooker or passenger, it would appear that the ferry is owned by that operator. In some instances, this may well be the case. However, it is not necessarily so. A while ago, while the author was a lecturer at Liverpool John Moores University, he made a visit to the port of Immingham with a group of students, and they were shown around not only the terminal facilities but we also were taken on board one of the ferries, the *Jutlandia Seaways* (25609 gt). They were introduced to some of her crew, including the captain, an Estonian. He explained to the group that although the ferry was operated by DFDS Seaways, it was chartered in from another company. She was owned by Snowdon Leasing of London, and is managed by Ellingsen Shipmanagement of Stockholm, Sweden. Her crew was also employed by Ellingsen Shipmanagement, and she sailed under the UK flag. She was chartered by Ellingsen to DFDS, in whose colours she sails, on a long-term charter basis. In reality, the charter arrangement for the ***Jutlandia Seaways*** is a hybrid, comprising a time charter combined with a bareboat charter. Under the time charter, the vessel operates for DFDS but is managed by Ellingsen under the terms of the charter. However, unlike a true time charter, the vessel sails not in the colours of Ellingsen, but rather in the colours of DFDS, in an agreement more akin to a bareboat charter. Other DFDS-operated vessels, such as the ***Princess Seaways*** and the ***King Seaways***, are also wholly-owned by DFDS.

DOI: 10.4324/9781003256359-8

The above scenario is not an unusual practice. The ill-fated container vessel ***MSC Napoli*** was owned by a consortium of different owners, but was chartered by a ship management company to MSC, which operated the vessel in their colours. After her foundering in the Channel in early 2007, the main challenge was to find the owners of the vessel in order to conclude a full salvage contract, and this proved a complex task. It is often the case that many people consort to purchase a ship, and then form a contract with a ship management company such as V.Ships to have the ship managed by the ship management company. In turn, the ship management company has the authority to charter the ship out to whichever company seeks to operate the vessel. Ship management in itself is a complex affair which requires significant expertise on the part of qualified shipbrokers to ensure that the ship is managed and chartered out properly. Another example of vessel chartering is a German company called Thomas Rickmers, which owns many vessels and charters them out to several container shipping lines. Many more shipping companies carry out similar ventures.

In essence, the rationale is simple. A shipping company may own a basic core fleet of vessels which it needs on a regular frequent basis, but charters in others according to the *ad hoc* need for other additional vessels, especially during peak times of the year when traffic increases according to demand. In general, the demand for operational vessels dictates the need to use more vessels, and when the demand decreases, the charter may be terminated. Also, where there is a specific project, such as the movement of specific cargoes from one place to another, specific vessels will be chartered for that purpose. This is very much the case with worldwide capital projects and oilfield projects, where specific amounts of material will be shipped to satisfy the needs of the project. Companies engaged in such charter contracts include UAL, BBC Chartering and Johannes Spliethoff. The shipping company Furness Withy, once a subject of an article in this magazine, was at one time a major shipowner, but over the years has changed to becoming a ship chartering company, chartering vessels from elsewhere according to demand.

Chartering is also a major element of bulk shipping. Bulk shipping, unlike liner shipping, does not rely on a specified frequency of routes and schedules; cargoes are shipped according to specific need, such as iron ore or coal, grain, fertilisers, raw sugar and forest products. The dry and liquid bulk sector relies on chartering to satisfy its needs, and there is a variety of bulk carriers, from handysize to capesize and VLOC dry bulk carriers sailing the seven seas loaded with a variety of dry bulk commodities. This is also the case with the oil tanker sector. Tankers are also chartered on a regular basis for the carriage of crude oil from the oilfields to the markets, and again tankers vary in size and deadweight capacity.

The term "**Chartering**" refers to the arrangement of the use of vessels and containers for the purpose of the transport of cargo by sea. There are several terms used for the purpose of chartering, which are:

- Bareboat (Demise);
- Voyage charter;

- Time charter;
- Slot chartering (Containers).

In general, the chartering principle refers to the carriage of bulk cargoes by dedicated bulk carriers, but it can also refer to the carriage of general or specific cargoes on a general cargo carrier, as well as the carriage of containers on a container vessel. The carriage of general or specific cargoes as well as container carriage is covered under the slot chartering arrangement, to be covered later in this section.

A vessel is owned by a shipping line, but is not necessarily managed by that company. That vessel may be managed by a separate vessel management company, whose responsibility is to crew and maintain the vessel, as well as ensuring that its operation remains profitable. The vessel management company (or the shipping line, whoever manages the vessel) then employs shipping agents to represent the vessel and the company when it arrives in port, and to ensure that its cargo is arranged, managed, loaded and unloaded correctly and efficiently. In many cases, the space on board the vessel is chartered by way of the slot chartering method, to be explained later in this section, but often the whole vessel is chartered by another trader wishing to arrange the transportation of a cargo or a series or group of cargoes from one port to another. In the main, such chartering concerns the use of bulk carriers for the purpose of the transportation of raw materials such as minerals, grain, petroleum, fertilisers or timber from one place to another. Equally, bulk shipments of finished products such as road vehicles, steel, aluminium, heavy machinery and refrigerated cargoes can be transported in consignment large enough to fill a ship to capacity. The contract made for carrying these bulk consignments is known by the generic title of "charterparty", a term derived from the Latin "Charta Partita", literally translated as "A Letter Divided". In the early days of such agreements, a contract was copied exactly, and the paper on which the two parts were written was then cut in half, so that each of the contracting parties could keep one segment which agreed entirely with the other. The present-day Charterparty is a maritime contract by which the charterer, a party other than the shipowner, obtains the use of a ship for one or more voyages (voyage charter), or for a specified period of time (Time charter).

Vessels transporting cargoes under the terms and conditions set out in a charterparty are known as "private carriers", in that they are operated to cater for the needs and schedules of the shipper and the vessel owner. In direct contrast to this arrangement, a carrier which offers transportation for all goods offered between the specific ports it serves is known as a "common carrier", given that it regularly operates on such routes, often as what is described as a "liner" service. The term "common carrier" can also be used to describe a company which owns or operates container and logistics services, as well as consolidating cargoes into containers, but does not own its own vessels; it uses the services of vessels owned by other shipping companies for the transportation of its containers. Such an entity is known as an NVOCC (Non-Vessel-Owning Common Carrier), and it charters slots, or spaces for the loading of containers, on container vessels operating on specific routes on an agency basis. Certain NVOCCs act as liner or shipping agencies for shipping lines in several ports worldwide, and in general they issue their own FIATA Bills of Lading for each cargo shipped.

An important distinction can be made between a private carrier and a common carrier. A ship loaded with cargoes belonging to a single shipper is a private carrier, whereas a vessel carrying the property of two or more shippers is a common carrier. In this respect, if a bulk carrier, such as the ***Berge Stahl***, is carrying a single load of iron ore, for example, between Brazil and Rotterdam, and that cargo is destined for a single buyer, then that vessel is a private carrier. On the other hand, if a vessel such as the ***Emma Maersk*** is carrying several thousand containers from the Far East to Rotterdam, with each container load destined for a variety of different importers, then the vessel is deemed to be a common carrier. The same is true for a vessel such as the *Toisa Polaris* carrying a variety of cargoes on her deck from the UK and Norway bound for the Brazilian offshore oilfields. A private carrier undertakes the service specified by the owner of the cargo, in that it loads the particular cargo at the place designated by the shipper, transports it to the destination named in the contract and delivers the cargo according to the conditions laid down in the contract or charterparty, including the specific International Term of Delivery (INCOTERM), usually FOB or CIF (the INCOTERMS are covered in another chapter of this text).

We can now analyse the three main types of charter available, and how they work. Chartering is a very important activity within the shipping industry, and indeed constitutes a major element of present-day shipping business. In some cases a charterer may own cargo and employ a shipbroker to find a ship to deliver the cargo for a certain price, called the freight rate. Freight rates may be on a per-ton basis over a certain route (e.g. for iron ore between Brazil and China, or for coal between Colombia and the UK) or may alternatively be expressed in terms of a total sum, normally expressed in US Dollars per day for the agreed duration of the charter. A charterer may also be a party without a cargo who takes a vessel on charter for a specified period from the owner and then trades the ship to carry cargoes at a profit above the hire rate, or even makes a profit in a rising market by re-letting the ship out to other charterers.

As a brief introduction, let us look at the abbreviated definitions of a typical charter.

- A **voyage charter** is the hiring of a vessel and crew for a voyage between a load port and a discharge port. The charterer pays the vessel owner on a per-ton or lump sum basis. The owner pays the port costs (excluding stevedoring), fuel costs and crew costs.
- A **time charter** is the hiring of a vessel for a specific period of time; the owner still manages the vessel but the charterer selects the ports and directs the vessel where to go. The charterer pays for all fuel the vessel consumes, port charges and a daily "hire" to the owner of the vessel.

- A **bareboat charter** is an arrangement for the hiring of a vessel whereby no administration or technical maintenance is included as part of the agreement. The charterer pays for all operating expenses, including fuel, crew, port expenses and hull insurance. Usually, the charter period (normally years) ends with the charterer obtaining title (ownership) in the hull. Effectively, the owners finance the purchase of the vessel.
- A **demise charter** shifts the control and possession of the vessel; the charterer takes full control of the vessel along with the legal and financial responsibility for it.

Depending on the type of ship and the type of charter, normally a standard contract form called a charterparty is used to record the exact rate, duration and terms agreed between the shipowner and the charterer. Examples of such forms can be found on the BIMCO (Baltic International Maritime Council) website.

The **voyage charter** is a maritime contract under which the shipowner agrees to transport, for an agreed amount of money (technically known as *freight*) per tonne of cargo loaded, a stipulated quantity of a named cargo between two or more designated ports. The shipowner retains full responsibility for the operation of the ship and costs relating to its voyage (its *Voyage Costs*). The charter agreement lasts for the duration of the voyage or specific number of voyages determined in the terms of the charter agreement deemed necessary to transport the specific consignment or consignments from one port to another.

Under the terms and provisions of a voyage charter, the shipowner is obliged to provide a fully operational and seaworthy vessel, and in all respects fitted to carry the proposed cargo on the proposed route. The charterer in turn is required to provide a full load of the named and described item or commodity and to that end may demand that the shipowner stipulate, as warranties or verifiable facts, the following details:

- The name and classification of the vessel;
- The flag and nationality of the vessel;
- The IMO registration number of the vessel;
- The deadweight tonnage and capacity (in cubic feet or metres) below decks.

Operational characteristics such as speed, fuel consumption and date of last drydocking are not a concern of the charterer, since these issues are only the concern of the shipowner, and therefore would normally be omitted from the warranties (additional details not otherwise specified as terms or conditions) of the voyage charter. The charterparty always stipulates the port in which the vessel is to be delivered or "tendered" by the owner. It also specifies the beginning and the ending of the period of days during which tender of the vessel may be made. This period is known as "lay days", as the vessel may well be lying idle while berthed at the quayside prior to being loaded in readiness for the voyage specified in the charter. In order to obtain maximum revenue from the voyage, the shipowner directs the Master of the vessel to accept as much cargo as the safety of the vessel will permit, up to the level permitted by the Load Line (the Plimsoll Line) marked on each side of the hull of the vessel. Once the vessel has been tendered or delivered, the charterer is expected to have the cargo waiting at the quayside so that no time is lost in loading once the vessel has been delivered to the charterer. Any delay incurred as a result of the cargo not being ready for loading is classed as "laytime" for the vessel, and may be incurred as costs against the charterer, known as "demurrage". The voyage charter must also specify and state precisely the responsibilities of the contracting parties for the loading, unloading and stowage of cargo aboard vessel, and thus which party is liable for costs incurred as a result of cargo handling by the port authority, in terms of the use of dockside cranes and quayside personnel. The "net form" of charter makes this task the responsibility of the charterer, whereas the "gross form" charter or "liner terms" contract simply states that the charterer is obliged only to provide the cargo at the loading port and to accept it at the port of destination, often under the terms of a CIF Contract. The freight cost charged includes the cost of stevedoring and all other voyage expenses. The shipowner bears full responsibility for the proper loading, stowage and discharge of the cargo, and passes these costs on to the charterer as part of the overall freight cost.

The **time charter** is a maritime contract setting out the terms under which a person or party other than the shipowner obtains the use of the vessel for a specified period of time to trade and transport cargoes within broad but defined limits, carrying any cargoes not positively barred or prohibited by the wording of the contract. Time charters normally contain restrictions concerning the types of cargo which may be carried aboard vessel. These restrictions range from any lawful cargo not deemed as being injurious or harmful to the vessel, to specific cargoes which may not be loaded aboard vessel, such as toxic substances or livestock. Compensation, known as *charter hire*, may be defined at an agreed sum per deadweight tonne per month or at a fixed amount per day. The shipowner remains in all aspects the operator of the vessel. The charterer, among other obligations, assumes responsibility for loading and discharging the cargoes, especially where certain INCOTERMS such as FAS, FOB, C&F, CIF and DAT are concerned. The charterer also pays the costs of vessel fuel (bunkering), pilotage, harbour and light dues, wharfage and dockage (berthing), among other items of operational cost such as port handling and conservancy charges.

The time charter (and, for that matter, the bareboat charter) directs where the vessel may sail. Because marine insurance underwriters are very definite as to the areas of the world where they will accept responsibility for damage sustained by vessels they insure, the time and bareboat charter parties provide a space in which the limits of the ship's voyaging are stipulated, including entry into sea areas vulnerable to icing up during winter months, for which an "ice clause" applies.

The **bareboat charter** (or **demise charter**) is a maritime contract by which the vessel itself is transferred in all but title from the owner to a separate party for a specified period of time. It is the least used, for the reasons that it imposes the heaviest burden upon the charterer, who becomes the *de facto* operator of the ship. Among members of the legal profession, it is referred to as a "demise charter". The charterer pays compensation (charter hire), either at an agreed amount per deadweight tonne per month or at a fixed sum per day. All burdens and responsibilities of operation, including hiring officers and other crew and maintaining the vessel in good condition, are assumed by the charterer, who legally is said to be the owner *pro hac vice* (for this period).

The term "bareboat" refers to the fact that the fully operational ship is delivered to the charterer in its "bare" state, i.e. that it has on board no crew, no stores, little or no fuel and no navigational charts. The term "demise" refers to the transfer of possession (but not ownership), command and control of the chartered vessel from the owner to the charterer for the length of time covered by the contract. Although this type of charter is the least used out of all the charter types, it is still a common occurrence where vessels are chartered out by one shipowner to other shipowners for the purposes of temporary expansion of their fleets in order to satisfy the demands of specific markets, such as container transportation. Under the bareboat charter, the shipowner is required to provide to present a fully seaworthy and operational vessel that is fit and suitable for the service intended. Once the vessel is accepted by the charterer, the responsibility of seaworthiness no longer rests with the owner but passes to the charterer. The charterer has the full right and responsibility of recruiting the officers and crew of the vessel, although they may be nominated by the shipowner if required. The vessel's entire crew thus become the employees of the charterer. All voyages undertaken by the vessel are specified by the charterer, and all associated costs per voyage are incurred by the charterer.

Documentation, such as Marine Bills of Lading or Sea Waybills, for the cargo carried by the vessel in question may be issued by the charterer. If the Master of the vessel is required to sign these Bills, as well as the Mate's Receipt, the documents must indicate or state that the vessel's Master is the agent of the charterers. The shipowner is not deemed responsible for loss or damage to the cargo, but the ship may be subject to liens (rights of possession) by cargo interests. Under the terms of the laws of Carriage of Goods at Sea, the carrier is deemed responsible for the cargo while it is on board vessel. In this case, the party accepting liability for the carriage of the cargo is the charterer, who has undertaken to perform the contract of carriage in agreement with the shipper or owner of the cargo.

Slot chartering is a term which refers to the chartering of space aboard a vessel for freight of various kinds. It is generally used to refer to containerised freight, as it concerns the "slotting" of a container on board a container vessel, and generally concerns the allotting of space on board a vessel of one shipping line for containers belonging to another partner, or other, shipping or container line.

A container load may be a single consignment destined for one buyer (FCL), or may be a groupage or consolidated consignment comprising several loads, each destined for a different buyer (LCL). In each case, each cargo belongs to a different owner, and may be booked aboard vessel separately from the other cargoes. However, the representative of each shipper or cargo owner, in this case a freight forwarder, arranges a space aboard the vessel by entering into contact with the shipping agent. The shipping agent may be the liner agent representing the shipping line, or may be an NVOCC, as described earlier in this text.

In the case of the container business, the shipping agent or NVOCC arranges for a container to be despatched to the premises of the shipper or consolidator, where the individual or consolidated consignment is loaded into the container. The space for that container is then arranged aboard a specific vessel in the form of a "slot", or space, either above or below deck depending upon the nature of the consignments concerned. That slot is effectively chartered from the shipowner or operator of the vessel, depending upon whether the vessel is chartered out under the terms of a bareboat charter or not. In reality, shipping agents may charter slots on a series of vessels depending upon their relationship with the shipping lines. In the case of shipping conferences, where several shipping lines pool their maritime resources and fleets together to operate on a specific set of routes, the shipping agents or container operators will be able to charter slots on several vessels, each of which belong to a different shipping line, but which operate collectively on the same set of routes, for example between the Far East and Europe. The shipping agent hires in the container at a fixed container (box) rate, which applies to any of the shipping lines operating on the specified routes, and then sells the space to the shipper either at a fixed box rate for the container or at groupage or consolidation rates, based on the volumetric weight of each of the consignments consolidated inside the container.

The slot refers to a specific single voyage, as once the container has been offloaded at the port of destination the terms of the charter cease to apply. Another slot charter arrangement will be made for the return of that container to its point of origin. The same is true of any consignment loaded directly aboard vessel without being containerised. In cases where the cargo is of an outsize nature, or is being despatched to a specific destination outside the scope of container operations on a general cargo vessel, the slot applies to the space booked aboard vessel. An example of this is the transportation of Oil and Gas equipment destined for offshore operations. A vessel belonging to a shipping line can be chartered under a voyage or time charter arrangement for the purposes of the shipment of such equipment to a particular customer located in the area where the offshore activities are being undertaken, e.g. Angola or Brazil. However, the deck or hold space on board that vessel may also be booked on a slot charter basis, i.e. that each cargo may be booked separately with the shipping agent by the supplier for loading aboard vessel. That slot charter only applies to the shipment of that consignment on a single specified voyage, and is completed once the vessel has been unloaded at its destination. Unless further shipments have been booked for the vessel's return voyage, it will return empty, although in reality it may well be loaded with equipment for return to the UK or Europe. As with container loads, each cargo is covered by a specific document, usually a bill of lading, which refers to either the container in which the cargo is loaded and the details of the cargo itself, or to the cargo itself where a container is not utilised. That bill of lading refers to the details of the consignment and/or container details shown on the Cargo Manifest, which is produced once all the slots have been arranged aboard vessel.

There are other specific terms used with charter arrangement depending upon the type of charter and what it contains.

The **Part Charter** is usually based on voyage charterparty model, and occurs when a shipowner cannot locate a charterer with a full load. Part charters can be very suitable if the cargo is too large or bulky to be carried on a liner vessel, but too small to justify a full vessel charter.

The **Recap** is a document transmitted when a fixture has been agreed, setting forth all of the negotiated terms and details. This is the operative document until the charterparty is drawn up.

In the case of **Hire**, the charterer compensates the owner for use of a vessel. The term "On hire" means that the ship is in service as contracted. The term "Off Hire" means that the ship is temporarily unavailable to the charterer.

The **Fixture** is the conclusion of charter negotiations between owner and charterer, when an agreement has been reached to charter a vessel.

Figure 7.1 **Marcalabria**, General Cargo Vessel, Seaforth Dock, Liverpool

Figure 7.2 **Apollogracht** (Spliethoff), General Cargo Vessel, Seaforth Dock, Liverpool

The **Disponent Owner** is the name used to describe a charterer who acts as an owner by sub-chartering a vessel, and assuming an owner's liability to the sub-charterer.

Freight is the compensation or consideration paid to the owner by the voyage charterer for use of a vessel, although this can be confused with the same term being used to describe the payment made by a cargo shipper to the bill of lading issuer.

The **Contract of Affreightment** is the contract reached between the shipowner and the charterer whereby the charterer agrees to pay the shipowner for the use of the vessel to carry cargo at an agreed fixed freight rate for the entire voyage. The shipowner agrees to carry a number of cargoes within a specified period of time on a specified route. The agreed frequencies of cargo may require the use of more than one ship.

Wharfage charges/dues/taxes can be a contentious issue but are usually considered to be for the Shippers/Receivers account and there may also be many other statutory levies on cargo or freight that may apply. Many Shippers/Receivers are unaware of these additional costs and do not include them into their costing and consequently may be left with an unexpected considerable expense at the completion of a project.

The application of charter terms is rather more explanatory. Let us suppose that an oil company needs to charter a series of vessels to carry a variety of oilfield materials from Europe to West Africa. The materials are too bulky to be containerised, and are of sufficient quantity to require a time charter basis for three vessels to carry the equipment over a period of two years between Europe and West Africa to support a major offshore drilling campaign.

The oil company enters into an agreement with a vessel-owning company based in Germany to arrange three vessels to carry the equipment to West Africa. The agreement covers the following:

- The three vessels required (including names and registry of vessels, tonnage etc.);
- The length of time the vessels will be required;
- The route the vessels will be employed on;
- The precise dates of start and finish of the agreement;
- The cargo specified;
- The agreed freight rate;
- Loading & unloading of the vessel;
- The agreed INCOTERM (e.g. FCA, FAS, FOB, CFR, CIF, DAT);
- Bunkering costs;
- Pilotage;
- Harbour dues;
- Wharfage;
- Berthing.

These costs must be agreed upon before the charterparty is agreed and signed, as these elements and who is liable for them constitute part of the contract. The oil company agrees with the shipowner all these factors plus any other clauses which will be included in the charterparty. These clauses include:

- **Bunker clauses** (where the charter agrees to pay for all bunker fuels required for the vessel's voyage);
- **Ship clauses** (stating that the ship is seaworthy);
- **Lighterage clauses** (showing as port of discharge any safe port in a certain range);
- **Negligence clause** (excluding the shipowner's or carrier's liability for loss or damage resulting from an act, default or neglect of the Master, mariner, pilot or the servants of the carrier in the navigation of manoeuvring of a ship, not resulting, however, from want of due diligence by the owners of the ship or any of them or by the ship's husband or manager);
- A **Ready Berth clause** (i.e. a stipulation to the effect that laydays (the days that a vessel lies inactive at a port)) will begin to count as soon as the vessel has arrived at the port of loading or discharge "whether in berth or not". It protects the shipowner's interests against delays which arise from ships having to wait for a berth.

The charterparty will only expire once the full term of the time charter has expired and the contract has been carried to the satisfaction of both parties.

Vessel chartering of any kind is a major global business, and accounts for a huge share of the international shipping sector. Given its importance, it is prudent to consider the extent to which charter contracts are being concluded every year, and how many of the vessels which we see are not owned by a shipping operator, but are in fact chartered in by them. Pass me the paint brush, will you?

CHAPTER 8

Chartering documentation

The Hague-Visby Rules

The Hague-Visby Rules (HVRs) are properly called the Hague Rules as Amended by the Brussels Protocol 1968 and apply to every bill of lading or any similar document of title relating to the carriage of goods between ports in two different states if:

i) the bill of lading or document is issued in a contracting State; or
ii) the carriage is from a port in a contracting State; or
iii) the contract contained in or evidenced by the bill of lading provides that the Hague-Visby Rules or the legislation of any State giving effect to them (e.g. the UK's Carriage of Goods by Sea Act 1971) are to govern the contract.

Under Article V, the Rules will not be applicable to charter parties, but if bills of lading are issued in the case of a ship under a charterparty, they must comply with the Rules. Many states, such as the UK, have legislation incorporating the Hague-Visby Rules into national law. Where no such national law applies, the Hague-Visby Rules may still apply to the carriage by agreement of the contracting parties. (See Clause Paramount in bill of lading, waybill or charterparty.)

Article II provides that, subject to the provisions of Article VI, under every contract of carriage of goods by sea, the carrier, in relation to the loading, handling, stowage, carriage, custody, care and discharge of such goods, will be subject to the responsibilities and liabilities, and entitled to the rights and immunities, set out in the Rules.

"Goods" is defined in Article I as including goods, wares, merchandise and articles of every kind whatsoever except live animals and cargo which by the contract of carriage is stated as being carried on deck and is so carried.

Carrier's responsibilities under the Hague-Visby Rules

The carrier has three basic obligations:

i) to ensure the vessel's seaworthiness;

 DOI: 10.4324/9781003256359-9

ii) to care for the cargo; and
iii) to issue a bill of lading where the shipper requests one.

Obligation in respect of seaworthiness

Article III paragraph 1 provides that the carrier must, before and at the beginning of the voyage (i.e. up to the moment of sailing), exercise due diligence to:

- make the ship seaworthy;
- properly man, equip and supply the ship; and
- make the holds, refrigerating and cool chambers and all other parts of the ship in which goods are carried, fit and safe for their reception, carriage and preservation.

"Exercising due diligence" means taking all reasonable precautions to see that the vessel is fit for the voyage contemplated. The carrier is not obliged to give an absolute guarantee of seaworthiness. The carrier may delegate his duty to exercise due diligence (e.g. to surveyors or repairers) but he will be responsible if his servants or contractors, etc. fail to exercise due diligence in carrying out their work.

"Seaworthy" in this context means that the hull must be in sound condition, the vessel must be mechanically sound, equipped with charts, etc., and crewed by a properly trained crew. She need only be seaworthy at the commencement of the voyage, which usually means when she leaves the berth, whether under her own motive power or with the aid of tugs.

If a cargo owner can show that his loss was caused by a failure of the carrier to exercise due diligence to make the vessel seaworthy, the carrier will not be able to rely on any other clauses in the Rules which reduce his liability (i.e. the exceptions from liability).

The holds must be fit and safe for the reception, carriage and preservation of the cargo and, in particular, the hatch covers must be tight and there must be no instability of the vessel through improper stowage. It has been held that the neglect to protect a water pipe in a hold from frost which could have been expected at the time of year showed lack of due diligence to make the vessel seaworthy.

Carrier's obligation in respect of the cargo

Article III paragraph 2 provides that, subject to the provisions of Article IV, the carrier must "properly and carefully load, handle, stow, carry, keep, care for and discharge any goods carried". Unlike seaworthiness, this duty extends throughout the voyage and implies a greater degree of care than exercising "due diligence".

The courts do not expect perfection from the carrier, but it has been held that stowage was improper where:

- contamination of other goods occurred;
- there was inadequate or no ventilation;
- dry cargo was damaged by liquid goods; and
- vehicles were secured only by their own brakes.

The carrier must have a proper system for looking after the cargo when stowed. He has a duty to use all reasonable means to ascertain the nature and characteristics of the cargo and to care for it accordingly, although the shipper should give special instructions where special care is required. (Where water in tractor radiators froze, it was held that the carrier should have been told of the risks.)

Obligation to issue a bill of lading

Article III paragraph 3 provides that after receiving the goods into his charge, the carrier, the Master or the carrier's agent must, if the shipper demands, issue a bill of lading to the shipper showing, among other things:

- all leading marks for identification of the goods, as stated by the shipper before loading (in his shipping note), provided these are visible on the goods or their coverings;
- either the number of packages or pieces, or the quantity, or weight, as stated by the shipper (in his shipping note); and
- the apparent order and condition of the goods.

The carrier, Master or agent need not insert any inaccurate statements on the bill of lading or give any details which he cannot reasonably check. (Hence the practice for statements to be made such as "said to weigh" and "shipper's load and count".)

Any bill of lading thus issued will be prima facie evidence of receipt of the goods by the carrier as described, but proof to the contrary will not be admissible if the bill of lading is transferred to a third party acting in good faith (Article III paragraph 4).

Any bill of lading issued after loading must be a "shipped" bill of lading if the shipper demands, provided he surrenders any previously issued document of title (e.g. a "received" bill of lading issued when the goods arrived at a warehouse or depot before shipment) (Article III paragraph 7).

Carrier's rights and immunities

- the carrier's exceptions from liability;
- the carrier's right to deviate; and
- the carrier's rights in respect of dangerous goods.

Article IV paragraph 2 grants 17 exceptions from liability to the carrier (compared with six under English common law). Neither the carrier or ship will be responsible for loss or damage arising or resulting from:

- act, neglect or default of the Master, mariner, pilot, or the servants of the carrier in the navigation or management of the ship;
- fire, unless caused by actual fault or privity of the carrier;
- perils, dangers and accidents of the sea or other navigable waters;
- act of God;
- act of war;
- act of public enemies;
- arrest or restraint of princes, rulers or people, or seizure under legal process;
- quarantine regulations;
- act or omission of the shipper or owner of the goods, his agent or representatives;
- strikes, lockouts, stoppage or restraint of labour;
- riots and civil commotions;
- saving or attempting to safe life or property at sea;
- wastage in bulk or weight or any other loss or damage arising from inherent defect, quality or vice of the goods;
- insufficiency of packing;
- insufficiency or inadequacy of marks;
- latent defects not discoverable by due diligence;
- any other cause arising without the actual fault or privity of the carrier, or without the fault or neglect of the agents or servants of the carrier (but the burden of proof will be on the carrier to show that his fault or privity or the fault or neglect of his agents or servants did not contribute to the loss or damage).

Article IV paragraph 4 provides that any deviation in saving or attempting to save life or property at sea, or any reasonable deviation, will not be an infringement or breach of the Hague-Visby Rules or of the contract of carriage, and the carrier will therefore not be liable for any resulting loss or damage.

Article IV paragraph 6 provides that goods of an inflammable, explosive or dangerous nature, if not properly marked, or if shipped without the knowledge or consent of the carrier, may be landed, destroyed, jettisoned or rendered innocuous at any time before discharge. Such goods, even when shipped with the carrier's knowledge and consent, may be dealt with in this way without liability to the carrier, should they become dangerous.

General average under the Hague-Visby Rules

Under Article V, nothing in the Rules may be held to prevent the insertion in a bill of lading of any lawful provision regarding General Average. (Most bills of lading have a clause making the merchant or shipper aware that he may become liable for a contribution in General Average.)

Exclusion of deck cargo and live animals from Hague-Visby Rules cover

Article II excludes from the items defined as "goods" live animals and cargo which by the contract of carriage is stated as being carried on deck and is so carried. Live animals are excluded from cover at all times. Cargo which is carried on deck without being stated as such in the contract will, therefore, be subject to the Rules, as will cargo which is stated as being carried on deck but which is, in fact, carried below deck.

Where the carrier's terms and conditions of carriage incorporate the Hague-Visby Rules, then in the absence of any term expressly providing to the contrary those terms will not cover live animals or deck cargo. A shipper of live animals or deck cargo should therefore make a special contract with the carrier, and should specifically state "FOR DECK CARRIAGE" on his shipping note.

The Hamburg Rules

International contracts of sea carriage

Hamburg Rules are properly called the United Nations Convention on the Carriage of Goods by Sea 1978, were drafted under the auspices of the UN agency UNCITRAL and introduced in 1992 in response to shippers' complaints that the Hague and Hague-Visby Rules were unfavourably weighted in favour of the carrier.

The Hamburg Rules are supported by very few states with any significant maritime trade. The main features of the Hamburg Rules of interest to a shipmaster are:

- The carrier is liable from the time he accepts the goods at the port of loading until he delivers them at the port of discharge. (Under the other rules the carrier is liable from "tackle to tackle".)
- The carrier is liable for loss, damage or delay to the goods occurring whilst in his charge unless he proves that "he, his servants or agents took all measures that could reasonably be required to avoid the occurrence and its consequences".
- The Hamburg Rules do not give the carrier so many exceptions from liability as the Hague and Hague-Visby Rules. In particular, the carrier is not exonerated from liability arising from negligence in navigation or management of the ship.
- The Hamburg Rules govern both inward and outward bills of lading, whereas the Hague and Hague-Visby Rules govern only outward bills of lading.

- The Hamburg Rules cover live animals, unlike the Hague and Hague-Visby Rules, but the carrier is not liable for loss, damage or delay in delivery resulting from any special risks inherent in their carriage.
- The carrier can only carry cargo on deck if there is a custom of the trade to do so or by an agreement with the shipper. If such an agreement exists the carrier must insert a statement to this effect on the bill of lading. Where goods are carried on deck without a custom of the trade or an agreement with the shipper, the carrier is liable for loss, damage or delay.

Bills of Lading

Bills of Lading are internationally respected documents on which banks and other institutions rely when advancing large sums of money. If a Master or agent signs a bill of lading knowing or suspecting that the cargo description is incorrect, or if a false date is deliberately inserted in the bill, a court will probably consider that a fraud has been committed. This will render worthless any guarantees or letters of indemnity that may have been tendered by the shipper and will expose the ship to liability for any loss that has been incurred.

The Master should be aware of the condition of cargo loaded to the extent that he can reasonably be expected to have inspected it. If it is impossible for him to properly inspect the cargo, the bill of lading should be qualified accordingly. Additionally, the Master will often be under a duty to state the quantity or weight or number of pieces of cargo shipped, and once he has signed bills to that effect it will be very difficult to claim that a different quantity was shipped. As it seldom, if indeed it ever, happens that the Master or his officers are in a position to check or vouch for the quantity of cargo shipped, Mate's Receipts and bills should always be claused "shipper's weight, quantity and quality unknown" or, in the case of bagged cargo "xxxx bags said to contain . . . weight, quantity and quality unknown"

The intrinsic value represented by a bill of lading tends to give rise to many disputes and accordingly, if there is any doubt about how a bill should be claused, advice of the owners or the P&I Club should be sought.

The bill of lading in the hands of a third party

At common law, a bill of lading is only prima facie evidence as to the quantity, weight and condition of goods shipped, i.e. if a bill is signed for a greater quantity of cargo than is actually shipped, it may be possible, provided the bill is not endorsed to a third party, for the carrier to refute the statements on it. Once the bill is endorsed to a third party, however, it becomes conclusive evidence of the shipment, i.e. the carrier will be bound by the bill of lading's terms and conditions, whether the goods were shipped or not. (Since Liner bills of lading are usually made out in a shore office and not on board, it is quite possible for bills to be issued for cargo that was not shipped for some reason.)

Section 4 of the Carriage of Goods by Sea Act 1992 (COGSA 92) underlines the common law position in the UK by providing that: "A bill of lading which:

(a) represents goods to have been shipped on board a vessel or to have been received for shipment on board a vessel; and
(b) has been signed by the Master of the vessel or by a person who was not the Master but had the express, implied or apparent authority of the carrier to sign bills of lading, shall, in favour of a person who has become the lawful holder of the bill, be conclusive evidence against the carrier of the shipment of the goods or, as the case may be, of their receipt for shipment. every bill of lading in the hands of a consignee or indorsee for valuable consideration becomes conclusive evidence of the shipment as against the Master or person signing the bill of lading, notwithstanding that such goods or part of them may not have been shipped".

A Conclusive Evidence Clause is inserted in some bills of lading stating that the contents of the bill will be conclusive evidence against the contracting parties. It is very important, therefore, for the Master to ensure, before signing a bill containing such a clause, that an accurate tally has been made of the goods received on board. (If there has been fraud on the part of the shipper, however, the clause will not be binding on the carrier.)

The bill of lading as a receipt for freight

If the bill of lading is endorsed with words such as "FREIGHT PAID" or "FREIGHT PREPAID", then once it is signed it becomes prima facie a receipt for the freight.

If the freight has not actually been paid, but the receipted bill of lading is endorsed to a third party, the carrier will probably lose his right to recover the freight, i.e. the statement becomes conclusive evidence that freight has been paid. It is important, therefore, to verify before signing such a bill of lading that freight has in fact been paid. (In practice the agent will normally do this.)

The bill of lading as a document of title

"Title", in the context of carriage of goods, means the right to possession, as distinct from the right to ownership.

A "document of title" is a document embodying the undertaking of a person holding goods (who is called a "bailee") to hold the goods for whoever is the current holder of the document and to deliver them to that person in exchange for the document.

Possession of an original bill of lading is equivalent in law to the right to possession of the goods described in the bill, i.e. it gives title or "constructive possession" to the goods it represents. In other words, an original bill of lading, being a "bearer document", is good evidence that its holder is the rightful possessor of the goods. This enables any holder to obtain delivery of the goods at the discharge port by production of an original bill of lading.

Title to the goods may be transferred after shipment to a third party, such as a bank under a Letter of Credit arrangement, by "negotiation" (i.e. transfer) of the full set of original bills of lading by the shipper, subject to the bills being made out in a way that permits this in law. A bill of lading made out so as to enable its negotiation is a "negotiable document of title". Bills which are not made out in a way that permits negotiation are termed "non-negotiable", and are often endorsed to clearly indicate this.

To make the original bills of lading negotiable they must either be made out with the words "to order" in the space allocated for the consignee's name, or "to (XYZ CONSIGNEE LTD.) or his order" in the same space, which allows the original consignee to transfer title to a third party, such as another buyer of the goods, if required.

Transfer of title from the shipper may be made by any one of three methods, as follows:

i) By means of a "blank endorsement", whereby the shipper stamps the back of each original bill with his company's stamp and adds his signature, but without inserting any transferee's name, before passing the set of bills to the transferee. A blank-endorsed "order" bill of lading (i.e. one made out "to order") is a bearer document, like a postal order or a cheque made out to "Cash", and the carrier must deliver the goods to whoever presents any one of the originals (unless he has reason to suspect fraud). Like a bearer cheque, a blank-endorsed bill of lading is a dangerous document but due to the requirements of banks which are asked by international traders to advance money against documents it is commonly used.
ii) By "specific endorsement" on the back of the bill of lading, e.g. "deliver to ABC Receivers Ltd", with the stamp and signature of the shipper. The person to whom title is thus transferred may be termed the "endorsee".
iii) By attaching authorised delivery instructions on the shipper's stationery, e.g. a Delivery Order from the shipper to the consignee.

Once a bill of lading has been negotiated, the endorsee or transferee becomes subject to the same liabilities and has the same rights against the carrier as if the contract of carriage had originally been made with the endorsee. This means that if freight or demurrage is payable before delivery of the cargo, the endorsee may be liable for the payment. To protect the endorsee the contract terms must be clear and unambiguous, and where some term in the original contract is not included in the bill of lading terms, it will not be binding on the endorsee.

The reason for making out a set of original bills of lading is that, if a single bill of lading were to be lost, the consignment of goods would have to be warehoused, a duplicate obtained (which would cause delay), or an indemnity given to the carrier, before the goods could be released. Since this would be time-consuming and costly, bills of lading are normally issued in sets of two or more "originals", the most common number of originals being three.

It is unwise to enclose a full set of bills of lading in one envelope, because of the danger of all the bills being lost together. Banks will therefore split a set into two envelopes, one being posted immediately and the second being held for two, three or four days and then posted, to avoid the possibility of both envelopes being in transit in the same bag.

Several non-negotiable, "copy" bills of lading will normally be made for filing and other purposes, and one of them is usually marked "CAPTAIN'S COPY" and travels on the ship in the Master's custody.

The bill of lading as an export compliance document

The exporter must, as a matter of course, keep copies of all transport documents as a means of the proof of export by way of proof of shipment. Although the charterer may themselves keep a copy of the bill of lading as a supplement to the charterparty, especially concerning a combination of a GENCON Charter Party and the requirements laid down by the Hague-Visby and Hamburg Rules, the charterer may have purchased the material to be shipped as part of an overall project, and indeed may have purchased different materials or equipment from different suppliers. Each supplier may therefore be an exporter in their own right, and will therefore require copies of the shipping document, i.e. the bill of lading, as proof of shipment. Although the C/P bill of lading is not of itself the evidence of the contract of carriage (the charterparty is), it still acts as a receipt for the goods and the evidence of the title (ownership) of the consignment.

In terms of export compliance, especially from a Customs perspective, the exporter is responsible for obtaining proof of shipment, hence the importance of the bill of lading. In addition, the exporter will also require a copy of the Export Customs Declaration, which will generally be raised by the shipping agent. The agent represents the shipowner or the charterer, or both, and therefore has a duty of care to ensure that a copy of the export declaration is sent to the exporter of the goods concerned. However, where the exporter allows the charterer to collect the consignment from the exporter's premises, as under the INCOTERM EXW (Ex Works), this does not happen in many cases, as the charterer is arranging the export shipment, despite the fact that the charterer may not have paid the exporter for the consignment at the time of shipment. Indeed, the charterer may act as the exporter given that the charterer arranged the carriage of the consignment by way of the charterparty arrangement and hence is the *de facto* owner of the consignment. Hence the need for clear payment terms under such circumstances. If, however, the exporter arranges the loading and securing of the shipment aboard vessel under FOB (Free On Board) terms, or ensures that the charterer acts on their behalf, then both a copy of the bill of lading and a copy of the Export Declaration should be sent to the exporter as proof of loading and shipment. Failure to do so can result in the exporter being charged the VAT by the Revenue Authority as a result of breach of the conditions for VAT zero-rating in terms of export compliance. In order to avoid this, the exporter (or producer of the consignment) should charge the charterer the VAT, as if the sale was subject to domestic national rules concerning VAT. If the exporter subsequently receives copies of the export documentation, then they may refund the VAT to the charterer.

For example, Oil and Gas companies charter vessels for the purpose of the shipment of materials to overseas Oil and Gas field locations. The consignments are shipped to the port of destination on a chartered vessel, and are then transported to the offshore fields. The Oil and Gas companies purchase materials from suppliers, such as subsea flowlines, subsea christmas trees, or drill pipes, and arrange consolidations of these materials in a single vessel or several vessels chartered in for the purpose. In reality, the suppliers of these materials are considered the actual de facto exporters, and must therefore obtain proof of shipment in order to comply with Export requirements as dictated by the national Revenue Authority. The oil/gas company may be the charterer of the vessels, but it may only become the actual owner of the property later, once that part of the contract has been paid for and settled. It is, therefore, the express responsibility of the charterer, i.e. the oil/gas producer, to ensure that such documentation is sent to the supplier as proof of export of the cargoes.

Outline of bill of lading contents

A bill of lading is a receipt for goods either received (before shipment) or shipped on board. It provides good evidence of the existence and terms of a contract between the shipper and carrier.

(However, a contract of carriage may exist without the issue of a bill of lading.)

Long-form bills of lading, as issued by carriers operating liner services, typically contain about 30 printed and numbered clauses. The majority of clauses are common to the bills of most major carriers, although the wording may differ. Additional clauses are added by carriers to address the special features of their particular trades.

A long-form Liner bill of lading will usually, when issued, contain the following details:

- a reference number;
- name and address of the shipper or his agent;
- name and address of the consignee, or "to order", or "to the order of (consignee's name inserted)";
- name and address of any notify party (e.g. a receiver taking delivery of the goods for the consignee);
- ports of loading and discharge;

- name of the carrying vessel;
- any leading marks for identification of the goods (as stated by the shipper);
- the number and kind of packages or pieces (as stated by the shipper);
- description of the goods (as stated by the shipper);
- gross weight or measurement (as stated by the shipper);
- the order and condition of the goods if not in "apparent good order and condition" on receipt;
- the place where freight is payable, if freight has not been paid;
- the number of original bills of lading forming the "set" (so that the consignee or any transferee, such as a bank, can determine whether all original documents in the set have been delivered, in case of fraud or mistake);
- the date of receipt of the goods for shipment or, on a "shipped" bill of lading, the date of shipment;
- the place and date of issue;
- the signature of the carrier, Master or carrier's agent; and
- the carrier's standard terms and conditions (on the back).

A typical bill of lading includes clauses numbered and named as follows:

1. Definitions;
2. Carrier's tariff;
3. Warranty;
4. Sub-contracting and indemnity;
5. Carrier's responsibility – port-to-port shipment;
6. Carrier's responsibility – combined transport;
7. Sundry liability provisions;
8. Shipper-packed containers;
9. Inspection of goods;
10. Carriage affected by condition of goods;
11. Description of goods;
12. Shipper's/merchant's responsibilities;
13. Freight;
14. Lien;
15. Optional stowage and deck cargo;
16. Live animals;
17. Methods and routes of carriage;
18. Matters affecting performance;
19. Dangerous goods;
20. Notification and delivery;
21. FCL multiple bills of lading;
22. General average and salvage;
23. Variations of the contract;

24. Law and jurisdiction;
25. Validity;
26. Limitation of liability;
27. USA clause paramount.

A Charter Party Bill of Lading will usually contain a clause to the effect that all terms and conditions of the charterparty identified in the bill of lading are incorporated in the bill.

The "CONGENBILL" Charter Party Bill of Lading (1994 edition) includes clauses numbered and named as follows:

1. Unnamed;
2. General Paramount Clause;
3. General Average;
4. New Jason Clause;
5. Both-to-Blame Collision Clause.

"CONGENBILL" Clause 1 states as follows:

> All terms and conditions, liberties and exceptions of the Charter Party, dated as overleaf, are herewith incorporated. The Carrier shall in no case be responsible for loss of or damage to cargo arisen prior to loading and after discharging.

The carrier's exceptions from liability are contained in the Hague or Hague-Visby Rules, which are normally applied to the contract by the Clause Paramount.

Stamped or hand-written clauses, e.g. "CLEAN ON BOARD" and "FREIGHT PREPAID", may be endorsed on a bill of lading, and will override any printed clauses. A bill of lading that has been surrendered at the discharge port may be endorsed by the carrier's agent with the word "ACCOMPLISHED".

The Charter Party Bill of Lading

If one shipper or a group of shippers arrange to charter their goods to final destination, a vessel is chartered. This chartered vessel is meant to move the goods exclusively for such shipper or shippers. In such cases, as a proof of receipt of goods, the charterer who charters the ship issues a document of title which is called a Charter Party Bill of Lading.

A Charter Party Bill of Lading is therefore a B/L issued by the hirer (charterer), and not by the owner, of the ship (vessel) transporting the shipment. Since the owners of the vessel often have the right to lay claim to the cargo aboard the ship, especially in case of a dispute with the charterer, banks generally refuse to accept such B/Ls as collateral for loans, or for payment under a letter of credit. Indeed, the only bill of lading accepted by the banks is a Shipped On Board bill of lading issued by the Shipping Line. This form of B/L is issued for liner contracts, where containers are being shipped on regular scheduled liner services.

A Charter Party Bill of Lading is a document issued by the charterer of a ship or vessel outlining certain information like the types of goods, quantity and conditions under which the goods are to be transported. The document is issued under different circumstances to a Liner bill of lading. The bill of lading is generally the proof or evidence that the cargo has been loaded onto a ship, the quantity of the cargo, the cost of the cargo and under what conditions the cargo is to be transported.

The main differences between a Liner (or Ocean/Marine) bill of lading and a Charter Party Bill of Lading are in the origin and disclosures. The Liner bill of lading comes from the Master of the vessel or the captain, indicating that he or she has received the goods. This document contains all the disclosures and written clauses relating to the conditions under which the cargo is transported. This is important because the goods on the vessel will be delivered to anyone with the bill of lading. If such a person has purchased the goods, he or she will be able to see if there are any restricting conditions attached to them.

The charterparty is anyone who charters a vessel. Such a person assumes authority over certain functions normally reserved for the ship Master or captain. The main responsibility of a ship captain under a charter is to safely steer the ship to its destination. The charterer is responsible for the goods on the ship, including signing the bill of lading for those goods.

The Charter Party Bill of Lading does not have all of the normal disclosures of the Liner bill of lading. This factor is important because anyone who purchases this cargo has no way of knowing all of the conditions attached to the goods until he or she receives them. Such a bill of lading will merely have a clause informing the recipient that the bill originates from a charterparty. The origin of the bill of lading matters because if there is a dispute, a Liner bill of lading will suffice as evidence of the transaction. A charter bill of lading, however, must be supported by other documents, including another copy of the bill of lading from the charterer.

The main differences between a Charter Party Bill of Lading and Marine bill of lading

Charter Party clause: The Charter Party Bill of Lading contains a clause stating that it is subject to a charterparty. The Marine bill of lading does not contain such a clause or similar wording.

Signatures

- Marine bills of lading can be signed by;
  - the carrier or a named agent for or on behalf of the carrier; or
  - the Master or a named agent for or on behalf of the Master.
- Charter Party Bills of Lading can be signed by;

- the Master or a named agent for or on behalf of the Master; or
- the owner or a named agent for or on behalf of the owner; or
- the charterer or a named agent for or on behalf of the charterer.

Usage

- Charter Party Bills of Lading will be used mainly for big bulk shipments such as 20,000 tons of soybean transportation from a US port to a Chinese port.
- Marine bills of lading mostly used for containerised cargo that is transported by regular line container vessels.

Unlike an Ocean (or Marine) bill of lading, the Charter Party Bill of Lading is not the evidence of the contract of shipment. This is because it is issued by the charterer, not the shipowner or the company owning and operating the vessel. In the case of an Ocean bill of lading, the B/L is issued by the Shipping Line, because such B/Ls are not subject to vessel charters but are concerned with the scheduled liner trades.

Examples of charterparty clauses

Below indications could turn a Marine bill of lading into a Charter Party Bill of Lading (Source: www.commerzbank.com).

- "Prepayable freight paid as per charter party dd. . .";
- "Freight payable as per charter party dd. . .";
- "Freight as agreed";
- "Bill of lading to be used with charter parties".

The Mate's Receipt

The Mate's Receipt is a receipt issued by the Commanding Officer (or Chief Officer) of the ship, or the ship's agent on behalf of the vessel's Chief Officer, once the received cargo has been loaded and secured on board the ship. It is a prima facie evidence that the goods are loaded in the vessel, and supports the vessel's cargo manifest.

It may be encountered in virtually any conventional trade (general cargo, dry bulk or tanker), but has been replaced in the liner trades (i.e. container and RO-RO shipping) by a more modern document, the Standard Shipping Note (SSN).

It is the document on which the details entered on the bill of lading are based; the information on both Mate's Receipt and bill of lading should therefore be identical. The Mate's Receipt should not be copied directly from the shipping note presented when the goods are brought alongside, but should be compiled from a ship's tally or measurement and show the actual quantity and condition of the goods as received should, when the condition or quantity of the cargo justifies it, be endorsed with remarks such as "torn bags", "stained bales", "rusty drums", etc. and should, where the ship's and shipper's tallies disagree, be made out for the smaller figure, with the clause "X more (drums) in dispute; if onboard to be delivered", "X" being the difference between the tallies.

It will normally be on the shipowner's form, in a triplicate pad or book kept on board. The original should be given to the person delivering the goods to the ship, a copy should go to the agent, and a second copy should be retained in the pad on the ship for comparing with bills of lading before signature, and for use in compiling the cargo plan.

It should be noted that the Mate's Receipt is not a document of title to the goods shipped and does not pass any title by its endorsement or transfer.

In ports and trades where Mate's Receipts are used, the shipper must usually present the signed Mate's Receipt to the agent in order to be issue with the signed set of original bills of lading before the vessel sails.

Function of Mate's Receipt defending claims

Goods or packages received in unsound condition clearly cannot be delivered in a sound condition. Therefore, it is essential to maintain a careful watch during loading for any packages which may have been tampered with, which are improperly or inadequately protected, broken, leaking, damaged, repaired, spilled, torn or stained. Such packages should be rejected unless reconditioning is an option. Care should, of course, be taken to see that any packages for which Mate's Receipts (see below) have been issued but for some reason have been returned ashore and then reloaded, are still in good condition.

The Mate's Receipt is given for goods actually received on board and is given up to the agent or broker authorised to issue the bill of lading.

The Mate's Receipts are often the shipowner's first line of defence in defending a cargo claim for damage or shortage. It is essential that the receipts are accurate and correctly reflect the quantity and condition of the cargo received on board.

Where it is practical for the ship's staff to carry out a tally, the total received on board may differ from charterers' or shippers' tallies. The lower quantity should be stated on the receipt and claused, for example, in the case of a contractual load of 24,000 bags, "23,850 bags received on board. 150 bags in dispute, to be delivered if found on board at discharge". Such tallies are mainly found in the case of vessels on charter carrying general or break bulk cargo, or Project Cargo. This should also verify the information on the cargoes to be loaded aboard vessel in accordance with the vessel's cargo manifest as produced by the ship's agent at the port of loading.

It is more difficult to verify the quantity of cargo on board a bulk carrier, particularly as it may be impossible for the Master to carry out a draft survey to compare with the shippers' figures. For example, the ship may be loading at a roadstead, where the weather and sea conditions would render the survey inaccurate. The only practical remedy is to endorse the Mate's Receipts showing shippers' figures, "weight, measure, quantity, quality, conditions, contents and value unknown to the vessel and owners". A partial, practical remedy may be for the ship's hatches and cargo accesses to be sealed and certified by an independent surveyor appointed by the owners P&I Club.

A surveyor should be appointed at the discharge port to certify that seals are intact before breaking bulk with receivers/charterers invited to attend the verification, although it may be found that the charterers' representative seldom appears. The Master should keep a written sequence of events at load ports and make annotations in the deck log book. His letter of authority to agents to sign bills of lading on his behalf must state that they are to be issued in strict conformity with remarks on the Mate's Receipts. Charterers' attempt to word the authority "Mate's Receipts or tallies" should be resisted as they may attempt to use the tallies issued clean rather than the claused Mate's Receipts.

Cargo arriving at shipside in a damaged condition should be rejected. It is fraud to sign Mate's Receipts that do not reflect the true condition of the cargo. The rejection of bagged cargo or packaged goods for mould, wet damage or leakage, is relatively straightforward. However, this may not always be practical with limited ship's staff and six hatches being loaded with bagged commodities.

Often, it is not possible to verify the condition of the contents within the packaging; rice may be infested, and coffee may be mouldy, for example. The best the ship's staff can do, is to be vigilant and exercise due diligence. If there is a problem, this should be drawn to the attention of the shipper or charterer. The Mate's Receipts should be signed in good faith and endorsed, "quality, condition, contents and value unknown".

Cargo tallying

It is impossible for ship's staff to efficiently tally loading and/or discharge of cargo except in circumstances involving small parcels such as mail or bullion. In some ports it will be sensible for the ship to employ tally clerks independent of any employed by the shipper or receiver to ensure that the ship has figures to defend any shortage claim. Even this may not be sufficient in some jurisdictions and the Master should consult his P&I Club to ensure that the best course of action is followed in a particular port.

If tally clerks are employed jointly by shipper and owner, the clerk's receipt may be accepted in place of the Mate's Receipt and spot checks by ship's staff on the accuracy of the tally are a sensible precaution. The ship's tally should be taken on board both for loading and discharge and not ashore or in a lighter as the ship's liability usually commences and ceases when the cargo passes over the ship's rail. Tally records should be retained on board for defence in the event of a claim against the ship.

Differences between Mate's Receipt and bill of lading

Mate's Receipt	*Bill of lading*
Mate's Receipt is issued when goods are placed on board ship after verification of quantity and condition.	Bill of lading is prepared & issued based on the Mate's Receipt.
Mate's Receipt is prepared and issued by chief officer.	B/L is issued by Master, or Agent, or Owner of the ship, or charterer.
Mate's Receipt simply acknowledges the receipt of goods inboard prior to carriage. It does not guarantee carriage of goods.	B/L acknowledges receipt of specified goods for carriage on board the particular ship.
Cargo may be refused to carriage even after preparation of Mate's Receipt.	Once B/L is prepared cargo must be carried unless refused for valid reasons. (Dangerous cargo, improper declaration, suspicious cargo, etc.)
Mate's Receipt is not evidence of existence of any contract of affreightment.	B/L is the evidence of existence of contract of affreightment.
Mate's Receipt is prepared by chief officer in capacity of servant of Master.	B/L is signed by the Master in capacity of Agent of carrier.
Mate's Receipt is not legal requirement but a procedural convenience.	B/L is a legal requirement in accordance with section 3 & 4 of Hague-Visby rules (COGSA 1925).
Mate's Receipt is not a legal document and is not admissible as evidence in court of law.	B/L is legal document. It is admissible in court of law even in absence of person who has signed it.
Mate's Receipt does not bind carrier.	B/L binds the carrier.
Mate's Receipt is a temporary document prepared for the purpose of verifying cargo when it is brought onboard.	B/L is a permanent document.
Mate's Receipt may be destroyed once B/L is prepared.	B/L must be preserved for a period of three years from the date of delivery of cargo or the cargo claims are settled whichever is later.
Mate's Receipt is not a negotiable document.	B/L is a negotiable document unless specifically barred.
Mate's Receipt is inferior document to B/L.	B/L is superior document to Mate's Receipt. In case of any disputes between Mate's Receipt and B/L as to quantity or quality of cargo, the B/L will prevail.
Cargo cannot be delivered against Mate's Receipt.	Cargo must be delivered against B/L.
Mate's Receipt does not give title to goods.	B/L gives right to title (ownership) to the goods.
Holder of Mate's Receipt is not owner of goods.	Bonafide holder of B/L is the owner of goods described therein.
Mate's Receipt does not give right to cargo claims.	B/L gives right to cargo claims.

Mate's Receipts can be clean or qualified

- **A) Clean Mate's Receipt:** Make of the ship issues a clean Mate's Receipt if the condition, quality of the goods and their packing are proper and free from defects.
- **B) Qualified Mate's Receipt:** If the Mate's Receipt contains any adverse remarks as to the quality or condition of the goods packing, it is known as "Qualified Mare's Receipt". If the goods are not packed properly and the Mate's Receipt contains any adverse remarks about the packing such as Poor Packing', the shipping company does not assume any responsibility in respect of the goods during transit. It is necessary for the exporter to secure the Mate's Receipt without any adverse remarks. On the basis of the Mate's Receipt, the bill of lading is prepared by the shipping agent. If there are adverse remarks in the Mate's Receipt, the same will he incorporated in the bill of lading, which may turn to become a claused (dirty/foul) bill of lading, and this may not be acceptable for negotiation.

The Mate's Receipt is first handed to the Port Trust Authorities who hands over to the exporter soon after he clears their dues. This procedure is adopted to facilitate for collection of port dues from the exporter.

Chartering procedures summary

The traditional chartering procedures require time and efforts. It is necessary to circulate the prospective charterer's position via emails, talk with other professionals continuously, filter hundreds of emails received every day, ask for ideas from other companies and try to find out whether one ship/cargo is matching with the other cargo/ship. It may sound fairly familiar, but when one considers the modern world with huge amounts of data which are usually stored in either our heads or our computers, this could be a very exhausted (and exhaustive) routine. After all, it is often the case that one does not always find the proper business within time or there is no time left for other operations.

In essence, the following set of stages is considered to be normal practice.

- A cargo owner needs cargo moved (or a ship operator needs an additional ship);
- He engages a shipbroker who finds suitable ships;
- After meticulous checking of the ships, the charterer chooses a ship, and via the broker, makes a First Offer;
- The first offer includes charter/freight rates and other conditions;
- The shipowner either accepts or rejects the offer;
- Further offers and counter-offers may lead to a charter being FIXED, i.e. the shipowner and the charterer agree to the charter, and a CHARTER PARTY (a special dedicated document) is signed by the owner and the

charterer, hence the origins of the term "Charter Party", i.e. a Charter Divided. All the details in the charterparty govern the charter.

Similarly, a shipowner may engage the services of a shipbroker to find cargo for his ship(s), or, for that matter, prospective charterers. The procedure is the same as outlined above.

Some details that are included in the charterparty

- Name and IMO number of the ship;
- Date of commencement and end of charter;
- Port (or range of ports) where the charter begins;
- Port (or range of ports) where the charter will end;
- Laycan date when the ship must be at a particular place and ready to load/discharge;
- Cargo to be carried (for voyage or time charters);
- Exclusions regarding areas of trade, cargoes;
- Insurance details;
- Rates applicable to the charter and payment details;
- Laytime agreement. (See below.)

Voyage instructions

These are issued by the shipowner to the Master, and contain all the basic information in the charterparty.

- Date of commencement and end of charter;
- Port (or range of ports) where the charter begins;
- Port (or range of ports) where the charter will end;
- Laycan date (*see below*) when the ship must be at a particular place and ready to load/discharge;
- Cargo to be carried (for voyage or time charters);
- Exclusions regarding areas of trade, cargoes;
- Insurance details;
- Specific instructions to the Master regarding the required ship's speed, fuel consumption, routeing, recording the weather, unusual incidents, etc.
- Laytime agreement.

Over and above this, there needs to be negotiation concerning the freight, i.e. the cost of the carriage of the cargo itself. It should never be forgotten that it is one thing to charter a vessel, and another to pay for the physical cost of moving the cargo, depending upon the nature, description, volume and mass of the cargo. In general, for chartering purposes, freight costs are based on the price per ton(ne), rather than per kilo, as the cargo is of such weight or volume that it occupies the whole of the vessel's holds.

Definitions

- ***Laycan*** – The dates between which a ship must be a given place (as agreed in the charterparty) to start her charter and be ready to load. If the ship is late, the charter can be cancelled or renegotiated. If the ship is early, the shipowner is responsible for all costs up to the starting date and time of the charter.
- ***Laytime*** – The agreed number of hours it will take to load or discharge a ship. This is included in the charterparty. If the cargowork, i.e. the loading/unloading of the vessel, takes more time than agreed, the charterer pays the shipowner an agreed amount per hour of delay, which is called ***demurrage***. If the cargowork takes less time than agreed, the shipowner pays the charterer an agreed amount per hour, which is called ***dispatch***. The number of hours and the amount of money paid are in accordance with the charterparty. Delays that are caused by factors that are the fault of no-one involved in the charter, i.e. external extenuating circumstances, are not subject to demurrage or dispatch. Rainfall during the loading or unloading of a weather-sensitive cargo (e.g. cement or grain) or a strike among shoreside workers, i.e. stevedores, would not be subject to demurrage of dispatch.
- ***Off Hire*** – If a ship does not meet her requirements in terms of the charterparty (e.g. she cannot maintain the agreed speed because of a machinery problem; she suffers an engine breakdown; a crane breaks down; the ship is detained) the charterer can put her Off Hire. This means that she will not earn money during the time she will be Off Hire. Some events do not count as time Off Hire e.g. a ship diverting to assist a vessel in distress or to land an injured crewmember, or weather-related delays.
- ***Notice of Readiness*** – When his ship has arrived at a given place to start the charter, the holds or tanks must be ready to receive the cargo. They should be clean and dry. The Master issues to the charterer a notice of readiness that his ship is ready to load. The charterer sends a surveyor to check the condition of the ship. If he is satisfied that the condition of the ship is satisfactory, the surveyor will inform the charterer and instructions will follow that loading can start. If the surveyor finds that the ship has deficiencies and cannot start loading, he will list the deficiencies and refuse to allow loading to start until the deficiencies have been put right.

Shipowners and charterers wishing to charter a vessel have to go through the complex and time-consuming manual process of reviewing thousands of emails with offers from shipbrokers in order to identify prospective matches.

Currently shipowners and charterers rely extensively on the information provided by the brokers with whom they cooperate regarding the prevailing market hire rates at given ports. To this extent, the shipbroker is an integral part of the whole chartering process, and needs to be aware of all the relevant information concerning the charterer, the prospective vessels required and the cargo to be transported, in order to reach informed decisions.

Choosing the right charterer or shipowner to cooperate with is a very sensitive process which needs to be executed in a very timely and appropriate manner. Time is often of the essence, given the combination of the need to transport the cargo at a certain time, the vessel charter rates at the time of the contract, i.e. spot or *ad hoc* charter, and also the freight costs depending upon the prevalent market.

The manual way in which chartering is currently processed and the number of different methods used makes it a very tedious process for both parties and does not allow either to effectively make the best possible informed decision. It is perhaps an unfortunate scenario that charter parties are still arranged on a manual basis by using specific charter contracts, e.g. GENCON 94, rather than by using electronic means, i.e. completing a charterparty online. This method has not yet become standard practice for reasons best known to those creating and arranging charters, or even the governing bodies of vessel chartering such as BIMCO. Hence the meticulous means of negotiating charter parties and the time taken to arrange such contracts.

CHAPTER 9

Break bulk and charterparty freight calculations

"Freight" is the remuneration payable by the charterers to the owners for the performance of the contract. It may be called charterparty freight in the contract.

Freight clause specifies the freight rate, how freight will be calculated, when it must be paid and the arrangements for payment. Details of bank accounts may be in a separate document annexed to the charterparty.

"Freight" is normally payable in US Dollars in the deep-sea trades, but may be payable in local currency in short-sea trades. It must be paid, under common law, and in the absence of any term to the contrary, on delivery of the cargo to the consignee or his receiver at the agreed destination. It is normally payable in accordance with the terms of a Freight Clause which stipulates the amount of freight, the time for payment and the method of payment.

"Freight" is often payable under charterparty terms partially in advance, e.g. on loading, or on the issue of bills of lading. It may depend in amount on the intaken weight of cargo, or (less commonly) on the outturn weight, the cargo volume, cargo value or on some other stipulated basis. It is not payable unless the entire cargo reaches the agreed destination, even if not the carrier's fault, e.g. if the voyage is abandoned after a General Average act. (The owners usually protect themselves by insuring against possible loss of freight, so that in a case of General Average the loss of freight insurers become a party to the "common maritime adventure".)

"Freight" is not payable where the owners have breached the contract. When cargo is delivered damaged, however, full freight is normally payable and a separate claim is presented by the cargo owners for the damage.

Freight, if payable in advance, is collected by the agent at the loading port before issue of bills of lading marked "FREIGHT PAID" or "FREIGHT PREPAID". And if payable on delivery of the goods, is collected from the consignee or his receiver by the port agent on the first presentation of an original bill of lading.

Freight is not payable on delivery if the goods have lost their "specie", i.e. changed their physical nature.

Freight may be of the following kinds:

- Ordinary or charterparty freight;
- Pro-rata freight;

DOI: 10.4324/9781003256359-10

- Advance or prepaid freight;
- Back freight;
- Ad valorem freight;
- Lumpsum freight;
- Bill of Lading freight;
- Ad valorem freight;
- Dead freight.

Ordinary or charterparty freight

"Freight" is the remuneration payable by the charterers to the owners for the performance of the contract. It may be called charterparty freight in the contract. Freight clause specifies the freight rate, how freight will be calculated, when it must be paid, and the arrangements for payment. Details of bank accounts may be in a separate document annexed to the charterparty.

Pro-rata freight

Pro-rata freight is payable in common law where only part of the voyage has been completed, e.g. when the voyage is abandoned following an outbreak of war or an accident, and the cargo is discharged at an intermediate port, or if the vessel had to leave port because of the onset of ice. It is not "freight" in the normal sense, but the shipowner's compensation for carrying the goods at least part-way to their destination.

Advance or prepaid freight

Advance or prepaid freight is often demanded by carriers of dry cargoes, and is the usual type of freight in the liner trades. It may be the total freight or an agreed proportion of it, payable in advance at the loading port, the balance being payable on delivery of the cargo. Freight is deemed to be earned as the cargo is loaded and is not refundable if the vessel and cargo are lost (albeit that the owners may be liable for damages to the charterer). It is commonly required where cargo is shipped under a negotiable bill of lading, as buyers of goods covered by a bill of lading often require a "freight paid" bill of lading.

Prepaid freight is not often seen in tanker charter parties, since tanker charterers are usually in a stronger bargaining position than dry cargo charterers, and tanker owners would have problems in storing large quantities of oil when exercising their lien for unpaid freight.

Back freight

Back freight is freight paid by a shipper for the return carriage of goods not delivered to or not accepted by their receiver or consignee.

It is normally not mentioned in charterparty terms. If the non-delivery or non-acceptance was the vessel's fault (e.g. due to over-carrying), no back freight will be payable.

Defining ad valorem freight

Ad valorem freight is charged at a rate stated as a percentage of the value of a shipment, usually of high-value goods, e.g. bullion. It is not normally used in voyage charter parties, generally being confined to liner shipments.

An ad valorem bill of lading is one on which the value of the cargo is recorded and under which the carrier waives his right to limit his liability to the goods owner under the package limitation provisions in the contract, usually in return for the higher ad valorem freight.

P&I clubs do not normally cover owners for liabilities in connection with high-value cargoes, and owners must usually make other insurance arrangements.

Dead freight

"Dead Freight" is not genuine freight, but owners' compensation for lost freight, payable by the charterers on a quantity of cargo short-shipped, i.e. a quantity which he agreed, but failed, to load. For example, if the charterparty agreement was that the charterers would load 50,000 tonnes of wheat, but he loaded only 40,000 tonnes, the shipowner will claim dead freight on 10,000 tonnes at the agreed rate of freight. (Some shipowners place dead freight claim forms on board, on which the Master quantifies the amount short-shipped.)

Lumpsum freight

Lumpsum freight is a fixed sum payable irrespective of the amount of cargo carried, the owners usually guaranteeing a specified cargo capacity for the charterer's use. It is useful in "mixed cargo" charters where cargoes are of varying densities. And is more common in the tanker trades than in dry cargo trades.

Examples

Break bulk cargo is cargo that is unitised, palletised or strapped. This cargo is measured along the greatest length, width and height of the entire shipment. The cargo is also weighed. Shipping lines quote break bulk cargo per "freight ton", which is either one metric ton or one cubic metre, whichever yields the greatest revenue.

Example

A case has a gross mass of 2 Mt (Metric Tonnes).

The dimensions of the cargo are:

2.5 × 1 × 2 metres

The tariff rate quoted by the shipping line is: US$110.00 weight or measure (freight ton)

Step 1

Multiply the metres 2.5 × 1 × 2 = 5 metres Compare to the mass = 2 Mt

Step 2

Calculate the freight with the greater amount either the mass or the dimension. 5 × US$110.00 = **US$550.00**

Freight would be paid on the measurement and not the weight. All shipping lines carrying cargo in a break bulk form insist on payment based on a minimum freight charge which is equivalent to one freight ton, one cubic metre or one metric ton.

Full container load calculations and surcharges

Freight rates for containers are based on the container as a unit of freight irrespective of the commodity or commodities loaded therein, Freight All Kinds (FAK). The shipping lines quote per box (container) either a six or 12 metre container. From time to time, abnormal or exceptional costs arise in respect of which no provision has been made in the tariffs. For example a shipping line cannot predict the movement of the US Dollar or the sudden increase of the international oil price. These increases have to be taken into account by the shipping line in order to ensure that the shipping line continues to operate at a profit. These increases are called surcharges. All shipping lines accordingly retain the right to impose an adjustment factor upon their rates taking into account these fluctuations. All surcharges are expressed as a percentage of the basic freight rate. Surcharges are regularly reviewed in the light of unforeseen circumstances, which may arise and bring cause for a surcharge increase.

Bunker Adjustment Factor (BAF)

"Bunkers" is the generic name given to fuels and lubricants that provide energy to power ships. The cost of bunker oil fluctuates continually and with comparatively little warning.

Example

Freight rate: Port Elizabeth to Singapore
Freight rate: US$1250.00 per 6-M container

+ BAF 5.2%
US$1,250.00 X 5.2% = US$65.00
Add the two amounts together, i.e. $65 + $1250
Freight rate: **US$1315.00**

Currency Adjustment Factor (CAF)

The currency adjustment factor is a mechanism for taking into account fluctuations in exchange rates, these fluctuations occur when expenses are paid in one currency and monies earned in another by a shipping company. The currency adjustment factor is a mechanism for taking into account these exchange rate fluctuations. It is always expressed as a percentage of the basic freight and is subject to regular review.

Example

Freight rate: Port Elizabeth to Singapore
Freight rate: US$1250.00 per 6-M container
+ CAF 6.3%
US$1250.00 X 6.3% = US$78.75
Add the two amounts together
Freight rate: US$1328.75

War surcharge

The outbreak of hostilities between nations can have a serious effect upon carriers servicing international trade even though they may sail under a neutral flag. Carriers sailing within the vicinity of a war zone may impose a war surcharge on freight to compensate for the higher risks involved and the higher levels of insurance premium, which they may be obliged to pay.

Example

Freight rate: Port Elizabeth to Singapore
Freight rate: US$1250.00 per 6-M container
+ WAR 5%
US$1250.00 X 5% = US$62.50
Add the two amounts together
Freight rate: US$135.50

All of the above surcharges may be applied to a single freight rate.

Example

Freight rate: Port Elizabeth to Singapore
Freight rate: US$1250.00 per 6-M container

+ BAF 5.2%
+ CAF 6.3%
+ WAR 5%
Total amount of surcharge 16.5%
US$1250.00 X 16.5% = US$206.25
(add to freight rate)
US$1456.25

Port congestion surcharge

Congestion in a port for a period of time can involve considerable idle time for vessels serving that port. When a ship lies idle, this creates a huge amount of loss for the ship's owner. Shipping lines therefore have the right to impose a surcharge on the freight to recover revenue lost. Another factor which influences port congestion surcharge would be labour disputes. Port congestion surcharges are calculated as a percentage of the freight rate as expressed in the previous examples.

Consolidation services

The consolidator or groupage operator hires a container from a shipping line and then sells that space to his clients/exporters. The benefit for the exporter is that small quantities which, would not fill a full container load, can be shipped by sea freight in a shipping container as an alternative to air freighting the goods. The consolidator would charge per metric ton or cubic metre, whichever yields the greatest. Example: US Dollar 89.00 Weight or Measure. The shipping line would have a contract of carriage with the consolidator and in turn the consolidator would have a contract of carriage with the exporter. The consolidator would be issued with a Combined Through Bill of Lading from the shipping line and then present the exporter with a house bill of lading (see bill of lading below).

The bill of lading

The bill of lading performs the following functions:

- A contract of carriage between the shipper of the cargo and the carrying shipping company (Ocean bill of lading) – N.B. A Charterparty bill of lading is NOT a Contract of Carriage, as it is agreed with the charterer of the vessel);
- The name of the shipper and the receiver of the goods the consignee;
- The contents of the packages as declared by the shipper;
- Shipping details such as: port of loading and the port of discharge;
- The bill of lading is a freight invoice and indicates if the freight costs have been prepaid by the exporter (Freight Prepaid) or will be paid by the importer, "Freight Collect";

- The bill of lading states the number of packages, weights and dimensions of the shipment;
- It is a document of title to the goods stated thereon.

Every original bill of lading signed by or on behalf of the shipping company is a document of title to the underlying goods. This special function of a bill of lading is achieved by a form of words which state: "In witness whereof the undersigned on behalf of the shipping company has signed three bills of lading all of this tenor and date, one of which being accomplished the others to stand void." "Accomplishing" the bill of lading requires the surrender to the shipping line or its agents in the port or place of destination one of the signed original bills of lading duly endorsed by the consignee/importer. Unless and until one of the original bills of lading as described above is surrendered, the shipping line will not release the cargo to the consignee/importer. Upon surrender of any one of the originals the other original bills of lading become void.

CHAPTER 10

Project Cargo management

Project Cargo, or project freight logistics, is a special type of freight shipping that suggests moving high-volume and high-price freight. Sometimes, Project Cargo is so complex to arrange that it requires changing the infrastructure, combination of modes, handling equipment, specific time frames and other intricate requirements.

Project freight can be national or global. The main difference in Project Cargo logistics from regular shipments is the unusual amounts and types of freight. Typically, mining, Oil and Gas and building industries are heavily saturated with Project Cargo shipments.

Project Cargo shipping can consist of single or multiple shipments, use several transportation modes, and cover a rather high value of cargo. Essentially, this type of logistics requires precise planning and logistics experts to be executed properly and on time.

The function of Project Cargo forwarders

People who plan and manage Project Cargo logistics must have a high level of industry expertise and connections. It requires the highest possible level of management skills due to the complexity of operations. Apart from that, the project freight forwarders must have exceptional communication skills to efficiently connect vendors, suppliers, shippers, and others involved in the supply chain. Ultimately, the Project Cargo forwarder needs to arrange the work among all people and polish processes.

In many cases, project forwarders are also shipbrokers, agents or ship management companies. They arrange vessels to carry Project Cargo, and therefore are engaged in vessel chartering, on either a voyage charter or time charter basis, depending upon the need for the use of one or more vessels in the whole project duration.

Handling of project freight transportation management

Advanced planning

Planning is crucial, the most important step in project freight logistics management. From securing capacity and equipment to risk management, every link of Project

DOI: 10.4324/9781003256359-11

Cargo matters. Apart from successful operations, proper planning can significantly reduce costs and eliminate risks during the transportation process.

Strategy

Risk management takes a prominent place in arranging Project Cargo as well. There's always a chance that something might go wrong, especially in such a complex supply chain. Thinking out all the possible outcomes and pitfalls in the process of transportation and project logistics is key to a smooth project finish.

Execution and compliance

For obvious reasons, the execution process must be as precise and organised as the planning. Once all of the strategy work is done, it's time to move to practice. Customs, compliance, paperwork and tracking must be organised, collected and managed properly. Maintaining clear communication, complete transparency and liability will help execute the Project Cargo logistics excellently.

The meaning of Project Cargo

"Project Cargo" is a term used to broadly describe the national or international transportation of large, heavy, high-value or complex pieces of equipment. The materials can be sourced globally, or from one individual location. The Oil and Gas, wind power, mining, engineering and construction industries are heavily involved in this level of transportation. Project Cargo requires a detailed engineering process in order to stay within the projected budget, and be completed on time.

It can consist of multiple or single shipments, and can both cover a wide range of freight volume and cargo value. It can mean single or multiple pieces of equipment being transported from point A to point B, or various destinations over a period of time. It can move by land, sea, or air, and can involve trucks, rail, cranes, ships, barges and/or planes.

Project Cargo is all about attention to detail. Pre-planning is the crucial step that leads to efficient operations. Maintaining efficiency in such complex cargo operations eliminate risks and reduce costs.

Background

This chapter will look deeper into the process of Project Cargo transportation, and will examine the best practices that can be applied to decrease expenses, and minimise the risks associated with Project Cargo shipments.

In the last few decades, the variety and number of sources grew dramatically, pushing companies to seek the most efficient transportation methods as they embark on large and expensive Project Cargo operations. As globalisation took over, the demand for large infrastructure projects increased worldwide, to fulfil the need of industries that supports refineries, power plants, mining operations and wind farms.

There was a major boom in manufacturing industries on almost every continent, and an increase in large infrastructure projects and building sites all around the globe. Now, the world experiences an era where massive structures, large-engineered-over-dimensional cargoes are being shipped from multiple origins to multiple international destinations.

As complex Project Cargo materials are procured, and transported internationally, it is crucial for companies (that engineer, construct and supply for infrastructure projects) to have transportation expertise on their side, too. Working with a transportation expert can add an immense amount of value at every single stage. The Project Cargo needs to be pre-planned, perhaps even before financing, cargo design and sourcing begins. The overall success of the project is directly related to how successfully the raw and finished Project Cargo is delivered.

Within this context, understanding cargo requirements and incorporating certain practices into the project process will prevent common problems, reduce risk and result in the best possible outcome as companies complete their project shipment requirements.

Industries involved in Project Cargo transportation

Project Cargo transportation is used within many industries, yet over the past few decades the transportation needs of specific industries continue to grow at a faster rate. Global tribune projects for Wind Farms are expected to grow in Asia, North America and Europe. Nuclear Plants in China, India, South America and the Middle East are also powering the growth. Demand for mining industry-related equipment is increasing, due to increasing demand for metal commodities. Natural gas consumption worldwide is projected to increase almost 50% by 2035. The United States' vast shale gas resources are also one of the most promising factors to count in as we look into the demand for Project Cargo arrangements.

Pre-planning and execution

Successful project transportation practices require a smart planning process from the preliminary stages. This can have direct effect on avoiding extra costs for transportation, duties and taxes. It requires expertise to provide a detailed projection of cost. Some cargoes can be highly valuable. At this stage, choosing a provider with a proven record of success in the transportation of Project Cargo is a must.

Countries have different regulations when it comes to Customs compliance, documentation, taxation, duties, exemptions, licenses and many other considerations. An analysis from a Project Cargo expert can help companies with all the regulative aspects, and the budgeting process. A Project Cargo expert can provide important insights into the cargo design process, can study the routing options based on the designed size of the cargo, and can work on the best suitable option for final delivery.

A Project Cargo expert can also advise on dimensional and weight restrictions, upon completion of a survey, by going through several variables by means of transportation to achieve successful performance, and the utmost optimisation during the shipment.

The execution of Project Cargo needs to be as detail-oriented as the pre-planning stage. According to transit time, delivery obligations and other requirements, the Project Cargo transportation provider carefully executes the pre-planned move, keeping accountability, proactive communication and transparency at the forefront of the operation.

Bringing it all together

A typical checklist in Project Cargo transportation

1) **Pre-planning is key** – initial transportation advice to move over-dimensional or overweight cargo can save shippers and costs, provide certainty and reduce unexpected events. When pre-planning, allow sufficient lead time to coordinate transportation details.
2) **Choose a quality transportation provider:**
   a) With a quality engineering team
   b) With the financial strength to assume a certain amount of risk and liability
   c) With a proven track record, on-hand experience, and country knowledge
   d) Stresses proactive communication that keeps the quick response time to changes/issues
   e) With broad knowledge of equipment, local haulers and manufacturers of equipment and materials, and fast, flexible access to specialised capacity
   f) Accuracy and honesty in pricing
   g) Impeccable execution
3) **Work on a contingency plan(s)** – Unexpected events can cause the initial transportation plan not to work out properly, and during these scenarios an alternative plan should be put in place to minimise and resolve issues.
4) **Work on constant improvement** – There is always room for improvement in Project Cargo transportation. Tracking the results of finished Project Cargo moves, and developing potential improvement areas, can help future shipments to produce better outcomes.

The following points are key services for Project Cargo management:

- Project planning, preparation and overall logistics control;
- Own fleet of special trucks and trailers;
- Long-term management of trucks and trailers of other subcontractors;
- Chartering of vessels;
- Rail forwarding;
- Planning stevedore activities at various sea port terminals;
- Unique solutions for cargo Customs clearance;
- Special cargo insurance for multimodal transport;
- Easy to use IT solutions which support project management on the daily basis;
- Route survey and preparation for transporting oversized and heavy weight cargoes;
- Making stowage plans and lashing schemes.

Oil and Gas

The Oil and Gas industry essentially involves exploring, utilising and transporting hazardous materials. Therefore, Oil and Gas safety compliance and risk management are crucial in such a complex sector. Unfortunately, disruptions and breakdowns in Oil and Gas supply chain lead to devastating consequences, such as the Piper Alpha and Deepwater Horizon disasters, that, apart from an environmental disaster, often cause numerous injuries and fatalities.

Risk management in the Oil and Gas industry has to be handled properly. However, it does not always work the right way. Sometimes, companies may underestimate the importance of safety measures while exploring and transporting crude Oil and Gas. It is critical to regularly check if your operations are in compliance with safety guides.

Practices for Oil and Gas project risk management

Risk management strategy

In the Oil and Gas industry, preventing an issue is much more important than solving the consequences. That's why proper project analysis and forecast of all dangerous situations is essential for the risk management strategy. Potential issues can occur on every stage of the process. So, it is important to outline all the possible scenarios before the execution begins.

Operational safety control

Unfortunately, the majority of accidents in the Oil and Gas industry are the result of human error. The first step to ensure safety compliance is developing a proper safety culture. Often, company leaders dismiss small signs that later might lead to an unwanted outcome. Also, make sure that employees that are responsible for operations and safety measures are doing it on practice, not just in their paperwork reports. Companies certainly should pay close attention to any changes in the system or processes.

Proper communication and analysis

In industries like Oil and Gas, it always seems like the disaster occurs randomly and with no possibility to be predicted. However, after some time of analysis, many minor warnings of danger come to the surface. Despite these factors, there was no proper communication or the importance of them was just underestimated. Make sure to structure the efficient communication strategy within the company and with all the parties involved to diminish the risks.

Ultimately, regular control and accurate planning can reduce the risk rate to a very low level. It's better to be safe than sorry, especially in the Oil and Gas industry, where being sorry costs a very high price.

The range of Project Cargo management services can include the following:

- Casing and tubing delivery;
- Long haul and flatbed trucking for freight of any size and weight;
- Line pipe and stringing;
- Rig site delivery;
- Transportation of oilfield equipment, supplies or production equipment, as well as exploration and development equipment;
- Storage and warehousing, including special storing needs;
- Processing and inspection facilities, including heat treating facilities;
- Barge shipments and port operations;
- Freight management and engineering;
- Rail logistics;
- Hot Shot services;
- Trans-loading services.

Casing/tubing deliveries

The transportation of extremely large or heavy equipment may be challenging, especially when it is line pipes, tubing, drilling and rig equipment, supplies, drilling fluid, bulky cargo, and similar commodities. It is essential to ensure safe delivery to the destination and precise attention to details. With more wells being drilled in unconventional places and hard-to-reach shale plays, rig locations can be tight or difficult to access. This can create issues when trying to locate trucks to make these deliveries. Our team will communicate with each site in advance to understand the specific delivery requirements of that location. That way, we ensure that the proper equipment is provided.

Oversized equipment delivery

With deadlines and strict schedules weighing on an already complex logistics environment, companies may face difficulties while managing the process of shipping by themselves. PLS Energy Services provides all of the required assistance to enhance your business efficiency and eliminate waste operations and costs. As more drilling sites appear, it may be hard to access rig locations and destinations. Teams of specialist professionals will communicate all of the details in advance to figure out all requirements to get your freight moved safely and on time. Whether you are shipping oilfield tools or equipment, valves, drill pipe, or general supplies, no load is too big for our Oil and Gas shipping service providers.

Line pipe delivery – stringing

Delivering line pipe to a location can be a very involved and specialised process that often requires attention to detail to ensure that everything runs as safely and efficiently as possible. Our team handles line pipe orders daily that require stringing services. We contract with several partners that can provide tow capable stringing trucks to deliver to ROW as well as stretch equipment to handle Triple Random and Quad Random lengths of a pipe if necessary. Our team is experienced in dealing with stringing contractors and inspectors to ensure that your job goes smoothly from the beginning to the end.

Hot shot

The service provider is constantly investing in people, equipment and technology to provide the quality priority services that its customers deserve, based on its reliability and reputation. The cargo management teams work closely with drilling contractors as well as Oil and Gas companies all across the globe to ensure that freight shipping and delivery needs are met. These teams always take the time to learn their customers' business to provide solutions that will exceed their transportation requirements in hopes of developing a transportation partnership for many years to come.

Warehousing and storing

The role of warehouses and storage is often underestimated when it comes to Oil and Gas logistics. We understand that there is a necessity for specially equipped facilities to keep and process oversized supplies and hazardous materials, and it is often hard for businesses to maintain warehouses on their own. Thanks to our broad network of storage and inspection facilities, PLS' Energy Services provides decent management for storing your materials. Our warehousing strategies help eliminate empty space and store the products with maximum efficiency. As for temperature-sensitive materials, we offer heat treating facilities as an excellent solution for freight storage.

Barge shipments and port operations

Barges and vessels play a significant role in expanding the capacity for moving oil cross-country and beyond. Regardless of how challenging your needs are, PLS Energy Services provide safe and convenient barge shipping. Our reliable carriers and advanced management tools will help make complex transportation seamless. Also, if you need to handle inbound shipments to various ports around the country, we can provide direct discharge services that include picking pipe and other steel products up from vessels located within ports and deliver the products throughout the United States, Mexico and Canada via truck or rail.

Pipe storage – processing – inspection

A reliable Project Cargo forwarder/service provider can assist the companies involved in any Oil and Gas project with pipe storage, processing or inspection needs. Many project forwarding teams work with a large network of storage and inspection facilities, heat treating facilities, coating plants and threading facilities throughout the world.

Freight management and visibility

Apart from operations management, the service provider provides tactical execution, shipment planning, tracking, metrics and reporting. Apart from the industry experts and professional service, we also offer our advanced transportation management system. It automates and simplifies the execution processes. Visibility into the supply chain is crucial to ensure shipping remains timely and efficient. As a result, the service provider's track and trace technology, in tandem with its automated tracking solutions, controls if the right shipment reaches the right destination in demanded time, and constantly keeps the project management team updated.

Trans-loading service

No matter how complicated the supply chain is, the service provider can generally provide all shipment modes, including Truckload, LTL, Flatbed and Multimodal. All of these modes can be combined with rail or barge shipping to match the project needs. Depending on freight type and route, the service provider can outline the best trans-loading strategy with a maximum result for fewer costs.

Other areas that must be considered include:

- The complexity of the cargo;
- Maximum weight and dimensions of pieces;

- Client delivery obligations;
- Origin facilities/routes;
- Consolidation points;
- The import/export regulations;
- Onsite delivery and installation requirements.

These elements must be considered when chartering vessels, as it is essential to ensure that the vessel being chartered can accommodate all of these factors, as well as the nature of the voyage concerned.

Finding a project logistics provider

The global recession took its toll on the logistics sector, causing many service providers to seek out new market opportunities. One segment gaining market share is project logistics. This specialisation, which requires expertise in handling and moving oversized or hazardous cargo from origin to final destination, represents an important and growing facet of the logistics sector.

Logistics has been traditionally viewed as encompassing warehousing, transporting and handling product at the least cost. However, the project logistics function does not automatically assume that cost is the prime factor. Project logistics can require years of planning for billion-dollar projects, and shippers cannot take logistics or monetary shortcuts.

Finding a partner

Shippers do, however, need to take special care when selecting a 3PL to handle project logistics. Any provider can claim it is able to tackle special projects, but specialists follow a unique business model with core competencies in global freight forwarding.

According to project managers, shippers typically do not have an adequate in-house logistics division to coordinate and plan all aspects of project logistics. They rely on 3PLs to handle the essential requirements of the job, craft a plan and a reasonable budget, then execute the plan effectively.

The search begins

When seeking a project logistics service provider, it is expedient to narrow the search to companies with financial stability, proper insurance and experience in handling various cargo projects. The most efficient way to find a competent partner is to ask for referrals, search the Internet for successful projects and contact organisations such as Project Professionals Group, whose members are made up of qualified and vetted freight forwarders. Once this has been carried out, interview the top three candidates to discuss company philosophy and project details, and solicit customer references.

According to project managers, flooding the market with numerous inquiries and not vetting forwarders in advance often results in higher rates. That is because providers will think that the potential customer is only looking for the cheapest solution, not quality, and will not take the inquiry seriously.

When selecting providers, it is necessary to be aware that the majority of true project forwarders tend to be smaller, specialist companies operating in local markets, effectively operating in niche markets, such as groups of independent companies specialising in international oversized, out-of-gauge and heavy-lift cargo projects. Indeed, shipbrokers and shipping agents are often more specialised in this business than are most average freight forwarders, which tend to deal in the high-frequency traffic of sea containers and road trailers. Shipbrokers and shipping agents are constantly involved in vessel chartering and cargo management, and are therefore more likely to have the credentials to deal with project forwarding. UK companies such as Union Transport, Cory Brothers, Pentagon Freight, OBC Shipping and John Good Shipping (now Good Logistics following its merger with Denholm) are classic examples of such forwarders, along with other specialist companies such as LV Shipping and Gillie & Blair. Gillie & Blair is based in Newcastle-upon-Tyne, whereas LV Shipping has offices around much of the UK, with its international headquarters based in Vlaardingen, the Netherlands.

However, most of the large, recognisable freight forwarding companies do not fit this category. Although some logistics organisations operate project departments in certain global markets, and attract business based solely on the reputation and popularity of their names, they are not necessarily the best providers available. For a true project company, it is often necessary look to local specialists.

It also pays to consider the provider's internal staff. It is widely known that some logistics companies might not have a dedicated Project Cargo department, but they might have recruited specialists with 20 years of project experience, in order to deal with such specialist projects. That said, using the services of a specific vessel-owning company such as Spliethoff or BBC Chartering will usually pay dividends concerning the value of the project and the ability to execute the logistics element of it smoothly and efficiently.

Eliminating surprises

All parties involved in a project logistics move need to feel comfortable with their role. Getting the logistics provider involved in the project as early as possible, namely some 30 to 45 days before the estimated ship date, is critical to success.

Before any project commences, it is crucial to ensure that everyone involved understands all the processes that will be required to move the cargo. In addition, the freight forwarder and the shipper need to work together to make sure the cargo is compatible with all the transportation vendors' equipment, especially cranes and lifting equipment, both on the vessel and on the quayside.

Bringing a 3PL into the project planning phase early allows it to provide input into transportation plans. For instance, conducting detailed route studies at the destination point will determine if the location has adequate infrastructure to move the cargo. Sometimes, obstructions such as toll booths or trees along the route can cause delays. Hence the need to become involved with the shipper as early as possible, even before an oversized piece of cargo is manufactured, especially in the case of offshore Oil and Gas equipment. The 3PL can tell the manufacturer if the product will be able to get where it needs to go, or if it has to be lighter and smaller, or maybe shipped in a disassembled form, to be re-assembled on-site.

It is always stated that there is no substitute for determining these details ahead of time. Airbus, for example, had to plan ahead and working out the best transport routes when it decided to have the wings fls A380 super-jumbo passenger aircraft manufactured at the BAE Systems Broughton plant, close to the city of Chester in North-West England. The wings had to be transported by dedicated barge to the RO-RO port of Mostyn, on the lower estuary of the River Dee, in North Wales, where they were transported to dedicated heavy-lift RO-RO service to Bordeaux, in south-western France, before being transferred to dedicated low-loading trailers for onward movement to the Airbus assembly plant at Toulouse Blagnac. The ferries had to be specially chartered to accommodate the huge wings, and the contract was based on a time charter to accommodate the full supply contract.

For some carriers, such as Atlantic Container Line (ACL), becoming involved just a few months before a project is reasonable lead time. ACL works with many large companies directly or with their freight forwarders. The ocean carrier receives and loads special Project Cargo on board its vessels, relying on roll on-roll off (RO-RO) equipment to handle and transport special Project Cargo while minimising cost and handling. RO-RO shipments often move as one piece, using specialised trailers from origin to port to destination. ACL also operates out of the port of Liverpool, and it is often the case that many Project Cargoes are shipped through the port because of the capacity of the ACL vessels.

ACL ships massive turbines, heavy machinery, aircraft fuselages and giant cranes on every voyage. In addition, the carrier transported a colossal high-voltage transformer from Antwerp, Belgium, to New York aboard its RO-RO/containership *Atlantic Compass*. The transformer weighed 255 tons and stood 30 feet tall, 11 feet wide, and 15 feet high. It was secured by ACL's cargo bridge system, in which loadbearing beams are bolted to steel pedestals for stowage into the vessel's RO-RO decks via a 460-ton-capacity stern ramp. For this voyage, specific space aboard the vessel had to be arranged on a voyage charter basis, albeit a partial charter to allow for other cargoes to be loaded as normal on what would otherwise have been a scheduled voyage allowing for the transport of containers and other cargoes.

If all the cargo dimensions and weights are not properly calculated, there may not have the necessary equipment on board to handle it, and that could present a significant problem. Involving the 3PL early in the project prevents problems from emerging later in the project. For instance, the provider can look at project drawings and suggest ways to reduce transport expenses, analyse timelines to be sure it can meet milestones and ensure that pricing is adequate to cover execution costs.

Treat cargo with care

Covering all elements is essential to avoiding project logistics pitfalls. The objective is to have the cargo shipped to its destination as quickly and safely as possible. Timing almost always influences cost. However, shippers looking to save money should discuss the best transportation mode with their 3PL, in order to optimise time and cost.

Also, as a result of the recession, many service providers are trying to secure Project Cargo contracts, but not all of them are qualified. For example, a company specialising in containers would not have adequate knowledge about how to handle oversized equipment, whereas experienced project logistics providers understand the details of moving this type of cargo. From this, using providers lacking in Project Cargo experience can negate the bargain price they offer. The 3PL might offer a good rate for using road transport to a jobsite from the port, but that does not mean that it will know to check whether engineering studies are required for permits. If not, that could mean be a rather costly surprise.

A specialist can also help to minimise or eliminate risks involved in project logistics. For example, a detailed method statement outlining the best way to lift and handle the cargo is particularly important when transporting hazardous materials.

The bottom line is that it pays to invest in the services of an experienced project logistics provider. Many shippers do not fully understand special project logistics, and given that this is cargo that requires extra care and attention, there is a need for crucial individual attention to detail and achieving maximum success with such projects.

Voyage charter vs time charter

A voyage charter is the hiring of a vessel and crew for a voyage between a load port and a discharge port. The charterer pays the vessel owner on a per-ton or lump sum basis. The owner pays the port costs (excluding stevedoring), fuel costs and crew costs. The payment for the use of the vessel is known as freight. A voyage charter specifies a period, known as laytime, for unloading the cargo. If laytime is exceeded, the charterer must pay demurrage. If laytime is saved, the charterparty may require the shipowner to pay despatch to the charterer.

A Contract of Affreightment is a contract similar to a voyage charter, but shipowner undertakes to carry a number of cargoes within a specified period of time on a specified route. Agreed frequency of cargoes may require more than one ship.

A time charter is the hiring of a vessel for a specific period of time; the owner still manages the vessel but the charterer selects the ports and directs the vessel where to go. The charterer pays for all fuel the vessel consumes, port charges, and a daily hire to the owner of the vessel.

A trip time charter is a comparatively short time charter agreed for a specified route only (as opposed to the standard time charter where charterer is free to employ the vessel within agreed trading areas).

It is possible to determine the comparison between Voyage and time chartering on a Project Contract by the traditional SWOT (Strengths, Weaknesses, Opportunities, Threats) analysis.

Strengths

Voyage charter

- Fixed Income Benefits;
- Eliminate the Risk of Weather Delays;
- Firm Control of Documentation when payments are delayed;
- Stronger Position on Cargo Lien (Ownership).

Time charter

- Confidentiality and Control of Access to Cargo;
- Firm control over the vessel and the Voyage;
- Access to varied tonnage while being asset light;
- Voyage flexibility;
- Source of Income and Profitability.

Weaknesses

Voyage charter

- Imprecise ability to evaluate the loss risks due to weather etc.;
- Delayed Receipt of Freight Payments;
- Possible Loss of Confidential Information to competitors on the identity of cargo owners and governing market freight levels.

Time charter

- Sizeable Capital requirement prior to receipt of Freight;
- Long Time-charter chain;

- Financial Responsibilities that can extend to the time charter operator that are primarily the fault of the shipowner;
- Extensive investment of time in determining voyage feasibility etc.

Opportunities

Voyage charter

- Maximising Revenue which is otherwise enjoyed by the time charter Operator;
- Once again having direct access to the beneficial cargo owners for future contracts/contacts;
- Beneficial Positioning of owned tonnage.

Time charter

- Business Opportunity with no Asset burden;
- Larger and more varied tonnage base;
- Secondary Trading in Freight Futures and Derivatives;
- High Revenue Opportunities in a volatile Market;
- Sub-letting Opportunities.

Threats

Voyage charter

- Practical Difficulties in managing cargo liens in case of non-payment of freight;
- Inability to secure payment of large demurrage claims from marginal charterers;
- Last-minute cancellations after long sailings to load port, citing dubious *force majeure* conditions.

Time charter

- Losses due to weather and port congestion;
- Integrity of the Cargo Supplier or Head charterer;
- Inflexible shipowners;
- Intermediate Voyage Risks in vessel readiness;
- Market Volatility;
- Especially spectacular crashes in cases of long-term period chartering.

The voyage charterer is

- Primarily the beneficial cargo owner;
- Prime focus is on the trade;
- Has covered his position with a fixed cost in the freight;
- Risk averse.

The time charterer is

- An Opportunist;
- Uses his extensive knowledge of the markets;
- Combines his finely-honed experience and entrepreneurial spirit . . . to make money and realise opportunities;
- Is nimble and asset light;
- Aggressive in his approach to making a success of the venture;
- Industrious and invests a large amount of time for preparation.

(Source: Capt. Richard Creet, 2014)

The main considerations in comparing the different types of charter are as follows:

1. Profile of the charterer:
    - Beneficial cargo owner;
    - Time charter Operator – Trip or Period.
2. Financial and Operational management.

It should be noted that for Project Cargo management, there is no absolute answer to the choice between voyage and time charters. Much of the issue depends upon the duration of the charter and the quantity/volume of materials to be transported. A single project could require several shipments of materials, and a long-term project, such as oil and/or gas field development, will require many shipments owing to the size and duration of the project.

Consolidations

Another issue to note in terms of project management concerns the extent to which products or materials are carried individually as unitised cargoes or are consolidated into groupage loads to be carried by a single vessel. For example, products such as boilers, rail locomotives/unitised trains or subsea flowlines for the offshore Oil and Gas sector are often carried as single loads owing to their outsize nature, particularly where there would be no space available for other cargoes aboard vessel.

In other cases, the products concerned may only occupy a single cargo hold aboard vessel, and therefore may be treated as "parcels". In such cases, other cargoes may also be loaded aboard vessel and stowed in the other cargo holds available. These cargoes may belong to different cargo owners, or they may be part of an overall project destined for one single organisation, i.e. the construction company building a particular specified project. In such cases, it is more than likely that the cargo owner, i.e. the project management company, will authorise the consolidation of several individual cargoes to be loaded on board the same vessel for a specific voyage, even in cases where such a voyage is part of an overall time charter contract involving a set of shipments over a prolonged period. This is particularly common in the offshore Oil and Gas sector, where oil companies such as BP or Shell will require the consolidations of materials such as drillpipes and other equipment to be loaded in the same vessel to avoid greater shipment costs, maximisation of the vessel's cargo capacity, and simply because all of the equipment is destined for the same location.

In such cases, the shipments will be managed by a project forwarder, usually a large global forwarding outfit such as Kuehne & Nagel, or a specialist shipping company such as BBC Chartering, or Shipbrokers and Forwarders such as Good Logistics or LV Shipping.

CHAPTER 11

Project Cargo insurance

Project Cargo is, quite simply, much bigger, heavier and more challenging to carry than the traditional goods that make up cargo in transit throughout the world. The items that make up Project Cargo are invariably large, heavy, sometimes having a higher centre of gravity than is ideal for any goods being moved but that is the risk the Project Cargo underwriter accepts.

Project Cargo requires a highly specialised form of marine cargo insurance, covering the national or international movements of equipment, materials or goods from manufacturing to construction site. These pieces of equipment/materials/goods are critical for the construction, operation and maintenance of various large-scale projects, and may be manufactured and delivered on a short or a long timescale, depending upon the nature and duration of the project. Given that each project may involve several suppliers and manufacturers, the project insurance must cover the materials supplied by each manufacturer, as well as the means of transport for each consignment of materials. Given that on overseas or offshore projects materials are carried by seagoing vessels under charter arrangements, the insurance must cover all elements of such transport.

The present-day supply chain for a modern infrastructure project can involve numerous manufacturers from several countries, a number of differing contractors and an array of supply routes that will involve any combination of land transport, sea, river, rail, road or air. Each party may have different insurance policies with different terms and conditions, deductibles and restrictive clauses. Hence the need for single integrated insurance policies covering all these aspects.

The Project Cargo business consists of the risks associated with the construction of engineering projects including (but not limited to):

- Power Generation Plants;
- Offshore and onshore Wind Farms;
- Offshore Oil and Gas projects;
- Oil and Gas refineries;
- Water treatment;
- Extraction of minerals, metals, ores, etc.;
- Railways;
- Infrastructure projects;

DOI: 10.4324/9781003256359-12

- Large items of plant, e.g. earth movers and cranes;
- Petrochemical Plants;
- Civil and Commercial properties.

As with general and break bulk cargo, Project Cargo is subject to many of the risks associated with the movement of goods, including the perils of the sea, loading and unloading to and from a variety of conveyances and, on land, all the perils that are usually found in transit by road or rail. The risk of theft is much less with Project Cargo but, to counter this, there are greater risks associated with its handling and general movement.

This type of cargo is also often described as heavy or large indivisible loads, and it usually requires specially adapted vehicles and ships for its carriage. The bigger risk, in terms of the stability of a typical load of Project Cargo, is that of the road carrier. This is because the load to be carried represents a great proportion of the weight of the carrying vehicle than such a load bears to the total weight of a ship.

A more comprehensive description would refer to cargo of all descriptions intended for use in the project works being undertaken. The cargo includes a wide range of machinery and equipment for use in the project when it is completed. Inevitably, much of the cargo falling within this description is large and, sometimes, indivisible into smaller constituent parts for easier carriage. These items of cargo may also have a high centre of gravity, making them prone to toppling or twisting during carriage and particularly during loading, transhipment or unloading.

However, Project Cargo is not necessarily always restricted to cargo that is large and difficult to handle. Smaller pieces of equipment, such as computers and similar electronic equipment, will usually form an integral part of the project, and may be critical to its whole operation. As severe weather episodes demonstrate, it doesn't take much to knock out a relatively small-sized piece of equipment, as seen in the example of heavy rain and flooding, which recently brought a whole airport complex to a grinding halt. So the lesson to be learned here is, large or small, the criticality of any one item for a project is a significant factor that the Project Cargo underwriter must bear in mind when assessing the risk.

Project Cargo insurance allows the principal to have one policy that protects against damage to equipment during transit to the project and, if required, can provide insurance to protect against delay in the project start-up as a result of a marine peril.

Project Cargo insurance is split between Cargo insurance (covering marine perils involving delays, loss or damage to materials, plant and machinery while in transit from manufacturer to project site) and cover for Delay in Start-Up (DSU) or Advance Loss of Profits (ALOP).

Issues that distinguish Project Cargo from ordinary cargo include the inherent instability of Project Cargo in transit and the greater claims costs, including the extra charges involved in establishing whether the cargo for the project has hidden damage, following any impact during transit or in handling.

Project Cargo also covers the costs involved in a delayed start to the project. This is known as Delayed Start-Up (DSU) insurance. It provides indemnity for the following factors:

(i) loss of anticipated gross profit, also known as ALOP;
(ii) additional costs to avoid or mitigate a delay;
(iii) debt servicing costs; or
(iv) increased cost of working.

The DSU section describes the criticality of any one item of the cargo for the project and its effect on the commencement of the project. This is an important issue for underwriters who insure Project Cargo risks.

Customers rely on the ALOP/DSU coverage to protect them from financial loss. This can result from business interruption caused by physical loss or damage to project-critical or key items while in transit to the project site. Damage to project-critical items can have a serious effect on the envisaged completion and operational start-up of a project. Project Cargo insurance also covers any resultant increased costs of working and continued payment of fixed costs and debt servicing.

Major parties, which usually purchase Project Cargo insurance, include the principal for whose benefit the project is undertaken, e.g. a private company, public corporation or government or state sponsored body, lenders who may be supplying the finance and the principal contractor employed to carry out the construction work.

Effective risk management is vital in ensuring customers are able to deliver ongoing and sustainable revenue, and requires the provision of robust and economically viable risk management services. A Risk Manager carries out the management and coordination of risk management services for a project.

Up to 70% of Project Cargo losses may be preventable. Risk Managers work with their customers' businesses to prevent these, but losses do inevitably occur. This is when insurers endeavour to keep their customers' businesses moving. Global Claims Teams are integral in minimising disruption to projects, and these teams provide a second-to-none claims service. All customers have access to a nominated claims contact to ensure a personalised and consistent service.

In terms of shipping Project Cargoes, insurance is vital to the contract. Project Cargo shipments are managed through shipbrokers, who arrange the vessels on a charter basis, be it voyage charters or time charters, depending upon the length of the project and the number of shipments involved. Therefore, Project Cargo insurance must be arranged for each shipment and hence for all the materials being shipped throughout the course of the contract. Although insurance primarily covers the maritime element of the shipment contract, provision must also be made for transporting the consignment from the manufacturing premises to the port of loading, and at the other end, from the port of destination to the final delivery point. Since the contract primarily involves seafreight, the INCOTERMS FCA (Free

Carrier), FOB (Free On Board) and CIF (Cost Insurance and Freight) are generally used, as the buyer is responsible for either the arrangement of the shipment from the point of manufacture, i.e. the manufacturer's factory gate, the consolidation of the consignments at the port of loading or a suitable inland consolidation terminal or unloading from the vessel itself into a nearby Transit Shed for Customs clearance. It is rare that a manufacturer would arrange the whole delivery right up to the customer's premises under a DAP (Delivered At Place) contract, as it is more than likely that the project management strategy would also cover the consolidation and groupage of several consignments from different manufacturers, all destined for the same project. Hence the reasons for the project managers or buyers of the material concerned to arrange the shipments from the manufacturers.

The London-based Chartered Insurance Institute has compiled a series of issues affecting and governing Project Cargo insurance. The primary areas are covered as follows.

How Project Cargo differs from traditional cargo risks

The sheer size of the material constituting the Project Cargo concerned means that:

- it is inherently unstable in transit;
- its centre of gravity must be kept as low as possible during carriage;
- lifting to and from conveyances must be planned with great care;
- each lift is a bespoke operation;
- road transit must be planned with great care; bridges must be strong enough to take the heavy load, which is concentrated in a relatively small area;
- adverse cambers must be avoided if the toppling risk is to be reduced.

How Project Cargo claims differ from those involving traditional cargo

- The cost of recovering the damaged Project Cargo is significantly higher than that for traditional cargo.
- Many of the claims are influenced by fear of hidden damage, fuelling additional and expensive inspection or survey costs.

Fear of hidden damage

Hidden damage is a fear – genuine or perceived – that further damage other than what is visible has been sustained to the item of cargo.

Following an accident during transit or lifting/moving the cargo, the owners of the Project Cargo will often insist upon a full inspection of the damaged item, to establish whether there is unseen damage. This might involve the use of X-ray or ultrasound examination or by the injection of nitrogen gas into a pressure vessel, such as a reactor, to establish whether any cracks – invisible to the naked eye – are apparent. In many cases this obligation to examine the damaged item in such detail may be incorporated into the contract of carriage between the carrier and the owner of the cargo. It may also be written into the cargo policy as a Sue and Labour expense.

There are several steps concerning the management of the cargo for insurance purposes. These are as follows:

1. Leaving the manufacturing plant

From the moment a project-critical item is uplifted from a supplier, the Risk Managers survey the condition of the cargo. They then check the quality and suitability of packaging and lifting gears, and supervise the loading of the vehicle at the manufacturer's premises, as well as the loading of the seagoing vessel, ensuring items are appropriately secured and covered on their transport. The insurance company also take steps in advance to ensure the carriers chosen to transport these goods have the necessary expertise.

2. Cargo at port

At the port of loading, the port's infrastructure and all lifting gears are surveyed to ensure they are suitable, and that the proposed loading and discharge points are adequate.

3. Shipping

The suitability of nominated vessels is also ascertained where necessary. Furthermore, pre-load surveys are utilised, along with the supervision of handling, loading, stowage and lashing on board vessels.

4. Offloading

At the location of discharge, further inspections of port infrastructure and all lifting gears are performed, along with pre-discharge surveys on board vessels. Unloading is also supervised, ensuring the proper degree of care is taken and vital details like centre of gravity are taken into consideration.

5. Transport to destination

From here, any inland transit route is surveyed. A surveyor looks at the suitability of roads, security issues such as the possibility of thefts or hijackings and whether the conveyance and its load can fit under any bridges and tunnels. If any problems are flagged up in advance, alternative routes are suggested. Solutions are formulated quickly when unforeseen issues arise. For projects involving the supply of heavy and voluminous materials to the project management teams on-site, these issues are crucial to the smooth and efficient movement of such materials.

6. Unloading at project site

Finally, at the project site, lifting gears and any storage facilities are inspected, unloading surveys are carried out and unloading is supervised.

As a project progresses, the Transportation Risk Managers working for the insurance company will carry out the following tasks:

- Coordinate surveys on a worldwide basis;
- Approve the choice of vessels and other transport methods;
- Following the study of method statements, make any necessary recommendations to reduce the risk for the principal.

In the event of loss, the local marine claims adjuster will handle the claim and progress any recovery action on behalf of the principal.

Key points relating to the transit of heavy and/or large machinery of all descriptions

- Specialist handling required.
- Large indivisible loads.
- Divisible large loads – one divisible load damaged will impact upon the undamaged load.
- Inherently unstable – must always be carried on a very low loader.
- Land routes must be pre-planned and agreed before transit to mitigate instability risks.
- Land routes may also be affected significantly by weather perils.
- By sea, large items of machinery etc. will usually be carried on deck and thus are vulnerable to even moderately heavy seas.
- By sea, items must be carefully protected against the effects of the salt water environment.
- Vehicle and load are especially vulnerable to uneven road surfaces and adverse cambers.
- Even minor knocks or shifting during transit may result in the need for specialist and costly surveying to confirm the integrity of the machinery.
- Machinery destined for nuclear installations will inevitably require costly inspection using specialist equipment, to confirm its integrity following any incident en route, before it can be accepted at the project site.

The Project Cargo policy

The Project Cargo policy is divided into two sections, covering:

1. Physical loss or damage during transit.
2. Delayed Start-Up (DSU) arising from physical loss or damage during transit.

Contract of insurance

1. There are several similar wordings available in the market.
2. Policy forms for Cargo and Project Cargo are both similar in some respects and equally different in others.
3. Cover is usually based on the Institute Cargo Clauses (A) 1/1/09.
4. The period of cover is usually on a facultative basis, with an end-date specified.

Typical description of a period of cover

"Facultative risks attaching and interest otherwise at risk from (stated date) Local Standard time until completion of contract estimated, but not limited, to be (stated date) – the expected date of commercial operation – both dates inclusive local."

Typical description of assured

"Projects Limited (as Principal and Project Manager, hereinafter called "the principal") and/or Sponsors and/or Shareholders and/or Partners and/or Parent/ Subsidiary companies and/or Affiliated companies and/or Partnerships and/or Joint Venture companies for their respective rights and interests of the foregoing and/or any new legal entities as they now exist and/or hereinafter be constituted having the ownership or management of the new facilities under construction."

Present and/or former directors, officers, or employees of the foregoing, while acting in their capacity as such.

Contractors or subcontractors of any tier.

Consultants, technical advisers, suppliers and/or any other company, firm, person or party with whom the assureds in 1 or 2 have, or in the past had, entered into written agreement(s) in connection with the Project.

All others for whom there may be an interest or responsibility to insure but only to the extent of their activities related to the Project.

Banks and other financial groups or individuals who are financing the Project.

Multiple assured clause

1. All entities comprising the Assured to be treated as one single party.
2. Representations by one are considered representations by all.

3. Breaches of warranties and/or conditions are treated as breaches by all.
4. Performance of duty or obligation by one party is considered performance by all.
5. All limits on the assured apply to all entities, not to each individually.

The voyage clause

At and from ports or places anywhere in the world to the Project Site – at the named place by direct shipment or ports or places in any order, including transits to, from and whilst at the premises of:

- the Assured;
- Forwarders;
- Packers;
- Consolidators;
- Hauliers;
- Warehousemen and other bailees;
- Fabricators, modification or assembly works (Process Clause applies);
- Specifically named premises en route – a Process Clause may also apply, depending upon the nature of any work done to the Project Cargo in such places, including loading, transhipment, unloading and returned shipments.

In the standard cargo clauses cover ceases:

1. On completion of unloading from the carrying vehicle or other conveyance in or at the final warehouse or place of storage at the destination named in the contract of insurance, or;
2. On completion of unloading from the carrying vehicle or other conveyance in or at any other warehouse or place of storage, whether prior to or at the destination named in the contract of insurance, which the Assured or their employees elect to use either for storage other than in the ordinary course of transit or for allocation or distribution, or;
3. When the Assured or their employees elect to use any carrying vehicle or other conveyance or any container for storage other than in the ordinary course of transit, or;
4. On the expiry of 60 days after completion of discharge overside of the subject matter insured from the oversea vessel at the final port of discharge;

whichever shall first occur.

Interest to be insured – section 1 of the policy – marine cargo risks

Goods, merchandise or cargo of every description incidental to the business of the Assured or otherwise, including duties, taxes or increased values of the

Property of the Assured or for which they have or assume a responsibility to insure or for which they have received instruction to insure prior to shipment or before known or reported loss or accident, consisting principally of but not limited to:

- Plant;
- Equipment;
- Materials;
- Machinery;
- Parts;
- Spare parts;
- Buildings, structures;
- Supplies, accessories;
- Process and general consumables;
- Office and Management Equipment, and all interests in connection with the Joe Bloggs Energy Ltd project located in and/or all other ancillary or associated facilities;
- Excluding Contractors' Plant and Equipment unless agreed by underwriters.

Conveyance or location limit defined – section 1 – marine cargo

Maximum any one Conveyance or Location £***

Accumulation Clause doubles this *** (when beyond Assured's control)

Location defined as: "each warehouse or place of storage or complex of buildings constituting one set of premises, including craft and rail or road conveyances at or alongside such premises". Wordings between policies of different insurers vary but the general thrust of the words is as above.

Interest to be insured – section 2 – marine Delayed Start-Up (DSU)

To indemnify the Assured for:

1. Loss of anticipated gross profit;
2. Additional expenditure (to avoid or reduce delay);
3. Debt servicing costs; or
4. Increased cost of working (ICOW) such as:
    - Safeguarding the profitability of a new manufacturing plant or production unit;
    - Protecting the potential loss of revenue from a commercial or residential development;
    - Covering the additional loan servicing costs resulting from a Delay in Start-Up of a commercial concern.

Basis of valuation clause – cargo and DSU

Section 1 – marine cargo

Cost, Insurance and Freight plus 10%, or
As stipulated in the contract of purchase or sale, or
As agreed by underwriters prior to known or reported loss.
NB: The 10% uplift is only for the benefit of the buyer. It does not represent the seller's profit. Such profit should have been included with the "Cost" element of the product.

Section 2 – marine DSU

To indemnify the Assured for up to a maximum of £*** for a ** month indemnity period.
The figures for sums assured and indemnity periods are set according to the individual requirements of each assured principal.

Deductibles

Section 1 – Marine cargo – usually not less than £25,000.
Section 2 – Marine DSU-typically:

- 60 days where delay caused by loss or damage to boilers, steam turbines, generator sets or transformers;
- 45 days for delays arising from other recoverable losses.

Unintentional Errors and Omissions in SMI, Conveyance or Voyage.
Subrogation-Assured assigning rights to insurers upon payment of claim.
Sue and Labour-To mitigate the cost of a loss.
Survey Fee-Payable in respect of survey following loss or damage.
Subrogation Waiver-Insurers not to subrogate against co-Assureds.
Wilful Misconduct – Applies only to issues arising from direct orders of the senior management or the Board of Directors of the Assured.

Provision of cover – to the project site

Cover is given principally by the standard cargo clauses of the London Market, suitably amended by additional policy clauses already detailed, with bespoke additional variations being adopted to suit individual situations.

The following London marine cargo clauses, introduced on 1 January 2009, providing internationally-recognised insurance cover, are to be found as standard in Project Cargo policies:

Institute Cargo Clauses (A) 1/1/09 CL382

Institute Cargo Clauses (B) 1/1/09 CL383

Institute Cargo Clauses (C) 1/1/09 CL384

Institute Cargo Clauses (Air) 1/1/09 CL387

Institute War Clauses (Cargo) 1/1/09 CL385

Institute Strikes Clauses (Cargo) 1/1/09 CL386

Institute War Clauses (Air Cargo) 1/1/09 CL388

Institute Strikes Clauses (Air Cargo) 1/1/09 CL389

Institute Classification Clause 1/1/01 CL354

Although the INCOTERMS 2020 allow for the use of Institute Cargo Clauses (C) to apply to CIF contracts, it is still advisable to use Institute Cargo Clauses (A) for the purposes of Project Cargo management, given the value of such projects and the nature of their management.

The cover given by cargo clauses (A), (B) and (C)

The (A) clauses cover all risks of loss or damage to the subject matter insured.

The (B) clauses cover a range of specified perils.

The (C) clauses cover a more limited range of perils.

All three clauses include cargo owners' liabilities for

- General Average;
- Salvage;
- "Both to Blame" collision liability -*NB*: this applies in **USA waters only**.

Cover under institute cargo clauses (A)

Cover is against All Risks of loss or damage. With this type of cover the loss is covered unless it is specifically excluded.

Cover under institute cargo clauses (B) and (C)

The (B) clauses cover loss or damage reasonably attributable to:

- fire or explosion;
- vessel being stranded, grounded, sunk or capsized;
- overturning or derailment of land conveyance;
- collision or contact of vessel or conveyance with any external object other than water;

- discharge of cargo at a port of distress;
- earthquake,* volcanic eruption* or lightning.

** They cause tsunamis.*

The (B) clauses also cover loss or damage to the subject matter insured caused by:

- General Average sacrifice;
- jettison or washing overboard;
- entry of sea lake or river water into vessel craft hold conveyance container or place of storage;
- total loss of any package lost overboard or dropped whilst loading on to, or unloading from, vessel or craft.

The (C) clauses cover loss or damage to which is reasonably attributable to:

- fire or explosion;
- vessel being stranded, grounded, sunk or capsized;
- overturning or derailment of land conveyance;
- collision or contact of vessel or conveyance with any external object other than water;
- discharge of cargo at a port of distress.

They also cover loss or damage caused by:

- General Average sacrifice;
- jettison.

Usual cover clauses for Project Cargo

(A) clauses are the usual ones used.

(B) or (C) are usually used only for damaged returned goods or pre-used goods but the (A) clauses can be used for damaged returned goods or pre-used goods provided underwriters are careful to so word their policies that they do not expose themselves to claims for existing damage, or wear, tear and depreciation.

Lifting operations

Any lifting operation represents one of the greatest risks of damage if the lift goes wrong. Great care in the planning of the lift must be taken before it commences. Due diligence must be exercised by the crane operators with regard to the securing of the crane and the load on a solid surface, the lifting capacity of the crane and the wind speeds at the time of the lifting operation.

In some lifts the weight or size of the object being lifted may demand the use of two cranes, to effect what is known as a dual lift. Great coordination between the two crane operators, and those supervising on the ground, must be exercised to ensure that each crane carries its portion of the weight and size equally. An unequal distribution of weight or size of the item being lifted will cause instability which, in itself, may cause the crane or cranes to topple over, taking the load with them and resulting in substantial damage.

In the example below, a reactor is lifted by crane from the overseas vessel using a horizontal lifting bar, which allows the lifting straps to be connected at each end of the reactor, spreading the weight evenly. On the ground other members of the lifting team hold onto guidance ropes in order to eliminate, or at least limit, any lateral movement.

Delayed start-up insurance

Originally known as Loss of Advanced Profits, its purpose is to provide indemnity against future loss of profits from a capital project that is under construction but whose start-up date, and consequent earning capacity, would be put back if the construction works were not completed in time for the launch date due to either a delay on-site or a delay in machinery and equipment in transit caused by an incident which results in loss or damage. Delayed Start-Up cover caters for such occurrences during the transit phase up to the site of the project.

It is written in a bespoke style and covers loss arising from specified perils or All Risks for the Transit section of the risk.

It is aimed at major capital projects.

The risk to the insurer increases the closer the major project gets to completion.

Unlike an annual policy, there is no "sigh of relief" as the final day of cover approaches. The Estimated Maximum Loss/Maximum Probable Loss (EML/PML) increases as the project nears completion.

Insurers may use a "GANNT" chart, Method Statement, or Work Breakdown Structure, in order to:

- establish an overall assessment of the risk;
- identify the criticality of any one or more items to the project.

The GANNT, Method Statement or Work Breakdown Structure tools are vital in identifying the criticality of any one item, as the delivery of a specific item or items, such as Power Generation equipment, may be time-sensitive and may significantly affect the overall timescale of the project concerned.

Marine insurers will try to avoid there being more than one piece of critical equipment or machinery on the same mode of transport (e.g. a ship) at any one time but it must be appreciated that this may not always be possible. Underwriters must therefore consider this accumulation of critical risk items in the premiums they charge and in any reinsurance arrangements, such as Excess of Loss, that they may choose so as to offer some form of mitigation of costs to the underwriting book.

Even though there is no legal requirement to obtain DSU insurance, in recent years it has been very much in demand following a shift from governmental funding programmes to Private Finance Initiatives (PFI) in respect of projects undertaken. DSU cover is of particular interest to the banks and financiers who are unlikely to put up funds and loans for major projects without there being such cover in force.

Delay in Start-Up – indemnity

Indemnity is payable for loss of revenue and/or debt servicing costs sustained during the indemnity period due to the production during such period falling short of the standard production as a consequence of physical loss or damage to the subject matter insured caused by:

- loss of or damage to subject matter insured in transit;
- loss of, mechanical breakdown of or damage to vessel or aircraft;
- loss of, mechanical breakdown of or damage to other conveyance.

Indemnity period

The indemnity period **starts** at a point in time when the goods are planned to be put into use and/or operation and **ends** at the point in time when the interruption ceases, or the last day of the agreed indemnification period, whichever comes first.

Normal indemnity period: 12–18 months.
Deductible: Rough Guide: 12 Month Indemnity – 30 Days
18 Month Indemnity – 45/60 Days

Delay in Start-Up – criticality

The following factors are significant in any assessment of the criticality of one or more items of Project Cargo in regard to how they may delay the start of the new completed project because of the time taken in repairing or replacing items that are critical to the commencement of the project:

- plant machinery and equipment;
- control systems;
- computer equipment;
- specific/specialised;
- essential/critical;
- long lead time for replacement or repair.

Delay in Start-Up – what other features do underwriters look at?

Client credentials – experience

Previous experience in the construction business and in the Assured's historic claims experience are factors that will greatly influence underwriters in deciding whether to write a risk.

If cargo is of specific or prototype design
A tried and tested cargo, for which its features in transit are proven by experience, is a more easily assessed risk than that of a prototype, for which an assessment of the risks in transit can only be theoretical.

Control systems/computer equipment
The quality of control systems and computer equipment are of vital importance in ensuring that the materials for the project can be sourced and delivered to site in the most efficient and timely manner.

Supply chain
The supply chain must provide a system that can respond readily to demands for new and replacement parts, to be delivered to site in a timely manner and in the order to which they are designed to be incorporated in the project.

Loading and discharge ports
These facilities must have the appropriate equipment for the loading, unloading and handling of all cargo destined for the project site.

Routing (especially with inland transits)
The chosen routes must be able to provide for free movement of the cargo for the project in a timely manner, and with the minimum risk.

Site details
The location of the project site, in particular, is a fact of material significance to underwriters in an objective assessment of the risk.

Bridge tolerances/route restrictions
The route must be planned with such factors in mind. With bridge tolerances account must be taken of whether the maximum allowed weight is spread over the whole span of the bridge or is the maximum that it can tolerate in any one area of the structure. A 100-tonne bridge cannot necessarily travel across a bridge with a weight limit of 100 tonnes evenly distributed over its whole length. The structure must be able to take the full 100 tonnes, without failing, should the conveying vehicle have to stop at any part of the bridge structure.

Alternative sources of supply and availability of spares
The risk is significantly reduced if there are alternative sources of supply which can replace an item lost or damaged in transit from off the shelf, if the original provider cannot do so. For any item that is bespoke manufactured for a specific purpose it will take time to supply a replacement, a factor which significantly affects the risk by increasing the chances of a DSU claim.

Basis of valuation
This must be made crystal clear in the policy from the outset. It is of particular importance in the case of second-hand machinery. Underwriters must make it clear to their Assured the extent to which they will provide indemnity in the event of loss or damage.

Ease of repair or replacement
Goods that are easy to repair or replace are a much better risk to underwriters.

The contract of insurance for Project Cargo and DSU insurances

While the basic cover provided by the Institute Cargo Clauses (A) 1/1/09 is the same as for ordinary cargo there are four significant differences:

1. The description of the Assured is much wider.
2. The cover is not open or annual. It is written on a facultative basis.
3. Premiums are much larger.
4. A large deductible is usually applied – US$25,000 is a norm.

Subrogation against carriers of Project Cargo

Recovering against carriers who are liable for loss or damage to goods in their custody has long been an important aspect of marine cargo insurance. If pursued properly, the amounts recovered over time can be significant in either reducing the loss ratio of an account or in improving its profitability. It is therefore necessary for underwriters and claims handlers alike to understand the basics involved in carriers' liabilities and how to effect a recovery in whole or, as in most cases, in part. Whether, and how much, an insurer is able to recover from a carrier is determined by the following factors:

- mode of transport used to carry the heavy machinery;
- the country in which carriage took place;
- whether it was a domestic or inter-country carriage;
- the weight of the cargo.

The amounts recoverable from carriers by rail or air are greater than those recoverable from a road carrier and even greater than from a carrier by sea.

In the United Kingdom, domestic carriage is usually done under the terms of the Road Haulage Association's (RHA) Conditions of Carriage 2009 for Abnormal Indivisible Loads. Under RHA terms, the carrier accepts responsibility for loss or damage to the Project Cargo between the time of collection and the time of delivery. There are few worthwhile defences to liability but the RHA carrier limits its liability to an amount not exceeding £1,300 per tonne on the weight of cargo lost or damaged, or pro rata for partial loss or damage. Higher levels of compensation can be negotiated but the cost of the carriage charges will be higher to cater for more generous compensation. Carriage charges are refundable in whole or in part.

Carriage between the United Kingdom and the Continent of Europe is governed by the CMR Convention (Convention on the Contract for the International Carriage of Goods by Road). Standard compensation set at up to 8.33 SDRs (Special Drawing Rights) per kilo of weight lost or damaged. This is about £7,500 per tonne, depending upon the prevailing rate of exchange. Carriage charges and Customs duties are also refundable. The standard level of compensation can be increased if both carrier and cargo owner agree to this before the CMR Contract is concluded.

The carrier can escape liability altogether if it can show that the loss or damage arose out of circumstances it could not avoid and the consequences of which it was unable to prevent. The CMR carrier is also not liable for the special risks inherent in the use of open unsheeted vehicles (provided it is specified on the consignment note).

If wilful misconduct by the carrier is proved, all the defences and the level of compensation are swept aside, leaving the carrier liable in full. This is a potentially valuable route in subrogation because it can allow for a full recovery if wilful misconduct can be proved. However, proving wilful misconduct in an English court is much more challenging than in some other jurisdictions. This can sometimes lead to forum shopping, in which one side seeks to recover in a jurisdiction that is more sympathetic to a claim of wilful misconduct whilst the defending carriers, and their insurers, wish to have the case heard in the court of a jurisdiction that is not so generously enamoured towards wilful misconduct.

International transit by rail between contracting countries is governed by the CIM Convention. The carrier by rail is liable in a similar way to the road-based CMR Convention and has similar defences to liability. Compensation is, however, set as standard at up to 17 SDRs per kilo of weight lost or damaged. This is around £15,300 per tonne, depending upon the prevailing rates of exchange at the time. Carriage charges and Customs duties are also refundable.

Carriage by deep-sea cargo carriers is mainly governed by the Hague-Visby Rules. These rules contain 17 defences to liability, including the negligent navigation of the ship by the officers or crew. Standard compensation is set at up to two SDRs per kilo of weight lost or damaged, which is currently worth about £1,700 per tonne, depending upon the exchange rate in force at the time.

In the USA, the United States Carriage of Goods by Sea Act 1936 governs international carriage between it and other countries. The liabilities under the American legislation are very similar to those of the internationally-recognised Hague-Visby Rules. Standard compensation, however, is set at US$500 per package.

International carriage of goods by air is governed by the Warsaw Convention – empowered in the United Kingdom by the Carriage by Air and Road Act 1979. Liability attaches to the air carrier if the loss or damage so sustained took place during the carriage by air. There are also some limited forms of defence but these relate to inherent vice, quality or defect of the cargo, defective packing, act of war or armed conflict and any act of a public authority carried out in connection with the entry, exit or transit of the cargo. Standard compensation is set at up to 17 SDRs per kilo of weight lost or damaged.

CHAPTER 12

Offshore supply vessel chartering

History of the offshore supply vessel

After the Second World War, the available units used to transport people, equipment and supplies to the offshore wells in the Gulf of Mexico were fishing vessels or retired military vessels. This was not their design function but, with some adaptations, it served their basic transport purpose.

In 1955, the first purpose-built vessel for the offshore industry entered service. The vessel *Ebb Tide*, with its bow wheelhouse and a long, flat afterdeck, pioneered a design which resisted the test of time, and become a standard for offshore support vessels.

This vessel's characteristics allowed her to be moored offshore for the discharge of cargo, manoeuvre and manhandle the cargo using equipment originally designed for fishing trawls. She was only 127 feet long and had a registered tonnage of 150 tons, which seems very small nowadays but, in fact, it was considerably larger than the previously used workboats.

Some of these very first OSVs were equipped with A-Frames and a small roller at the stern, for handling anchors and allowing the wire to be paid out. It was a model with multiple applications, depending on the required support, very well adapted to the conditions of the Gulf of Mexico.

The discovery in 1959 of the Groningen land gas field in the Netherlands, followed by the discovery of gas off the east coast of the UK, confirmed that the Southern North Sea was a potentially interesting area for the offshore industry. Oil exploration in this geographical area started during the 1960s but only in 1969 did the first oil strike in the Forties field produce enough oil to convince the major oil companies to invest in it.

At that time, the only available experience and technology of the offshore industry was acquired and designed to be operated in the Gulf of Mexico, especially the offshore supply vessels. With the weather conditions of the North Sea, producing large waves driven by winds often exceeding 180 km/h at its worst, the ideal GoM OSV design was no longer large enough or suitable enough for the new operations, especially in the deeper and less clement waters of the North Sea continental shelf.

Most of these ships that followed the accommodation forward, clear deck aft design with two funnels right aft, minimum freeboard aft (in some cases, inches

DOI: 10.4324/9781003256359-13

above the waterline), steel decks and rudimentary equipment as bolted standalone winches for towing and anchor handling, could not cope with the harsh conditions of the North Sea. Many suffered major power losses caused by water cascading down the funnels that completely stopped the main engines, their steels decks allowed the cargo to slide and, consequently, affecting the stability, and their crews were almost always working in a wet and slippery deck. To respond to the special needs of European waters, UK shipowners took the basic design and developed it further to better suit the environmental conditions and were shortly after followed by the Norwegians.

The first vessels produced followed the accommodation forward, low working deck aft types but with amidships funnels and the electric or hydraulic powered winch, many times undercover in a separate winch room, similar to deep-sea tugs. However, it was only with the entry into service of the Ulstein UT 704 design AHTS vessel that the standard European Offshore Support Vessel is more closely defined. This vessel was equipped with two Nohab main engines producing around 7040 BHP and with a 500 HP bow thruster which provided a remarkable and innovating manoeuvrability; the winch control was now carried out from the bridge, with an improved view of the working deck, leading to safer operations. The abilities of this design included an increased bollard pull of some 80+ tons, a semi-enclosed hydraulic towing winch and a workable deck of 124 feet long by 36 feet width built to take a cargo load of 850 tons with a strength rate of five tons/m^2 on wooden sheathed decks. It was, also, the first vessel of its type built with rounded quarters, allowing the free movement of the tow wire during turns, and provided with hydraulic pins which rose from the deck and trapped the tow wire.

The characteristics of these new vessels served the multi-task requirements of offshore support. Both rig owners and charterers liked the design and between 1975 and 1987 a total of 91 such vessels were built. The UT704 is called the original workhorse of the industry and can be said to be a major benchmark in the technological development of the Offshore Marine Industry.

From 1945 to 1975, the demand for oil increased rapidly, tripling in the United States, becoming 15 times bigger in Europe and being enormously multiplied by 147 times in Japan. This fact, combined with the rise of OPEC and the high oil prices, boosted the investment in the North Sea and led to the greater exploration for larger fields in deeper waters in the Gulf of Mexico.

The emergence of new technologies during the 1980s has contributed to breaking the 1,000 feet barrier of the "Deep Water" accepted definition. With the better understanding of the geological movements, namely of the deposit of turbidite sands and of the complex relationships to subsea salt, the deep-sea reservoirs have been revealed to be above all expectations. And once again the offshore industry shows to have an incredible ability to solve problems . . .

Parallel to the growing of the industry, the lessons given by tragic accidents like the Santa Barbara spill of approximately 80,000 barrels of oil in 1969 or the explosion and fire of the Piper Alpha in 1988, with the loss of 167 workers, has led to the adoption and implementation of tighter safety measures. The safety requirements for the installations increased and the OSVs added to their features emergency response equipment such as the FRC (Fast Rescue Craft), anti-pollution and containment barriers and firefighting assistance. Today it is recognised that the offshore industry needs to be very safety conscious, for it depends on this for its very survival.

With the advances into the deeper offshore and the increased exploration, other requirements of support emerge. The vessels need higher engine horsepower (to handle heavy Rig anchoring gear), greater cargo capacity (more quantity is needed per voyage) and to be faster (longer distances from shore) in order to meet all kinds of demands of the new generation deepwater rigs.

They will have to be larger and more powerful and, meanwhile, the use of Dynamic Positioning (DP) has almost become the norm.

The new generation of OSVs are indeed larger in size, in order to provide bigger cargo deck areas and to optimise the under-deck spaces with increased number of bulk tanks for liquid mud, brine and cement. The higher specification for towing and anchor handling, has led to the introduction of sophisticated anchor handling equipment and thrusters for dynamic positioning capabilities. Requirement for higher Bollard Pull has raised the trend to a range of 150 to 200 tonnes.

As illustrative example of the evolution status of OSVs, the current high-horsepower AHTS vessels have a total main engine exceeding 25,000 BHP, Bollard Pull above 300 tonnes and stern roller diameter greater than four metres. The anchors that they have to handle require winches of at least 600 T brake capacity and chain lockers enough to store around 1,000 m^3. The introduction of robotic cranes for handling of the outsize gear is being tested, mainly consisting of one crane on each crash rail, with their booms and robotic arms adjustable to reach and work in any part of the main deck.

Despite the fact that the accommodation and navigation bridge position remain almost unchanged, a greater emphasis in the crew's comfort and good ergonomics is integrated in the new generation of OSVs. Recently, new designs have made the deckhouse bulkhead rake aft, consequently reducing wind resistance and green sea loads. Navigation Bridge's new design concept is similar to that of airport control towers, aiming to achieve all-round visibility, and hull forms tend to pass from straight chimes to streamlined curves.

With the move into deeper waters, the subsea systems have become an essential part of offshore E&P mainly due to their improved technology and achieved cost savings. The Capex requirements differ between a topside production platform and four subsea wells installation might be on the order of 100%, and the time required to install it is often inferior to one year. In accordance with the subsea installation, intervention and maintenance requirements, some of the new generation of OSVs are equipped with ROV for underwater operations and lifting appliances with high working loads and heave compensators for cargo/equipment handling.

In addition, the Diesel Electrical Propulsion evolution has contributed with significant changes in the possible layout of the OSVs. The long propeller intermediate shaft can be eliminated and the main engines are replaced by alternator engines, being placed at a higher level, therefore improving bulk capacities. The motor is cost-effective and suitable for straight shaft or Azimuth propeller drives. It also features higher fuel efficiency and produces lower emissions which meet the needs of sustainable development.

In summary, the evolution of the offshore exploration was guided into progressively deeper waters and conducted the development of the Offshore Marine Industry to bigger, longer and deeper vessels, more powerful, with more cargo space, greater space efficiency, technologically very sophisticated and with increased versatility.

In the beginning of the offshore industry, the classification of support vessels comprised hull structural, essential propulsion and auxiliary machinery requirements. Any special function, such as towing, was not covered by the class regulations. Only in 1981, when IMO adopted the Resolution A.469(XII) "Guidelines for the design and construction of Offshore Supply Vessels", was it recognised that the particular features and service characteristics of OSVs could not be fully covered by the criteria applied to conventional cargo ships and specific safety requirements were introduced.

These guidelines refer to SOLAS 1974 standard of safety but introduce certain provisions to suit the nature of OSVs, namely in respect of stability criteria. Alternative stability criteria are prescribed and a minimum freeboard at the stern of, at least, 0.005L is recommended. In addition, as safeguard against collision damage, the Res. A. 469(XII) introduces damage stability requirements with assumed longitudinal, vertical and transverse damage extents. But, despite this new approach, the IMO resolution did not address other statutory aspects, obligating ship designers to find compromise solutions and Flag Administrations to issue exemptions in a case-by-case basis.

As the application of this resolution was not mandatory, its impact in the new builds was not promptly felt. Over the years, the IMO and other recognised institutions such as the IMCA have issued and adopted several documents, mostly of voluntary compliance. Operators in the offshore industry have gladly welcomed the guidance and their application has become part of the Industry recommended practices.

The Classification Societies began to incorporate the notions contained in the referred guidance in their own rules. Vessels specialised functions, like towing, firefighting, oil recovery and safety standby, are introduced and proposed as optional class notations. Similar measures are taken for specific vessel's performance capabilities as the DP, habitability and bridge ergonomics.

Today, most of the respected Classification Societies are adopting the OSV notation, as well as the specialised function notations (e.g. FiFi 1). The Offshore Support Vessel is starting to have a dedicated regulatory regime necessary to face the next demanding challenges of safe operations in increasingly harsher environments. The recovery of oil prices and the high number of undeveloped deepwater discoveries appears to have assured a secure future for the OSVs on the demand side.

Around 2005, the offshore industry had an aged OSV fleet with 45% older than 25 years and 29% aged between 20 and 25 years old. In 2010, the statistics changed and the average age of the fleet was already lower than 18 years. The OSV fleet's age structure analysis revealed the existence of two distinct fleets, being the old fleet comprising the larger number of vessels and the new fleet comprising the largest portion of tonnage.

This confirms the trend to build larger, heavier and more powerful vessels. In addition, the order book size and composition, with an obvious shift from supply vessel to anchor handler (AHTS) construction, indicate that owners and operators are willing to invest in more capital-intensive vessels for the perspective of obtaining additional charter rates in the market.

OSV chartering

The chartering of Offshore Supply Vessels (OSVs) is, in many ways, similar to the chartering of break bulk and general cargo vessels, as the principle of an offshore supply vessel, be it an AHTS (Anchor Handling Towage and Supply Vessel) or a

Figure 12.1 **EMEA**, Offshore Supply Vessel, ASCO Quay, Aberdeen

PSV (Platform Supply Vessel), revolves around the carriage of loose equipment and materials from a supply base adjacent to a quayside to an offshore installation used for the purposes of drilling for and the production of oil and/or gas. Vessels are sometimes chartered on an *ad hoc* basis, but in general, the use of OSVs is governed by time charters. These time charters are formulated by the BIMCO (Baltic and International Maritime Council). It should also be noted that the operation of offshore supply vessels is much more specialist than for conventional break bulk and general cargo vessels, but in many cases both types of charter operate in parallel, as much of the offshore Oil and Gas industry relies on the supply and transportation of Project Cargo, partly by break bulk and general cargo vessels, and partly by offshore supply vessels. Where break bulk and general cargo vessels operate globally, transporting cargoes from one international seaport to another, offshore supply vessels operate between offshore supply bases attached to international seaports and offshore installations on a much more limited and regional basis, e.g. the Gulf of Mexico, the North Sea, West Africa and Australasia.

An OECD Report on Permanent Establishments and the Offshore Oil and Gas Industry (July 2016) determined the nature of Permanent Establishments with reference to Offshore Drilling and Production Platforms and their operations, especially concerning tax liability on offshore operations and the income derived therefrom. It also referred to chartering arrangements for such establishments, including semi-submersibles and drillships, which, although not permanently fixed to the seabed, are moored in a static position for a significant length of time as part of offshore Oil and Gas drilling and production projects.

According to the OECD, whether mobile drilling rigs are considered to be fixed depends on the circumstances, a way of stating that there is no fixed or predetermined global fiscal rule on the issue. A drilling rig, e.g., a semi-submersible platform, a Jackup rig or even a drillship, that is anchored to the seabed for a long period of time could meet the fixed criterion in the same way as a permanent production platform which is fixed to the seabed. This rule applies to semi-submersible rigs and drill ships, which, even though they might not be anchored to the seabed as other types of drilling installations, can remain in the same place for a long time on the same contract with the same customer under a very long-term charter basis. In these circumstances, such drilling rigs can meet the geographical and commercial criteria and can therefore be considered to be fixed. It is suggested that this issue should be approached by considering each oil field to be one geographical area; a floating platform or rig moving around in the same oil field would, therefore, satisfy the geographically-fixed criterion, even though it is not fixed to the ground. Contrary to this argument, the Danish State's Tax Directorate (*Statsskattedirektoratet*, "SD") held that a Norwegian company operating two drilling rigs on the Danish continental shelf for more than 12 months had a PE (Permanent Establishment), as defined by the description of "Artificial Islands" according to the UN Convention of the Law of the Sea (UNCLOS), even though the drilling rigs were operating in different locations on the Danish continental shelf. In this respect, both the intended duration and the actual duration of a contract must be considered. Consequently, in analysing article 5(1) of the OECD Model, if a contract is intended to last for more than six months, but only lasts for four months, the activity should still be considered to be fixed given the nature and intention of the contract.

The way in which drilling activity is structured may have an effect on whether the owner is considered to be carrying on a business through the drilling rig. Common sense tells us that this is indeed the case; such actions are definitely not philanthropic, nor are they charitable. The purpose of the exercise is ultimately the generation of revenue through the production of oil and/or gas in the offshore field concerned, and the drilling exercise is part of this venture, seen as investment in the venture or project itself. After all, the oil company is paying for the services of the drilling contractors within the upstream element of this kind of project. An owner of a drilling rig may provide a drilling service to its customer, by way of a time charter, whereby the owner provides the drilling rig with a full crew to operate the rig, or the owner may rent out the rig, often to a related company, on bareboat or even time charter terms. In the case of the time charter, the owner of the drilling rig provides the drilling service to the oil company on a time charter basis, using its own rigs and operating crews. In these cases, the bareboat or time charterer, i.e. the oil company, takes possession of the drilling rig and is therefore the disponent owner of the equipment.

Service and supply ships cover a wide range of maritime support services provided to Oil and Gas and drilling companies. These vessels are regarded as mobile assets not fixed to the seabed, and indeed are actually marine vessels employed in the carriage of materials to the offshore platforms. A number of examples of these types of vessels from the industry are listed below:

- **Platform Supply Vessels** (PSVs): these are used for transporting supplies from a port to a drilling rig or other installation in an oil field. PSV activity is often carried out in a single jurisdiction. When these vessels are contracted for a longer period of time to support the same drilling rig, they are typically sailing the same route to and from a port and drilling rig over a long period of time.
- **Anchor Handling Tug Supply Vessels** (AHTSVs, or AHTS): these are used for towing drilling rigs and performing anchor handling for drilling rigs as well as PSV duties for the drilling rigs. The towing of drilling rigs may be from one jurisdiction to another. Once the transport of the rig is completed, the vessel sails on to the next customer in another jurisdiction.
- **Construction Support Vessels** (CSVs), **Dive Support Vessels** (DSVs) and **Multi-purpose Support Vessels** (MSVs): these are used for supporting or performing subsea construction work. Subsea construction includes activities such as dredging and/or ploughing on the seabed, laying pipelines, subsea oilfield installations and/or construction, diving support, supporting remotely operated vehicles (ROVs) operating on the seabed, etc.

- **Emergency Response Rescue Vessels** (ERRVs): these are vessels that operate along offshore installations in an oil field. The purpose of these vessels is to perform rescue services in the event of emergencies, such as transporting personnel away from the place of emergency. Alternatively, ERRVs may provide warning services and pollution control. The presence of ERRVs alongside offshore installations is legally required in many jurisdictions. ERRVs are not fixed to the seabed, but, by their nature, can be present in an offshore field in one geographical area on a more permanent basis than other types of support vessels.
- **Salvage vessels**: these are used for recovering or removing other vessels or equipment in the sea or on the seabed. Similar to the ERRVs, these vessels can work in the same area of the sea for a long period of time. In addition, the object, which a salvage vessel has been contracted to recover, can, in itself, be in a given area of sea for a long time.

As well as activities performed by these vessels, many other activities are carried on in the offshore industry, such as floating production storage and offloading (FPSO) units, towage and tug boats, accommodation vessels, crew change vessels, catering services, manning services, etc.

As at the beginning of 2021, the maritime organisation Clarksons reported the number of offshore vessels presently in operation as:

- OSVs (Offshore Supply Vessels, including AHTS) – 5301;
- OSV orderbook – 602;
- Fleet growth over last 10 years – 7%.

Charter rates fluctuate, but in general the charter rates for PSVs (Platform Supply Vessels) are lower than those for AHTS (Anchor Handling Towage & Supply) vessels. These can be illustrated as follows:

North Sea Average Rates (Rates/Day) January 2021

Category	*Avg rate Jan 2021*	*Avg rate Jan 2020*	*% Change*	*Minimum*	*Maximum*
PSVs <900m^2	£11.012	£6308	74.57%	£5250	£20,000
PSVs >900m^2	£9861	£8014	23.05%	£5250	£15,995
AHTS <22,000 bhp	£10,928	£18,562	41.13%	£6108	£27,132
AHTS >22,000 bhp	£20,121	£16,901	19.05%	£9327	£46,633

Source: Seabrokers Group (www.seabrokers.com)

It should be noted that for the PSVs and the AHTS of greater than 22,000 bhp, the charter rates have increased between 2020 and 2021, whereas for the AHTS of less than 22,000 bhp, the charter rates have decreased. It should also be noted that AHTS vessels attract significantly higher charter rates than do PSVs, on the grounds that AHTS vessels are more versatile, in that they can two drilling and production rigs to their locations as well as supplying materials to these offshore rigs, whereas PSVs are limited to simply supplying materials to these rigs and are therefore not as versatile, hence their lower charter rates.

Offshore drilling rigs are also chartered on a daily basis, and these charter rates vary according to the type, size and age of the rig, as well as demand for such rigs. As with offshore supply vessels, drilling rigs vary in types, such as:

- Jackup;
- Semi-submersible;
- Drillship.

Jackup rigs are located in projects located in shallower waters, for example on the continental shelf, whereas semi-submersible rigs are located in projects further out into the ocean, generally in deeper waters off the continental shelf. The same is true of drillships, which are effectively conventional self-propelled ships equipped with drilling rigs. For example, drillship rates rose from US$170,000/day in 2018 to US$193,000/day in 2019, then to US$250,000/day in 2020. However, such rates are average, with specific cases such as the Diamond Offshore drillships *Ocean BlackHawk* and *Ocean BlackRhino*, each securing rates around US$280,000/day to operate in the SNE offshore field off Senegal in West Africa (www.rystadenergy.com).

Similar to drilling rigs, how a vessel is chartered may have an effect on whether the owner is considered to be carrying on business through its asset. An owner of a vessel often provides a service to its customer or charters the vessel by way of a time charter, whereby the owner provides a vessel with a full crew to operate the vessel according to the customer's instructions. The owner may also rent out the vessel on bareboat or time charter terms, whereby the bareboat charterer takes possession of the vessel and becomes the disponent owner of the equipment. This can most often be seen between two related companies or in the context of a financial lease.

Whether a bareboat charter of a vessel may constitute a Permanent Establishment (PE) for the owner was considered by the Income Tax Rulings Directorate, Legislative Policy and Regulatory Affairs Branch of Canada ("ITRD") in an advance income tax ruling. The ITRD concluded that entering into a bareboat charter agreement for a ship to be used in Canadian waters could not be regarded as carrying on business. The ITRD also noted that the activity was not covered by the offshore provision in the Canada – Norway Income and Capital Tax Treaty (2002). Consequently, the bareboat charter agreement was insufficient for the foreign owners to have a PE in Canada according to the general rules of article 5 of the tax treaty. The ITRD decision did not address the remuneration under the contract, but, instead, defined a bareboat charter as:

> a contract under which a ship is leased or rented for a period of time on an unmanned basis. The person chartering the ship is responsible for manning and operating the ship and paying all expenses related thereto.

However, the ruling would suggest that if a time charter had been entered into, the person chartering the ship would also be responsible to the vessel owners for the costs of the vessel's crew and its overall operations. In other words, the charterer would pay the charter rates relating to the overall operation of the vessel, crewing, and operational costs including bunkering, victualling, vessel maintenance etc. This is why there is a definitive need to establish whether the charter arrangement is for bareboat or time charters.

By defining a bareboat charter as a type of contract where all of the operational risk is passed on to the lessee, the question of how remuneration is calculated was, therefore, less important. Indeed, the same would apply to time charters, as a time charter contract means that the vessel and its crew are employed by the lessee to carry out specific operations according to the lessee's requirements. For example, BP or Shell require the operations of a set of offshore drilling rigs as well as the services of the supply vessels. These oil companies will therefore charter the service of the drilling rigs from one owner, e.g. Transocean or Diamond Offshore and the services of several supply vessels from other supply vessel owners such as Bourbon Offshore or Skandi. The oil companies do not provide their own crews for these operations; such activities are left to the owners of the drilling rigs and the supply vessels themselves. As noted in section 5.2. of the OECD Model, the proposed amendments to the Commentary on Article 5

Figure 12.2 **KL Barentsfjord**, Offshore Supply Vessel, ASCO Quay, Aberdeen

of the OECD Model suggested including the following wording with regard to article 5(1) of the OECD Model:

> a ship or boat that navigates in international waters or within one or more States is not fixed and does not, therefore, constitute a fixed place of business (unless the operation of the ship or boat is restricted to a particular area that has commercial and geographical coherence)

The supplytime charter contract

The main charterparty that had been created by BIMCO for the offshore supply sector and used for some time was the 2005 time charter for Offshore Supply Vessels, more commonly referred to as SUPPLYTIME 2005. The purpose of this time charter form was to ensure that all aspects of the use of Offshore Supply Vessels were predetermined in the time charter contract, and for its time it was considered adequately comprehensive in its scope. It did not, of course, stipulate daily charter rates; these were determined by the market for Offshore Supply Vessels. Since the AHTS is a more versatile supply vessel, in that it can be used for a variety of functions, namely towage, anchor handling and the supply of materials to offshore installations, it is constantly in demand, and can therefore command high daily rates, in the region of £15,000/day. The Platform Supply Vessel, although larger than the AHTS, is, however, more limited in its function in that it is used solely for the supply of materials and equipment to offshore installations, and therefore commands daily charter rates of approximately £4000–£8000/day. In time, it was felt that the SUPPLYTIME Charter arrangement required revision and updating, and in due course, a new version was issued, with significant updates and revisions, especially covering insurance liability, but also covering other issues, including vessel lay-ups for maintenance and repair.

Overview

On 6 June 2017, the documentary committee at the Baltic and International Maritime Council adopted the revised and updated version of its Supplytime charter contract for chartering offshore support vessels, namely Supplytime 2017. Supplytime 2017 is the fourth version of this charterparty for offshore support vessels (OSVs), and has become, arguably, the most successful offshore vessel contract in use today, as it is more comprehensive and fundamental than its predecessor.

Supplytime 2005

BIMCO's SUPPLYTIME 2005 Charter Party contract is a basic fundamental of offshore supply vessel services, and is used for ships ranging from crew transfer vessels and tugs to modern offshore service vessels (OSVs), including AHTS (Anchor Handling, Towage and Supply) vessels, PSV (Platform Supply Vessels), and DSV (Dive Support Vessels). Because of the nature of the services provided by these vessels on a long-term basis for most offshore Oil and Gas projects, and, more recently, offshore wind farm projects, the charter contract is based on time charters alone. The versatility of the time charter contract is, however, the result of its complexity. Perhaps as a way of categorising and providing a more detailed analysis of the market, BIMCO has released more specifically-tailored contracts such as WINDTIME for crew transfer vessels, especially those involved in offshore wind farm projects, as well as wind farm supply vessels, PROJECTCON for heavy lift cargo, in particular where barges and tugs are involved in such projects, and an updated TOWHIRE 2008, specifically for towage vessels.

However, those contracts are definitely secondary to the SUPPLYTIME charter in terms of their industry scope, and hence the application and frequency of their practical application. In order to obtain a clear view of the SUPPLYTIME charter, the analysis must address, first, the multitude of boxes on the face of the contract to, second, APPENDIX A for a detailed assessment of the ship's capabilities and statistics and, third, to APPENDIX B for the various insurances to be obtained by the charterer and owner respectively. Finally, it must address the 38 clauses in the terms section of the document that govern the material legal aspects. It is consequently not an easy charterparty to handle in practice, owing to its complexity, but with care and due attention, it can be completed with the full confidence and details of both parties involved.

In general, the SUPPLYTIME charter provides for a reasonable balance of the interests of the owner and charterer. However, given the varied nature of offshore services, the liability regime will necessarily be shifted slightly in favour of the owner, since the charter rate presented to the vessel owner for the use of the vessel and crew is generally disproportionately small compared to the value of the project (and hence to the potential scope of liability) in which the vessel owner is involved. In broad terms, the value of the project contract will amount to millions, if not billions, of US Dollars depending upon the extent of offshore exploration and production.

The boxes contained in the charterparty

The first element to address is the number and nature of the boxes embedded in the contract. It should be remembered as a matter of importance that in the past, such charter parties were written in long-form. That means that there were no specific boxes. Instead, there were blank sections of contract clauses, which had to be filled in with the relevant information. Today, boxes and references (e.g., "as stated in Box 17") provide the same functionality but a different aesthetic approach. Indeed, the completion of the boxes provided makes it easier for all parties concerned to ensure that the right information is provided in simple form to enable the other parties to correctly understand and apply the charter parties to their full extent.

It is important to understand that the boxes are essentially used to fill in contract clauses. The information placed in the box is later used by the clause that references it, so it is necessary to consider the boxes as making changes to the operative text of the charterparty.

In practice, the terms "N/A" or "TBA" can be inserted into these boxes when SUPPLYTIME contracts are negotiated. However, these terms essentially avoid specific information, and are generally terms which should be avoided, as "N/A" (Not Applicable) will, in general, negate the clause (i.e., make it inoperative) while "TBA" (To Be Announced) has the potential to generate disclosure obligations at a future date. Neither of the parties generally desires this result. Indeed, TBA can prejudice a charter contract, as it may lead to information which may be detrimental, rather than beneficial, to the charter contract. Instead, the parties are trying to negotiate their way through the contract as quickly and efficiently as possible, typically due to time pressures, but are not content with leaving certain clauses blank. Furthermore, this lack of satisfaction is perhaps justifiable, since it indicates that the parties are, at least in principle, aware that what they are doing or negotiating contains a considerable risk of arriving at a less-than-optimal legal result for either party.

APPENDIX A

APPENDIX A is another section of the charterparty where mistakes can often be found. Or worse, it is often discovered that APPENDIX A is not even completed at all. While in principle data sheets about the chartered vessel can be relied on to function in place of APPENDIX A, it is important to remember that the text of the charterparty treats APPENDIX A as the operative section containing information about the nature and attributes of the vessel. Indeed, in any contract, the terms and conditions of the contract must always be adhered to, and these often will be referred to in the Appendices of the contract, sometimes seen as the "small print".

On this basis, the parties need to make certain that they have validly and unambiguously incorporated the vessel's data sheet into the charterparty instead of leaving open questions by, for example, allowing APPENDIX A to continue to exist parallel to the ship's data sheet and failing to specify which has priority.

SUPPLYTIME is often an excuse for an excess in legal terms and bureaucracy. One kind of arrangement that can be found refers to massive numbers of rider clauses or codicils appended to the charterparty, which deal with points that were often already discussed, often in a pedantic way. These are sometimes struck from the face, but not always. It is believed that such rider clauses are used because they are more clearly set out than the charterparty itself and its references to boxes, which actually demands a high level of legal skill to fill out correctly.

In this respect, rider clauses and striking the BIMCO standard language provide a way to generate a text which appears more definitive and even bespoke. Working with the BIMCO charterparty and making the necessary adjustments takes more effort, but it can also provide more security. When possible, it is always encouraged that less text be struck and that it is possible to work within the language of the BIMCO form to ensure that the goals of the parties are adequately addressed. Equally in this respect, the BIMCO SUPPLYTIME charter bears many similarities to the average GENCON Charter Party, which is designed to deal with vessel Charters pertaining to the use of general cargo vessels, and which can, to a degree, operate in parallel with the SUPPLYTIME Charter contract.

Another risk that needs to be taken into consideration is that making adjustments and modifications to the BIMCO standard forms, even if done innocently, can lead to problems further on. Courts of Law do not look favourably upon parties that do not make such modifications clear. Therefore, appending rider clauses and deleting the main text, rather than striking it through, can run the risk of fraud, especially where such clauses are designed to manipulate or falsify the value of the contract. There are certain charterparty forms which appear essentially as if they are from BIMCO, but upon careful comparison with the original BIMCO form, it is evident that some boxes and language on the face of the contract are missing entirely and that the form has been manipulated or distorted.

APPENDIX B

APPENDIX B is also an essential part of SUPPLYTIME, especially given the knock-for-knock rule concerning accidents and collisions. Essentially, knock-for-knock is a "shorthand" way to assign insurance risk. APPENDIX B then provides the parties a platform for apportioning this risk and specifying which policies need to be purchased.

It is essential that the form be filled out and that rider clauses not be used without unambiguously striking through the language in APPENDIX B that the rider clauses are designed to replace. Great caution and prudence must be exercised, since otherwise it is possible to create a self-contradicting or unclear contract, which is a direct opening to litigation.

Supplytime 2017

The Supplytime 2017 charter and its predecessors are the benchmark contracts of choice for the OSV industry as well as others seeking a comprehensive knock-for-knock charterparty, where insurance disputes may be resolved in a definitive manner. However, as the industry is changing and evolving over time, so must Supplytime, and in 2015, the Baltic and International Maritime Council (BIMCO) decided that Supplytime was due for its periodic revision. Two years later, Supplytime 2017 has become the industry's contract of choice.

Apart from the changes to the overall liability regime, various other amendments have been introduced to SUPPLYTIME 2017 to modernise the standard form and take account of day-to-day practice in the industry.

SUPPLYTIME 2005 had a reputation for being owner-friendly, particularly due to the set-up of the liability regime and certain exceptions only applying to the owners' liability. By contrast, SUPPLYTIME 2017, with only very few exceptions, aims to level the playing field by introducing an almost "pure" knock-for-knock with very few carve-outs and a widening of the definition of the charterers' Group. The consequential loss clause has also been amended to make it clearer in light of recent court decisions. The charterers also have to name the owners as co-insureds under their insurance policies if they choose to take out insurance, just as the owners have to include the charterers under their policies.

Central to the SUPPLYTIME charter form has always been its adherence to the offshore industry's general use of a knock-for-knock liability and indemnity regime in terms of insurance claims in the event of collisions or accidents. While almost all OSV charter parties use the principle of mutual indemnification, they all still give some degree of favourable treatment to one party or the other. This includes all charterers' own forms as well as past versions of Supplytime.

Supplytime 2017 changes that in attempting to treat both parties equally and, through the knock-for-knock regime, provides a properly balanced set of liabilities and indemnities with almost no exceptions. While the knock-for-knock regime is often criticised and misunderstood, the reasons for its existence within the offshore industry should be self-evident and work for the benefit of everyone involved. Supplytime 2017 recognises this fact and, further, that the cleaner the mutual indemnification regime, the more effective it is.

This attempt by Supplytime 2017 to treat both parties fairly and equally now runs through the entire contract, and where an issue or clause previously showed undue bias one way or the other, it was reviewed and, if necessary, amended so as to remove that bias as much as possible. The contract was also reviewed in the light of past legal judgments, its use sometimes of overly complex language, its practical application in real-world situations and known areas of conflict and misinterpretation. The result is that Supplytime 2017 contains numerous small changes from the 2015 version as well as a number of more significant and fundamental changes.

There are expanded provisions dealing with on- and off-hire surveys, audits, inspections and assessments, including condition of liquid mud and brine tanks to reflect what charterers have, for some time now, increasingly demanded. The importance of these onboard tanks cannot be underestimated, since offshore supply vessels must be able to carry large quantities of liquid drilling mud and even cement, for the purposes of the drilling and cementation stages in the well-drilling and casing processes, without any risk of contamination in the tanks, or, for that matter, any risk of leakage or pollution of the oceans, as stipulated in the MARPOL Conventions.

The wording regarding the right to suspend and/or terminate the contract for non-payment of hire and other sums due has been clarified to remove ambiguity. The owners can suspend performance of their obligations at any time after payment falls due and while it remains unpaid. During such suspension, the ship will remain on-hire. There is no requirement on the owners to give notice to the charterers before exercising their right to suspend performance. The owners retain the right to terminate the charterparty if the charterers have still not paid five days after the required notice of failure to pay has been given. It should be noted however, that if the charterers pay after the five days' grace period has elapsed, but before the owners have sent the written termination notice, the owners lose the right to terminate.

The charterers' right to terminate for convenience (against the payment of an agreed fee) remains unchanged, however the charterers' right to terminate for cause, which was criticised in the previous edition, has now been clarified. While the right to terminate for cause remains, breakdown, which was previously a termination event, has been removed. Breakdown now falls within the wider term "off-hire" for which there is a right to terminate if the off-hire exceeds defined periods.

With regard to the handful of standard BIMCO clauses that have always been included within SUPPLYTIME, the latest versions have been incorporated and three more have been added: Sanctions, Designated Entities and the MLC (Maritime Labour Convention) clause. At the same time, the Both-to-Blame collision clause and the General Average clauses have been removed as they are not relevant in an offshore support vessel context as they deal with cargo-related matters and are inconsistent with a purer knock-for-knock. Vessels operating in the US may, however, want to consider reinstating the Both-to-Blame collision clause.

The details

The following are some of the more notable changes to be taken into consideration.

The term "fuel" now replaces "bunkers", given that, on the majority of Offshore Supply Vessels (OSVs), a common fuel system is used for both bunkers and cargo. The payment for fuel on delivery and on redelivery has been amended to reflect what really happens in most cases, and two options are set out for the parties to choose which one applies. Liability for engine damage due to incorrect fuel has been redrafted to give owners greater control over the fuel coming on board while retaining the liability for engine damage, which was previously an exception to the knock-for-knock.

On and Off Hire surveys, audits, inspects and assessments are expanded to reflect what charterers have for some time increasingly demanded, including condition of liquid mud and brine tanks. How, where and when all these can be applied is more clearly defined along with references to the Offshore Vessel Inspection Database and Common Marine Inspection Document.

Explosive and International Maritime Dangerous Goods Code (IMDG) cargoes have always been permitted to be carried provided they are packed, marked and stowed in accordance with the appropriate IMDG regulations. This requirement has not changed, but the liability associated with their carriage, which was previously another exception to the knock-for-knock provision, has now been amended.

The wording and application of the right to suspend and then terminate the charterparty for the non-payment of any money owed has been clarified to remove any ambiguity.

Maintenance days are still earned and accumulated as previously, and their use is more clearly defined as being solely at the owner's discretion. However, days not used may no longer be cashed in upon the final redelivery of the vessel except in certain circumstances.

Various issues surrounding how, where and when a vessel shall be dry-docked during the period of the charterparty have been clarified, including when control of the vessel passes between owners and charterers.

Where charterers take out appropriate insurances to cover their liabilities under the contract, they must now name the owners as co-insureds, and their insurers must waive rights of subrogation in exactly the same way this has always applied to owners' insurers.

A completely new layup clause is included that recognises first that vessels rarely now go into "cold" layup and second that the issues surrounding the warm layup of a vessel are far more complex than with a cold layup. Consequently, the new clause seeks to identify the key elements that the parties need to address and agree before a vessel can enter layup. One additional note on layup is that maintenance days will no longer be earned during any period spent in layup.

HSE health and safety issues will always be important, but it now recognises that under no circumstances may the owner's legal obligations in respect to the International Safety Management (ISM) Code, Standards of Certification, Training and Watchkeeping (SCTW) and so on be compromised when agreeing to the standards and policies of others.

The charterer's right to terminate for convenience (against the payment of an agreed fee) remains unchanged. However, the charterer's right to terminate for cause has previously attracted attention because of the notice mechanism to be used. This mechanism has now been clarified, and while the right to terminate for cause remains, breakdown, which was previously a specific reason, has been removed.

Breakdown now falls within the wider term "off-hire" whereby part of any charter negotiation will be an agreement on the total number of off-hire days permitted and arising for whatever reasons, being recorded in a new Box (32) of Part 1 of the charterparty.

With regard to the handful of standard BIMCO clauses that have always been included within Supplytime, these are the latest versions, and three more have been added: sanctions, designated entities and the Maritime Labour Convention clause. At the same time, the both-to-blame collision clause and the general average clauses have been removed.

Finally, Annex A, referring to vessel specification, has also been brought up to date.

SUPPLYTIME 2005, the standard form of charterparty for offshore vessels, has therefore undergone a significant update to modernise and improve the form. At first glance, the revised 2017 form is very similar to its predecessor; however, it contains some important changes, some of which are more apparent than others.

The changes reflected in the revised 2017 form not only aim to provide a more balanced contract, from what has traditionally been seen as an owner-friendly form, but also update the form to reflect modern practices and developments in case law. The overriding aim of the 2017 form is to "make it as appealing to charterers as it is already to owners".

Liability

Arguably the most significant change is to the "knock-for-knock" regime. The principle behind "knock-for-knock" is that each party bears responsibility for any damage or loss to its own property or accident or injury to its own staff, without making a claim against the other party, even if the other party is at fault. The principle provides the contracting parties and their insurers with some certainty. Not that any accident or collision is wilful or accepted as a matter of course, but in the offshore industry, accidents concerning installations or supply vessels do occur, and must be accounted for according to their severity depending upon the gravity of the event, hence the element of risk and how it is assessed.

The 2005 form, however, contains numerous exceptions (contained within 16 clauses) where the "knock-for-knock" regime is not applied. Examples include (a) where damage or loss is incurred in circumstances where undeclared explosives or dangerous cargo are shipped by the charterers on board the vessel and (b) in the event of pollution claims. These exceptions in the 2005 form water down the "knock-for-knock" regime, many of which favour owners.

The 2017 form removes the vast majority of the exceptions, strengthening the "knock-for-knock" regime; applying it in a truer/more balanced form, with the only remaining exceptions being for owners' and charterers' towing wires, limitation of liability at law and salvage of charterers' property.

The remit of the "knock-for-knock" regime has also been extended to capture a broader range of the contracting parties' interests, with a view to ensuring that it covers all entities working on the offshore site. This has been achieved by expanding the definition of "charterers' Group" to now include charterers' clients (of any tier), and also affiliates of the entities referred to within the definition. Similar changes have been applied to the definition of "owners' Group".

The exclusion of consequential loss has been updated to bring it in line with the latest case law; the list of excluded losses is extended, and consequential and indirect loss is set out as a separate category.

The owners' liability for the vessel not working, which remains limited to the suspension of hire is, in the 2017 form, expressly stated to apply where caused by negligence on the part of a member of the Owners' Group. The owners' limitation of liability is also now stated to apply whether or not the vessel is off-hire.

Delivery/redelivery survey

The clause dealing with delivery and redelivery surveys has been revised in the 2017 form. The role of the independent surveyor (jointly appointed) is now limited to determining and recording (i) the type and quantity of fuel, (ii) the quantity of potable water on board and (iii) the cleanliness and condition of the cargo tanks. Charterers have the right in the 2017 form (with owners' consent, not to be unreasonably withheld) to conduct a vessel audit, assessment, survey and inspection of the vessel in the period prior to delivery, providing charterers with the opportunity to check that the vessel is compliant with the terms of the charterparty.

Fuel

The provisions relating to payment for fuel (the term "fuel" replacing the word "bunkers") have been amended to reflect current industry practice. There are also changes to the provisions on payment for fuel at delivery and redelivery, reflecting what more usually happens in practice. Under the 2005 form, charterers purchase fuel remaining on board at the time of delivery, with owners purchasing fuel remaining on board at redelivery at the price prevailing at the port of delivery and redelivery respectively.

Also, in line with a purer knock-for-knock regime, risk of damage to the engine caused by the use of unsuitable fuel now lies with the owners. This was thought to be fairer since the owners exercise control over the risks associated with fuelling operations through more developed sampling and testing provisions. In return, however, the owners are now given more time while the vessel remains on-hire to check the fuel for compliance and to stop fuelling operations, if necessary.

The process in the 2017 form provides two alternatives, either (i) the parties account for the fuel as aforesaid but at a substantiated price paid by the owners at the last loading of the fuel on board, or (ii) the difference in the quantity of fuel on board between delivery and redelivery by reference to delivery and redelivery surveys is paid, either at a pre-agreed rate or the substantiated price paid at the vessel's last loading of fuel.

The 2017 form provides the chief engineer with a right to stop the loading of fuel if it is suspected that it is off-specification, i.e. sub-standard and low quality, or at risk of damaging the vessel's engines because of contamination. This replaces the charterers' indemnity for off-specification fuel that exists in the 2005 form.

Maintenance and dry-docking

Maintenance days are a unique feature of offshore support vessel time charters. Under SUPPLYTIME 2017 they are still earned and accumulated as previously, but their use is more clearly defined. Days not used may no longer be "cashed in", i.e. redeemed, on the redelivery of the vessel to its operators except where the charterers have specifically asked the owners not to use them.

In addition, a new clause dealing with the layup of the vessel has been included. The clause recognises the fact that, currently, cold, i.e. *ad hoc* unplanned lay-ups, are rare, and warm lay-ups, i.e. those pre-arranged and planned for vessel maintenance and servicing, require a more sophisticated provision than was previously included in SUPPLYTIME 2005.

The maintenance provisions are more clearly stated in the 2017 form, including a definition for "Maintenance Days". Owners are no longer entitled to payment for unused Maintenance Days at redelivery, unless they have not been used at charterers' request, when they would be payable on redelivery or earlier termination of the charterparty.

The regularity of the dry-docking provisions in the 2017 form is now linked to Class society requirements (with owners required to provide vessel's Class dry-docking schedule at the start of the charter period). Additional provisions have also been added to the process, to remove ambiguity and ensure any dry dock location is reasonable, with regards to time and cost, for owners and charterers.

Various issues surrounding how, where and when a vessel is to be dry-docked during the period of the charterparty have been clarified, including when control of the vessel passes between the owners and the charterers. Unless being carried out using accumulated Maintenance Days, the ship will be off-hire during such dry-dockings and, in the 2017 revision, the opportunity has been taken to clarify where and when the ship goes off-hire and comes back on-hire again. This is particularly necessary considering the length of time that the vessel is operating on a time charter, which could be several years depending upon the duration of the oil/gas field supply contract.

The 2017 edition now states that the owners' choice of dry-dock location should always be reasonable, to both parties, when it comes to time and cost. To promote collaboration between the parties, the owners must provide the charterers with the ship's scheduled dry-docking programme for the entire charter period.

Termination

The rights to terminate for cause have been clarified in the 2017 form. Requisition, confiscation, loss of vessel and *force majeure* are now stated to be events of termination giving either party the right of termination, while bankruptcy and owners' failure to take out insurance only gives the non-defaulting party a right of termination.

The separate right of termination in the event of breakdown of the vessel after a stipulated period of time which appears in the 2005 form has been removed in the 2017 form. Breakdown in the 2017 form now falls solely within the off-hire regime for which there is a clearer termination right linked to prolonged off-hire for a single consecutive period or combined periods. The notification requirements for termination have also been clarified.

BIMCO clauses

The standard BIMCO clauses that are contained within the 2005 form have been updated in the 2017 form with the latest versions of the clauses included. These include the war risks clause and the dispute resolution clause. Additional standard BIMCO clauses have been included in the 2017 form to cover issues that contracting parties often look to address, namely the BIMCO infectious or contagious disease clause (clause 25), the BIMCO anti-corruption clause (clause 28), the MLC 2006 clause (clause 29), the BIMCO sanctions clause (clause 30) and the BIMCO designated entities clause (clause 31).

The both-to-blame and the general average clauses have been removed from the 2017 form, on grounds that the clauses are contrary to a pure "knock-for-knock" regime.

Conclusions

The SUPPLYTIME form provides a framework of the key rights, obligations and liabilities for parties wishing to contract in the offshore sector. It is a document that is well understood in the offshore industry and as a result has been widely used, and its use has undoubtedly extended beyond the remit of what the original drafting committee of SUPPLYTIME would have anticipated.

Users of the form should be aware that while the revised SUPPLYTIME 2017 form is an improved version, and is welcomed, it remains a generic standard form charterparty. In its non-amended form, SUPPLYTIME does not cater for the specific needs of particular projects. For example, in the offshore wind farm sector the SUPPLYTIME form is often used for the charter of Jackup installation vessels. However, SUPPLYTIME does not address specific issues that come with chartering a Jackup vessel, e.g. risks relating to the planting of the vessel's legs which result in issues such as responsibility for ground risk and surveys for unexploded ordnance.

Where SUPPLYTIME is used to contract for floating accommodation (for offshore projects or otherwise), additional provisions need to be considered to cover such areas as the services to be provided to those using the accommodation and their rights of access to the vessel. Caution should therefore be taken to ensure that it meets the needs for which it is being applied, and appropriate amendments are made to cover particular risks and issues that may apply to specific sectors and to align it to the needs of the parties.

It should be noted that because of the nature of many offshore platforms, i.e. semi-submersible rigs and self-propelled drillships, these can be included in such charter contracts, as they are not deemed to be permanent fixed offshore installations and can be moved from one offshore location to another with comparative ease. Given their manoeuvrability, they are considered to be on a par with supply vessels in terms of chartering, although charter rates for offshore rigs can be as much as US$700,000 per day depending upon location, as opposed to US$17,000 per day for an Offshore Supply Vessel. Daily charter rates for drillships can be as much as US$300,000. This is why much planning is needed when budgeting for offshore Oil and Gas field operations, as vessel and installation chartering is one of the prime elements of such operations. All of these operations are based on time charter operations, which can last from months to years, depending upon the size and complexity of the offshore operations involved, and indeed such operations will involve the chartering of several vessels and rigs at any time, amounting to millions of US Dollars per project contract. It is therefore very important to ensure that the nature of the contract is carefully planned and executed to encompass such costs and ensure that charter contracts are correctly and properly arranged.

The WINDTIME charter

WINDTIME is a standard time charterparty for the transfer of wind farm personnel and equipment to and from offshore wind farm installations. The latest edition of this contract is WINDTIME, issued in 2013. A recent article details how the WINDTIME Charter Party is designed to function.

This charterparty has been specifically designed to meet the increasing demand for small high-speed craft capable of transferring personnel and equipment to carry out the maintenance of offshore wind turbines. Until now, the wind farm sector has tended to rely upon amended SUPPLYTIME 2005 contracts to charter these support vessels. WINDTIME has been the result of two years' work by a team of industry experts representing workboat and windfarm operators, with additional guidance from legal and P&I representatives, including Fabien Lerede, the Standard Club's Offshore Syndicate Claims Director. Based on BIMCO's SUPPLYTIME 2005 charterparty, it provides for a knock-for-knock allocation of liability regardless of fault whereby owners and charterers are each responsible for and provide an indemnity in respect of the loss and/or damage to its property and the injury and/or death of its contractors and contractors (and client in the case of charterers) without recourse to the other party. Unlike SUPPLYTIME 2005, the knock-for-knock indemnities under WINDTIME apply regardless of gross negligence as well as simple negligence. However, it differs from SUPPLYTIME 2005 in that if a member of the owners or charterers Group intentionally or recklessly causes loss, damage, injury or death, with knowledge that such consequences would probably result (i.e. if there has been wilful misconduct), the knock-for-knock indemnity provisions will not apply, which may lead to an increased risk of litigation.

Another major difference to SUPPLYTIME 2005 is the cancellation provisions. Under SUPPLYTIME 2005, if owners miss the cancellation date and charterers elect to cancel the charterparty, charterers have no recourse against owners for losses that might arise during the project preparation phase, such as the cost of standby machinery, equipment and personnel. Under WINDTIME, if owners know that they will be unable to deliver the vessel by the cancelling date, they are required to notify the charterers in writing, stating the date by which they will be able to deliver the vessel. This reflects the critical importance of the vessel arriving when expected, given the costly and lengthy project preparation involved in wind farm projects. Charterers are entitled within three days of receiving such notice to cancel the charterparty. There is also an option to require owners to pay liquidated damages if they fail to deliver the vessel from the original cancelling date until such time as owners have delivered the vessel or a substitute vessel or charterers elect to cancel the charterparty. Further details can be found in the explanatory notes to WINDTIME which is available on the BIMCO website (www.BIMCO.org).

Similar to many other new industries which have learnt from older similar industries, the emerging offshore wind industry has taken much inspiration from the more mature offshore Oil and Gas industry, including on legal concepts and contracting formats, such as the use of SUPPLYTIME, the offshore Supply Vessel time charter arrangement. There is an interesting reverse trend of cross pollination back to the Oil and Gas industry from renewables, including a recent initiative by BIMCO to update and possibly rebalance the owner/charterer risk split in the SUPPLYTIME Charter Party arrangement on the back of the success of the new BIMCO WINDTIME Charter Party. It remains to be seen to what extent this cross pollination and "tail wagging the dog" phenomenon between the two industries will migrate to other legal areas.

The offshore wind industry arguably currently is at a similar stage of development to where offshore Oil and Gas was in the mid-1970s. Both migrated from onshore and faced similar additional challenges when they went to sea. Even if there are large differences between the industries, such as in environmental risks, climate impact, market price sensitivity, risk and reward etc., there are many similarities, in particular the marine, energy and construction aspects. Oil and Gas looked a lot to shipping for guidance in its early days. Due to the additional common energy and construction elements, the offshore wind industry arguably has been able to piggy-back on Oil and Gas to an even larger extent.

In both industries there has been a general tension between the original onshore and newer maritime culture and thinking. One of the most prominent examples thereof is the two fundamentally different liability profiles in the two main types of contract format commonly used at different levels in the contract chain on an offshore wind project. Inspired by Oil and Gas, Supplytime has generally been used for time chartering of vessels further down the contracting chain and sometimes in heavily amended form for lump sum-like installation work. FIDIC-like contracts, normally Yellow Book, are generally used for construction and main component supply higher up the chain. (**FIDIC** is a French language acronym for **F**édération **I**nternationale **D**es **I**ngénieurs-**C**onseils, which means the International Federation of Consulting Engineers.)

In Supplytime, the owner faces limited or no liability if he does not deliver the vessel on time or it does not operate properly. Property damage and personal injury/death is dealt with through a knock-for-knock concept. There is a consequential loss disclaimer, but no cap. By contrast, the contractor under a FIDIC-like contract faces heavy financial liabilities if he does not deliver the project on time or there are defects (liquidated damages for delay and breach of performance or availability warranties). There are negligence-based indemnities for property damage and personal injury/death. There is a consequential loss disclaimer and caps (overall and sub-caps for liquidated damages). The tension is much less prominent in Oil and Gas, which over time has developed industry-specific construction and service contracts, such as the LOGIC suite of contracts in the UK sector and the Norwegian forms (NF, NTK etc.) in the Norwegian sector of the North Sea. These include FIDIC-like liability for delay and defects and Supplytime-like knock-for-knock negotiations for damages and injuries.

As a result of various offshore wind industry participants expressing an interest in BIMCO developing a wind industry-specific time charterparty, BIMCO developed WINDTIME, which was released in 2013. A driving factor for the initiative was the concern of certain owners, including of crew transfer vessels, who felt that they were forced to accept charterer-developed charter-friendly forms. This is similar to BIMCO's development of the original SUPPLYTIME Charter in the mid-1970s, largely in response to the use by major operators of their own heavily-structured charter-friendly forms.

WINDTIME is a Supplytime-based wind industry-specific time charterparty for crew transfer and other service vessels. It can easily be adapted for other and larger vessels, in particular the 12-hour operation needs to be adjusted to 24/7 operation, such as Jackup installation vessels. In the same way that the Supplytime charterparty is used in offshore Oil and Gas projects, in theory the WINDTIME charterparty could also be used in Oil and Gas.

WINDTIME fundamentally rebalanced the risk split between owners and charterers. As a default, owners face liquidated damages in the amount of the day rate for late delivery and risk paying damages if the vessel is not as agreed. As a counterbalance, WINDTIME introduced a monetary cap on liability. It maintains a traditional knock-for-knock. WINDTIME also includes clarified drafting on several points, including the details and mechanics of the termination clause and an update of the knock-for-knock and consequential losses clauses in order to bring them in line with recent case law and current practices.

The WINDTIME Charter Party has been well received in the market. It appears that any fears that it would not be accepted by owners due to the increased potential liabilities were not warranted and have been dispelled. By contrast, it has led certain main charterers, such as Siemens, to generally shift from internally-developed charter-friendly forms to the more balanced WINDTIME Charter, at least for crew transfer vessels, reducing time for negotiating and, arguably, the risk that owners accept risks that they cannot manage or terms that they do not understand, which can be pernicious in terms of Charter Agreements and which can lead to costly litigation.

Following immediately from the success of WINDTIME, a revision of Supplytime 2005 was scheduled to begin later in 2015. BIMCO believes that WINDTIME introduced a number of useful amendments to the Supplytime charter wording that may be worthwhile incorporating into Supplytime itself. It would appear that there is an increasing perception at BIMCO and in the industry that the owner/charterer risk balance in the Supplytime charter is in urgent need of a review and overhaul. Many of the updates resulting from recent legal developments, clarifying drafting and other minor changes should be relatively uncontroversial. One must conjecture as to what extent the WINDTIME concepts will be ultimately fed back into the "mother" SUPPLYTIME form, as, inevitably, there is a significant overlap between both forms of charterparty.

Offshore wind and renewables projects can be expected to continue to implement legal concepts stemming from Oil and Gas charter contracts. For example, the knock-for-knock concept may become embraced more generally, which should be beneficial for the industry as a whole. One step in that direction would be if FIDIC would adopt a knock-for-knock concept in any new contract format or principles it may develop as part of its currently ongoing Renewables Contracting Initiative. It remains to be seen to what extent the recent trend of cross pollination, rather than one-way fertilisation, will continue in more general. It is expected that this will take place on a case-by-case basis when there are good reasons and mutual benefit in both industries, rather as a wholesale measure. It also proves that the development of both SUPPLYTIME and WINDTIME Charter Parties are subject to further development and adaptation, given their creation out of a whole new maritime dimension of offshore Oil and Gas and renewables management.

GLOSSARY OF TERMS AND ABBREVIATIONS

AHTS: Anchor Handling Towage and Supply vessel
ASN: Anti-Smuggling Net
B/L: Bill of Lading
BAF: Bunker Adjustment Factor
BDI: Baltic Dry Index
BHP: Brake Horse Power
BHSI: Baltic Exchange Handysize Index
BIMCO: Baltic & International Maritime Council
C/P: Charterparty
CAF: Currency Adjustment Factor
CBM: Cubic Metre
CCP: Customs Civil Penalty
CCS UK: Cargo Community Systems UK
CFR: Cost & Freight
CHIEF: Customs Handling of Import & Export Freight (HMRC Customs Computer, soon to be replaced by CDS: Customs Declaration System)
CIF: Cost Insurance Freight
CNS: Community Network Services
COA: Contract of Affreightment
COGSA: Carriage of Goods by Sea Act (UK)
CONGENBILL: Charter Party Bill of Lading
CSP: Community Systems Provider
CSPLO: Community Systems Provider Liaison Officer (HMRC)
DFDS: Det Forenede Dampskibs-Selskab: Danish Shipping Line
DP: Dynamic Positioning
DSV: Dive Support Vessel
Dwt: Deadweight
E&P: Exploration and Production (Oil and Gas)
ECSA: European Community Shipowners Associations
ERTS: Enhanced Remote Transit Shed
ETSF: External Temporary Storage Facility
ETSFAD: External Temporary Storage Facility Approved Depository

EU: European Union
FAS: Free Alongside Ship
FFA: Forward Freight Agreement
FOB: Free On Board
FPSO: Floating Production and Storage Offshore vessel
FRC: Fast Rescue Craft
Freight Collect: The Buyer pays for and arranges the Freight
Freight Prepaid: The Seller pays for and arranges the Freight
GoM: Gulf of Mexico
Handysize: Designation of the smallest size of ocean-going general/bulk cargo vessel
HMC&E: HM Customs & Excise
HMRC: HM Revenue & Customs
HP: Horse Power
IMCA: International Marine Contractors Association
IMDG: International Movement of Dangerous Goods
IMO: International Maritime Organization
INCOTERMS (2020): The International Commercial Terms of Delivery, 2020 Version
IT: Information Technology
ITSF: Internal Temporary Storage Facility
LASH: **L**ighter **A**board **Sh**ip
LCL: Less-than Container Load
LNG: Liquefied Natural Gas
LOGIC: Leading Oil and Gas Industry Competitiveness
LPG: Liquefied Petroleum Gas
LTL: Less Than Truckload
MCP: Maritime Cargo Processing
MPV: Multi-Purpose Vessel
NCTS: New Community Transit System
OCX: Officer of Customs & Excise
OECD: Organisation for Economic Co-operation and Development
OPEC: Organization of Petroleum Exporting Countries
OSV: Offshore Supply Vessel
P&I Clubs: Protection and Indemnity Clubs (Marine Insurance)
Panamax: The largest ships capable of transiting the Panama Canal (until the reconstruction of part of the Canal)
PSV: Platform Supply Vessel
RO/RO: Roll On: Roll Off
SARS-CoV: Covid-19 (Coronavirus)
SDR: Special Drawing Rights
SGX: The Singapore Exchange
SOLAS: Safety of Lives at Sea Convention
SSN: Standard Shipping Note
SCTW: Standards of Certification, Training and Watchkeeping

SWL: Safe Working Load
TAD: Transit Accompanying Document
TBA: To be Announced
Tramp Shipping: *Ad hoc* shipping, where ships carry cargoes on an *ad hoc* (i.e. non-scheduled) basis
UCC: Union Customs Code
UK: United Kingdom
UNCLOS: UN Convention of the Law of the Sea
US: United States
VAT: Value Added Tax
VLOC: Very Large Ore Carrier

INDEX

Note: Page numbers in *italic* indicate a figure on the corresponding page.

Made in the USA
Monee, IL
13 September 2026

62977689R00118